Emma Donoghue

Room

Annotationen von
Ursula Hermes

Ernst Klett Sprachen
Stuttgart

1. Auflage 1 10 9 8 7 6 | 2024 23 22 21 20

Annotationen und Zusatztexte: Ursula Hermes
Redaktion: Paul Newcomb
Layoutkonzeption: Elmar Feuerbach
Gestaltung und Satz: bostext, 71229 Leonberg
Umschlaggestaltung: Elmar Feuerbach
Titelbild: Alamy Images (Jack Maguire), Abingdon, Oxon
Druck und Bindung: CPI – Clausen & Bosse, Leck

Printed in Germany

ISBN 978-3-12-579880-9

Contents

About the author 6
About the book 8

ROOM

Presents 11
Unlying 59
Dying 105
After 160
Living 255

Additional material

1. Review from *The Guardian* 328
2. Journalist's account of the trial of Josef Fritzl 332
3. Interviews with Emma Donoghue about *Room* 336

Abbreviations used in the annotations

abb	abbreviation
adj	adjective
AD	anno domini
AE	American English
ca	circa
derog	derogative
e.g.	for example
esp	especially
etc.	et cetera
fml	formal
Fr	French
i.e.	id est (that is)
inf	informal
Lat	Latin
n	noun
old	old-fashioned
opp of	opposite of
pl	plural
sb	somebody
sl	slang
sth	something
USA	United States of America
usu	usually
vulg	vulgar

Emma Donoghue; © Andrew Bainbridge

About the author

Born in Dublin, Ireland, in October 1969, Emma Donoghue is the youngest of eight children. She went to Catholic convent schools in Dublin, spending a year in New York at the age of ten. In 1990 she left University College Dublin with a very good BA in English and French. Then she moved to England, and in 1997 received a PhD from the University of Cambridge. She has earned her living as a writer since the age of 23, and never had an 'honest job' (as she says it!) ever since she was once sacked after a month as a chambermaid. After years of moving between England, Ireland and Canada, in 1998 she settled in London, Ontario, where she lives with Chris Roulston and their children, Finn and Una.

Her first novels, STIR-FRY (1994) and HOOD (1995) were set in Dublin. The book that got her well known was SLAMMERKIN (2000), a historical novel inspired by a 1763 murder. It became a finalist for the 2001 Irish Times Irish Fiction Prize. This was followed by a sequence of short stories about real incidents from the fourteenth century to the nineteenth, including LIFE MASK (2004, a finalist for the Ferro-Grumley Award), which tells the startling true story of a love triangle in 1790s London. THE SEALED LETTER (2008) is a domestic thriller about an 1860s cause celebre (the Codrington Divorce), and was the joint winner of the Lambda Literary Award for Lesbian Fiction. These stories form a trilogy about the British class system, from the desperation of poverty in SLAMMERKIN, though the complexities of the genteel in LIFE MASK, to the bourgeois embarrassments of THE SEALED LETTER.

7 **PhD** advanced, post-graduate degree exam (*vergleichbar mit einem Doktorat, bzw. einer (akademischen) Promotion*) – 27 **the genteel** rich and refined people

Emma has also written drama, radio plays and literary history, been involved in film-making and furthermore taught creative writing in the UK and Canada.

Her novels have been translated into more than forty languages.

adapted from: www.emmadonoghue.com

About the book

ROOM is the story of a five-year-old called Jack, who lives in a single room with his Ma and has never been outside. When he turns five, he starts to ask questions, and his mother reveals to him that there is a world outside. Told entirely in Jack's voice, ROOM is no horror story or tearjerker, but a celebration of resilience and the love between parent and child.

An international bestseller as soon as it was published in August 2010, ROOM has now sold well over a million copies. It won several prizes, and was shortlisted for both the Orange Prize and the Man Booker Prize, which is generally regarded in the English-speaking world as the most prestigious prize in contemporary English literature. Only six books were on the "shortlist" in 2010, so "Room" was judged to be one of the six best books of that year in English.

adapted from: www.emmadonoghue.com/room.htm

Emma Donoghue dedicates the book to her children. She writes, as a prologue:

"*Room* is for Finn and Una, my best works."

7 **resilience** *Widerstand*

My child

Such trouble I have.
And you sleep, your heart is placid;
you dream in the joyless wood;
in the night nailed in bronze,
in the blue dark you lie still and shine.

Simonides (c. 556–468 BCE), "Danaë"

7 **BCE** "Before the Christian Era" (also known as: "BC" (Before Christ)

Presents

Today I'm five. I was four last night going to sleep in Wardrobe, but when I wake up in Bed in the dark I'm changed to five, abracadabra. Before that I was three, then two, then one, then zero. "Was I minus numbers?"

"Hmm?" Ma does a big stretch.

"Up in Heaven. Was I minus one, minus two, minus three—?" "Nah, the numbers didn't start till you zoomed down." "Through Skylight. You were all sad till I happened in your tummy."

"You said it." Ma leans out of Bed to switch on Lamp, he makes everything light up *whoosh*.

I shut my eyes just in time, then open one a crack, then both.

"I cried till I didn't have any tears left," she tells me. "I just lay here counting the seconds."

"How many seconds?" I ask her.

"Millions and millions of them."

"No, but how many exactly?"

"I lost count," says Ma.

"Then you wished and wished on your egg till you got fat." She grins. "I could feel you kicking."

"What was I kicking?"

"Me, of course."

I always laugh at that bit.

"From the inside, *boom boom.* " Ma lifts her sleep T-shirt and makes her tummy jump. "I thought, *Jack's on his way*. First thing in the morning, you slid out onto the rug with your eyes wide open."

I look down at Rug with her red and brown and black all zigging around each other. There's the stain I spilled by mistake

2 **Wardrobe** ['wɔːrdroʊb] cupboard in which clothes are kept ("Wardrobe", "Skylight", etc. start with capital letters because they are the names that Jack gives them, and not just the objects) – 9 **Skylight** window in the roof – 18 **to lose count** to count, but then forget how far you have counted to – 26 **rug** *Teppich* – 29 **stain** [steɪn] mark (*usu* messy or dirty)

getting born. "You cutted the cord and I was free," I tell Ma. "Then I turned into a boy."

"Actually, you were a boy already." She gets out of Bed and goes to Thermostat to hot the air.

I don't think he came last night after nine, the air's always different if he came. I don't ask because she doesn't like saying about him.

"Tell me, Mr. Five, would you like your present now or after breakfast?"

"What is it, what is it?"

"I know you're excited," she says, "but remember not to nibble your finger, germs could sneak in the hole."

"To sick me like when I was three with throw-up and diarrhea?"

"Even worse than that," says Ma, "germs could make you die." "And go back to Heaven early?"

"You're still biting it." She pulls my hand away.

"Sorry." I sit on the bad hand. "Call me Mr. Five again." "So, Mr. Five," she says, "now or later?"

I jump onto Rocker to look at Watch, he says 07:14. I can skateboard on Rocker without holding on to her, then I *whee* back onto Duvet and I'm snowboarding instead. "When are presents meant to open?"

"Either way would be fun. Will I choose for you?" asks Ma. "Now I'm five, I have to choose." My finger's in my mouth again, I put it in my armpit and lock shut. "I choose—now."

She pulls a something out from under her pillow, I think it was hiding all night invisibly. It's a tube of ruled paper, with the purple ribbon all around from the thousand chocolates we got the time Christmas happened. "Open it up," she tells me. "Gently."

I figure out to do off the knot, I make the paper flat, it's a drawing, just pencil, no colors. I don't know what it's about,

1 **cutted** Jack makes many mistakes in his language. Here he means, of course, "cut" – 3 **actually** really – 12 **to nibble** to chew – 13 **to sick** Jack means "to make ill" – 13 **to throw up** *sich übergeben* – 14 **diarrhea** [daɪə'riːə] *Durchfall* – 20 **Rocker** rocking chair

then I turn it. "Me!" Like in Mirror but more, my head and arm and shoulder in my sleep T-shirt. "Why are the eyes of the me shut?"

"You were asleep," says Ma.

"How you did a picture asleep?"

"No, I was awake. Yesterday morning and the day before and the day before that, I put the lamp on and drew you." She stops smiling. "What's up, Jack? You don't like it?"

"Not—when you're on at the same time I'm off."

"Well, I couldn't draw you while you were awake, or it wouldn't be a surprise, would it?" Ma waits. "I thought you'd like a surprise."

"I prefer a surprise and me knowing."

She kind of laughs.

I get on Rocker to take a pin from Kit on Shelf, minus one means now there'll be zero left of the five. There used to be six but one disappeared. One is holding up *Great Masterpieces of Western Art No. 3: The Virgin and Child with St. Anne and St. John the Baptist* behind Rocker, and one is holding up *Great Masterpieces of Western Art No. 8: Impression: Sunrise* beside Bath, and one is holding up the blue octopus, and one the crazy horse picture called *Great Masterpieces of Western Art No. 11: Guernica*. The masterpieces came with the oatmeal but I did the octopus, that's my best of March, he's going a bit curly from the steamy air over Bath. I pin Ma's surprise drawing on the very middle cork tile over Bed.

She shakes her head. "Not there."

She doesn't want Old Nick to see. "Maybe in Wardrobe, on the back?" I ask.

"Good idea."

Wardrobe is wood, so I have to push the pin an extra lot. I shut her silly doors, they always squeak, even after we put corn oil on the hinges. I look through the slats but it's too dark. I open her a bit to peek, the secret drawing is white except the

15 **pin** *Reißbrettstift* – 15 **Kit** a box with useful articles – 23 **oatmeal** *eine Art Haferflocken* – 32 **to squeak** to make a very high sound – 33 **slat** *Latte*

little lines of gray. Ma's blue dress is hanging over a bit of my sleeping eye, I mean the eye in the picture but the dress for real in Wardrobe.

I can smell Ma beside me, I've got the best nose in the family. "Oh, I forgetted to have some when I woke up."

"That's OK. Maybe we could skip it once in a while, now you're five?"

"No way Jose."

So she lies down on the white of Duvet and me too and I have lots.

* * *

I count one hundred cereal and waterfall the milk that's nearly the same white as the bowls, no splashing, we thank Baby Jesus. I choose Meltedy Spoon with the white all blobby on his handle when he leaned on the pan of boiling pasta by accident. Ma doesn't like Meltedy Spoon but he's my favorite because he's not the same.

I stroke Table's scratches to make them better, she's a circle all white except gray in the scratches from chopping foods. While we're eating we play Hum because that doesn't need mouths. I guess "Macarena" and "She'll Be Coming 'Round the Mountain" and "Swing Low, Sweet Chariot" but that's actually "Stormy Weather." So my score is two, I get two kisses.

I hum "Row, Row, Row Your Boat," Ma guesses that right away. Then I do "Tubthumping," she makes a face and says, "Argh, I know it, it's the one about getting knocked down and getting up again, what's it called?" In the very end she remembers right. For my third turn I do "Can't Get You out of My Head," Ma has no idea. "You've chosen such a tricky one… . Did you hear it on TV?"

5 **forgetted** Jack means "forgot" – 12 **cereal** ['sɪriəl] e.g. cornflakes – 14 **Meltedy Spoon** Jack's plastic spoon that got too hot and melted – 18 **scratch** a mark or small wound – 20 **Hum** bees hum

"No, on you." I burst out singing the chorus, Ma says she's a dumbo.

"Numbskull." I give her her two kisses.

I move my chair to Sink to wash up, with bowls I have to do gently but spoons I can *cling clang clong*. I stick out my tongue in Mirror. Ma's behind me, I can see my face stuck over hers like a mask we made when Halloween happened. "I wish the drawing was better," she says, "but at least it shows what you're like."

"What am I like?"

She taps Mirror where's my forehead, her finger leaves a circle. "The dead spit of me."

"Why I'm your dead spit?" The circle's disappearing.

"It just means you look like me. I guess because you're made of me, like my spit is. Same brown eyes, same big mouth, same pointy chin …"

I'm staring at us at the same time and the us in Mirror are staring back. "Not same nose."

"Well, you've got a kid nose right now."

I hold it. "Will it fall off and an adult nose grow?"

"No, no, it'll just get bigger. Same brown hair—"

"But mine goes all the way down to my middle and yours just goes on your shoulders."

"That's true," says Ma, reaching for Toothpaste. "All your cells are twice as alive as mine."

I didn't know things could be just half alive. I look again in Mirror. Our sleep T-shirts are different as well and our underwear, hers has no bears.

When she spits the second time it's my go with Toothbrush, I scrub each my teeth all the way around. Ma's spit in Sink doesn't look a bit like me, mine doesn't either. I wash them away and make a vampire smile.

"Argh." Ma covers her eyes. "Your teeth are so clean, they're dazzling me."

2 **dumbo** a silly person – 3 **numbskull** *Hohlkopf* – 22 **middle** waist

Her ones are pretty rotted because she forgetted to brush them, she's sorry and she doesn't forget anymore but they're still rotted.

I flat the chairs and put them beside Door against Clothes Horse. He always grumbles and says there's no room but there's plenty if he stands up really straight. I can fold up flat too but not quite as flat because of my muscles, from being alive. Door's made of shiny magic metal, he goes *beep beep* after nine when I'm meant to be switched off in Wardrobe.

God's yellow face isn't coming in today, Ma says he's having trouble squeezing through the snow.

"What snow?"

"See," she says, pointing up.

There's a little bit of light at Skylight's top, the rest of her is all dark. TV snow's white but the real isn't, that's weird. "Why it doesn't fall on us?"

"Because it's on the outside."

"In Outer Space? I wish it was inside so I can play with it."

"Ah, but then it would melt, because it's nice and warm in here." She starts humming, I guess right away it's "Let It Snow." I sing the second verse. Then I do "Winter Wonderland" and Ma joins in higher.

We have thousands of things to do every morning, like give Plant a cup of water in Sink for no spilling, then put her back on her saucer on Dresser. Plant used to live on Table but God's face burned a leaf of her off. She has nine left, they're the wide of my hand with furriness all over, like Ma says dogs are. But dogs are only TV. I don't like nine. I find a tiny leaf coming, that counts as ten.

Spider's real. I've seen her two times. I look for her now but there's only a web between Table's leg and her flat. Table balances good, that's pretty tricky, when I go on one leg I can do

1 **rotted** Jack means "rotten, bad" – 4 **Clothes Horse** *Kleiderständer* – 11 **to squeeze** *here*: to get in – 15 **weird** [wɪrd] strange – 24 **for no spilling** Jack means "in order not to spill water" – 26 **wide** Jack means "width" (*Länge*) – 27 **furriness** Jack means "hairiness"

it for ages but then I always fall over. I don't tell Ma about Spider. She brushes webs away, she says they're dirty but they look like extra-thin silver to me. Ma likes the animals that run around eating each other on the wildlife planet, but not real ones. When I was four I was watching ants walking up Stove and she ran and splatted them all so they wouldn't eat our food. One minute they were alive and the next minute they were dirt. I cried so my eyes nearly melted off. Also another time there was a thing in the night *nnnnng nnnnng nnnnng* biting me and Ma banged him against Door Wall below Shelf, he was a mosquito. The mark is still there on the cork even though she scrubbed, it was my blood the mosquito was stealing, like a teeny vampire. That's the only time my blood ever came out of me.

Ma takes her pill from the silver pack that has twenty-eight little spaceships and I take a vitamin from the bottle with the boy doing a handstand and she takes one from the big bottle with a picture of a woman doing Tennis. Vitamins are medicine for not getting sick and going back to Heaven yet. I never want to go, I don't like dying but Ma says it might be OK when we're a hundred and tired of playing. Also she takes a killer. Sometimes she takes two, never more than two, because some things are good for us but too much is suddenly bad.

"Is it Bad Tooth?" I ask. He's on the top near the back of her mouth, he's the worst.

Ma nods.

"Why you don't take two killers all the bits of every day?" She makes a face. "Then I'd be hooked."

"What's—?"

"Like stuck on a hook, because I'd need them all the time. Actually I might need more and more."

"What's wrong with needing?"

"It's hard to explain."

5 **Stove** oven – 20 **killer** *here*: painkiller

Ma knows everything except the things she doesn't remember right, or sometimes she says I'm too young for her to explain a thing.

"My teeth feel a bit better if I stop thinking about them," she tells me.

"How come?"

"It's called mind over matter. If we don't mind, it doesn't matter."

When a bit of me hurts, I always mind. Ma's rubbing my shoulder but my shoulder's not hurting, I like it anyway.

I still don't tell her about the web. It's weird to have something that's mine-not-Ma's. Everything else is both of ours. I guess my body is mine and the ideas that happen in my head. But my cells are made out of her cells so I'm kind of hers. Also when I tell her what I'm thinking and she tells me what she's thinking, our each ideas jump into our other's head, like coloring blue crayon on top of yellow that makes green.

At 08:30 I press the button on TV and try between the three. I find *Dora the Explorer,* yippee. Ma moves Bunny around real slow to better the picture with his ears and head. One day when I was four TV died and I cried, but in the night Old Nick brung a magic converter box to make TV back to life. The other channels after the three are totally fuzzy so we don't watch them because of hurting our eyes, only if there's music we put Blanket over and just listen through the gray of her and shake our booties.

Today I put my fingers on Dora's head for a hug and tell her about my superpowers now I'm five, she smiles. She has the most huge hair that's like a really brown helmet with pointy bits cutted out, it's as big as the rest of her. I sit back on Bed in Ma's lap to watch, I wriggle till I'm not on her pointy bones. She doesn't have many soft bits but they're super soft.

Dora says bits that aren't in real language, they're Spanish, like *lo hicimos.* She always wears Backpack who's more inside than out, with everything Dora needs like ladders and space

19 **Dora the Explorer** children's TV program – 21 **brung** Jack means "brought" – 30 **to wriggle** to move back and forth

suits, for her dancing and playing soccer and flute and having adventures with Boots her best friend monkey. Dora always says she's going to need *my* help, like can I find a magic thing, she waits for me to say, "Yeah." I shout out, "Behind the palm tree," and the blue arrow clicks right behind the palm tree, she says, "Thank you." Every TV person else doesn't listen. The Map shows three places every time, we have to go to the first to get to the second to get to the third. I walk with Dora and Boots, holding their hands, I join in all the songs especially with somersaults or high-fives or the Silly Chicken Dance. We have to watch out for that sneaky Swiper, we shout, "Swiper, no swiping," three times so he gets all mad and says, "Oh man!" and runs away. One time Swiper made a remote-controlled robot butterfly, but it went wrong, it swiped his mask and gloves instead, that was hilarious. Sometimes we catch the stars and put them in Backpack's pocket, I'd choose the Noisy Star that wakes up anything and the Switchy Star that can transform to all shapes.

On the other planets it's mostly persons that hundreds can fit into the screen, except often one gets all big and near. They have clothes instead of skin, their faces are pink or yellow or brown or patchy or hairy, with very red mouths and big eyes with black edges. They laugh and shout a lot. I'd love to watch TV all the time, but it rots our brains. Before I came down from Heaven Ma left it on all day long and got turned into a zombie that's like a ghost but walks *thump thump*. So now she always switches off after one show, then the cells multiply again in the day and we can watch another show after dinner and grow more brains in our sleep.

"Just one more, because it's my birthday? Please?"

Ma opens her mouth, then shuts it. Then she says, "Why not?" She mutes the commercials because they mush our brains even faster so they'd drip out our ears.

10 **somersault** *Rolle vorwärts* – 12 **to be mad at sb** *AE* angry with – 15 **hilarious** very funny – 24 **to rot** *here*: to corrupt – 32 **mute** Jack means "to make silent"

I watch the toys, there's an excellent truck and a trampoline and Bionicles. Two boys are fighting with Transformers in their hands but they're friendly not like bad guys.

Then the show comes, it's *SpongeBob SquarePants*. I run over to touch him and Patrick the starfish, but not Squidward, he's creepy. It's a spooky story about a giant pencil, I watch through Ma's fingers that are all twice longer than mine.

Nothing makes Ma scared. Except Old Nick maybe. Mostly she calls him just *him*, I didn't even know the name for him till I saw a cartoon about a guy that comes in the night called Old Nick. I call the real one that because he comes in the night, but he doesn't look like the TV guy with a beard and horns and stuff. I asked Ma once is he old, and she said he's nearly double her which is pretty old.

She gets up to switch TV off as soon as it's the credits.

My pee's yellow from the vitamins. I sit to poo, I tell it, "Bye-bye, off to the sea." After I flush I watch the tank filling up going *bubble gurgle wurble*. Then I scrub my hands till it feels like my skin's going to come off, that's how to know I've washed enough.

"There's a web under Table," I say, I didn't know I was going to. "It's of Spider, she's real. I've seen her two times."

Ma smiles but not really.

"Will you not brush it away, please? Because she isn't even there even, but she might come back."

Ma's down on her knees looking under Table. I can't see her face till she pushes her hair behind her ear. "Tell you what, I'll leave it till we clean, OK?"

That's Tuesday, that's three days. "OK."

"You know what?" She stands up. "We've got to mark how tall you are, now you're five."

I jump way in the air.

Usually I'm not allowed draw on any bits of Room or furnitures. When I was two I scribbled on the leg of Bed, her

15 **credits** list at the end of a film with the names of the actors

one near Wardrobe, so whenever we're cleaning Ma taps the scribble and says, "Look, we have to live with that forever." But my birthday tall is different, it's tiny numbers beside Door, a black 4, and a black 3 underneath, and a red 2 that was the color our old Pen was till he ran out, and at the bottom a red 1.

"Stand up straight," says Ma. Pen tickles the top of my head. When I step away there's a black 5 a little bit over the 4. I love five the best of every number, I have five fingers each hand and the same of toes and so does Ma, we're our dead spits. Nine is my worst favorite number. "What's my tall?"

"Your height. Well, I don't know exactly," she says. "Maybe we could ask for a measuring tape sometime, for Sunday treat."

I thought measuring tapes were just TV. "Nah, let's ask for chocolates." I put my finger on the 4 and stand with my face against it, my finger's on my hair. "I didn't get taller much this time."

"That's normal."

"What's normal?"

"It's—" Ma chews her mouth. "It means it's OK. *No hay problema.*"

"Look how big my muscles, though." I bounce on Bed, I'm Jack the Giant Killer in his seven-league boots.

"Vast," says Ma.

"Gigantic."

"Massive."

"Huge."

"Enormous," says Ma.

"Hugeormous." That's word sandwich when we squish two together.

"Good one."

"You know what?" I tell her. "When I'm ten I'll be growed up."

"Oh yeah?"

1 **to tap** to hit lightly – 12 **Sunday treat** sth special – 22 **seven-league boots** boots in which you walk go seven miles in one step (*Siebenmeilenstiefel*) – 31 **growed up** Jack means "grown up" *erwachsen*

"I'll get bigger and bigger and bigger till I turn into a human."

"Actually, you're human already," says Ma. "Human's what we both are."

I thought the word for us was real. The persons in TV are made just of colors.

"Did you mean a woman, with a *w*?"

"Yeah," I say, "a woman with a boy in an egg in my tummy and he'll be a real one too. Or I'm going to grow to a giant, but a nice one, up to here." I jump to touch Bed Wall way high, nearly where Roof starts slanting up.

"Sounds great," says Ma.

Her face is gone flat, that means I said a wrong thing but I don't know which.

"I'll burst through Skylight into Outer Space and go *boing boing* between each the planets," I tell her. "I'll visit Dora and SpongeBob and all my friends, I'll have a dog called Lucky."

Ma's put a smile on. She's tidying Pen back on Shelf.

I ask her, "How old are you going to be on your birthday?"

"Twenty-seven."

"Wow."

I don't think that cheered her up.

While Bath is running, Ma gets Labyrinth and Fort down from on top of Wardrobe. We've been making Labyrinth since I was two, she's all toilet roll insides taped together in tunnels that twist lots of ways. Bouncy Ball loves to get lost in Labyrinth and hide, I have to call out to him and shake her and turn her sideways and upside down before he rolls out, whew. Then I send other things into Labyrinth like a peanut and a broken bit of Blue Crayon and a short spaghetti not cooked. They chase each other in the tunnels and sneak up and shout *Boo,* I can't see them but I listen against the cardboard and I can figure out where they are. Toothbrush wants a turn but I tell him sorry, he's too long. He jumps in Fort instead to guard a tower. Fort's made of cans and vitamin bottles, we build him bigger every

10 **to slant up** to be at an angle, *die Schräge des Daches*

time we have an empty. Fort can see all ways, he squirts out boiling oil at the enemies, they don't know about his secret knife-slits, ha ha. I'd like to bring him into Bath to be an island but Ma says the water would make his tape unsticky.

We undo our ponytails and let our hair swim. I lie on Ma not even talking, I like the bang of her heart. When she breathes we go up and down a little bit. Penis floats.

Because of my birthday I get to choose what we wear both. Ma's live in the higher drawer of Dresser and mine in the lower. I choose her favorite blue jeans with the red stitches that she only puts on for special occasions because they're getting strings at the knees. For me I choose my yellow hoody, I'm careful of the drawer but the right edge still comes out and Ma has to bang it back in. We pull down on my hoody together and it chews my face but then pop it's on.

"What if I cut it just a little in the middle of the *V*?" says Ma.

"No way Jose."

For Phys Ed we leave our socks off because bare feet are grippier. Today I choose Track first, we lift Table upside down onto Bed and Rocker on her with Rug over the both. Track goes around Bed from Wardrobe to Lamp, the shape on Floor is a black *C*. "Hey, look, I can do a there-and-back in sixteen steps."

"Wow. When you were four it was eighteen steps, wasn't it?" says Ma. "How many there-and-backs do you think you can run today?" "Five."

"What about five times five? That would be your favorite squared."

We times it on our fingers, I get twenty-six but Ma says twenty-five so I do it again and get twenty-five too. She counts me on Watch. "Twelve," she shouts out. "Seventeen. You're doing great."

I'm breathing *whoo whoo whoo*.

"Faster—"

1 **to squirt** *herausspritzen* – 4 **unsticky** it will no longer stick – 5 **ponytail** *Pferdeschwanz* – 12 **hoody** pullover with a hood – 18 **Phys Ed** sports – 28 **to time** Jack means "to count"

I go even fasterer like Superman flying.

When it's Ma's turn to run, I have to write down on the College Ruled Pad the number at the start and the number when she's finished, then we take them apart to see how fast she went. Today hers is nine seconds bigger than mine, that means I winned, so I jump up and down and blow raspberries. "Let's do a race at the same time."

"Sounds like fun, doesn't it," she says, "but remember once we tried it and I banged my shoulder on the dresser?"

Sometimes when I forget things, Ma tells me and I remember them after that.

We take down all the furnitures from Bed and put Rug back where she was to cover Track so Old Nick won't see the dirty *C*.

Ma chooses Trampoline, it's just me that bounces on Bed because Ma might break her. She does the commentary: "A daring midair twist from the young U.S. champion ..."

My next pick is Simon Says, then Ma says to put our socks back on for Corpse, that's lying like starfish with floppy toenails, floppy belly button, floppy tongue, floppy brain even. Ma gets an itch behind her knee and moves, I win again.

It's 12:13, so it can be lunch. My favorite bit of the prayer is the daily bread. I'm the boss of play but Ma's the boss of meals, like she doesn't let us have cereal for breakfast and lunch and dinner in case we'd get sick and anyway that would use it up too fast. When I was zero and one, Ma used to chop and chew up my food for me, but then I got all my twenty teeth and I can gnash up anything. This lunch is tuna on crackers, my job is to roll back the lid of the can because Ma's wrist can't manage it.

I'm a bit jiggly so Ma says let's play Orchestra, where we run around seeing what noises we can bang out of things. I drum on Table and Ma goes *knock knock* on the legs of Bed, then *floomf floomf* on the pillows, I use a fork and spoon on Door *ding ding* and our toes go *bam* on Stove, but my favorite is stomping on the pedal of Trash because that pops his lid open

6 **to blow raspberries** *prusten* – 27 **to gnash** [næʃ] *here*: to bite – 27 **tuna** *Tunfisch* – 29 **jiggly** *here*: *zappelig* – 34 **Trash** rubbish bin

with a *bing*. My best instrument is Twang that's a cereal box I collaged with all different colored legs and shoes and coats and heads from the old catalog, then I stretched three rubber bands across his middle. Old Nick doesn't bring catalogs anymore for us to pick our own clothes, Ma says he's getting meaner.

I climb on Rocker to get the books from Shelf and I make a ten-story skyscraper on Rug. "Ten stories," says Ma and laughs, that wasn't very funny.

We used to have nine books but only four with pictures inside—

My Big Book of Nursery Rhymes
Dylan the Digger
The Runaway Bunny
Pop-Up Airport

Also five with pictures only on the front—

The Shack
Twilight
The Guardian
Bittersweet Love
The Da Vinci Code

Ma hardly ever reads the no-pictures ones except if she's desperate. When I was four we asked for one more with pictures for Sundaytreat and *Alice in Wonderland* came, I like her but she's got too many words and lots of them are old.

Today I choose *Dylan the Digger,* he's near the bottom so he does a demolition on the skyscraper *crashhhhhh.*

"Dylan again." Ma makes a face, then she puts on her biggest voice:

5 **mean** *geizig* – 22 **desperate** feeling awful – 26 **demolition** destruction

" 'Heeeeeeeeere's Dylan, the sturdy digger! The loads he shovels get bigger and bigger. Watch his long arm delve into the earth, No excavator so loves to munch dirt.

This mega-hoe rolls and pivots round the site, Scooping and grading by day and night.' "

There's a cat in the second picture, in the third it's on the pile of rocks. Rocks are stones, that means heavy like ceramic that Bath and Sink and Toilet are of, but not so smooth. Cats and rocks are only TV. In the fifth picture the cat falls down, but cats have nine lives, not like me and Ma with just one each.

Ma nearly always chooses *The Runaway Bunny* because of how the mother bunny catches the baby bunny in the end and says, "Have a carrot." Bunnies are TV but carrots are real, I like their loudness. My favorite picture is the baby bunny turned into a rock on the mountain and the mother bunny has to climb up up up to find him. Mountains are too big to be real, I saw one in TV that has a woman hanging on it by ropes. Women aren't real like Ma is, and girls and boys not either. Men aren't real except Old Nick, and I'm not actually sure if he's real for real. Maybe half? He brings groceries and Sundaytreat and disappears the trash, but he's not human like us. He only happens in the night, like bats. Maybe Door makes him up with a *beep beep* and the air changes. I think Ma doesn't like to talk about him in case he gets realer.

I wriggle around on her lap now to look at my favorite painting of Baby Jesus playing with John the Baptist that's his friend and big cousin at the same time. Mary's there too, she's cuddled in her Ma's lap that's Baby Jesus's Grandma, like Dora's *abuela*. It's a weird picture with no colors and some of the hands and feet aren't there, Ma says it's not finished. What started Baby Jesus growing in Mary's tummy was an angel zoomed down, like a ghost but a really cool one with feathers. Mary was all surprised, she said, "How can this be?" and then,

1 **digger** a person or a machine that moves earth – 3 **to munch** to eat, making a noise – 4 **hoe** *Hacke* – 4 **to pivot** ['pɪvət] to turn round – 21 **to disappear** Jack means "to take away" – 22 **bat** *Fledermaus* – 24 **realer** Jack means "more real"

"OK let it be." When Baby Jesus popped out of her vagina on Christmas she put him in a manger but not for the cows to chew, only warm him up with their blowing because he was magic.

Ma switches Lamp off now and we lie down, first we say the shepherd prayer about green pastures, I think they're like Duvet but fluffy and green instead of white and flat. (The cup overflowing must make an awful mess.) I have some now, the right because the left hasn't much in it. When I was three I still had lots anytime, but since I was four I'm so busy doing stuff I only have some a few times in the day and the night. I wish I could talk and have some at the same time but I only have one mouth.

I nearly switch off but not actually. I think Ma does because of her breath.

* * *

After nap Ma says she's figured out that we don't need to ask for a measuring tape, we can make a ruler ourselves.

We recycle the cereal box from Ancient Egyptian Pyramid, Ma shows me to cut a strip that's as big as her foot, that's why it's called a foot, then she puts twelve little lines. I measure her nose that's two inches long. My nose is one inch and a quarter, I write it down. Ma makes Ruler flip slo-mo somersaults up Door Wall where my talls are, she says I'm three feet three inches.

"Hey," I say, "let's measure Room."

"What, all of it?"

"Do we have something else to do?"

She looks at me strange. "I guess not."

I write down all the numbers, like the tall of Door Wall to the line where Roof starts equals six feet seven inches. "Guess

2 **manger** ['meɪndʒɚ] *Futtertrog* – 6 **pasture** grassy farm land – 17 **nap** a short sleep – 22 **inch** 25.4 mm. 12 inches = 1 foot = 30.48 cm – 23 **slo-mo** slow motion

what," I tell Ma, "every cork tile is nearly a bit bigger than Ruler."

"Doh," she says, slapping her head, "I guess they're a foot square, I must have made the ruler a little too short. Let's just count the tiles, then, that's easier."

I start counting the tall of Bed Wall, but Ma says all the walls are the same. Another rule is, the wide of the walls is the same as the wide of Floor, I count eleven feet going both ways, that means Floor is a square. Table is a circle so I'm confused, but Ma measures her across the middle where she's the very widest, that's three feet nine inches. My chair is three feet two inches tall and Ma's is the exact same, that's one less than me. Then Ma's a bit sick of measuring so we stop.

I color behind the numbers all different with our five crayons that are blue, orange, green, red, brown, when I'm all done the page looks like Rug but crazier, Ma says why don't I use it as my place mat for dinner.

I choose spaghetti tonight, there's a fresh broccoli as well that I don't choose, it's just good for us. I chop the broccoli into pieces with Zigzag Knife, sometimes I swallow some when Ma's not looking and she says, "Oh, no, where's that big bit gone?" but she isn't really mad because raw things make us extra alive.

Ma does the hotting up on the two rings of Stove that go red, I'm not allowed touch the knobs because it's Ma's job to make sure there's never a fire like in TV. If the rings ever go against something like a dish towel or our clothes even, flames would run all over with orange tongues and burn Room to ashes with us coughing and choking and screaming with the worst pain ever.

I don't like the smell of broccoli cooking, but it's not as bad as green beans. Vegetables are all real but ice cream is TV, I wish it was real too. "Is Plant a raw thing?"

"Well, yeah, but not the kind to eat."

"Why she doesn't have flowers anymore?"

1 **tile** [taɪl] *Fliese* – 21 **bit** piece – 22 **raw** [rɑː] uncooked – 23 **hotting up** Jack means "heating up" – 24 **knob** *Knopf, Regler*

Ma shrugs and stirs the spaghetti. “She got tired.”

“She should go to sleep.”

“She’s still tired when she wakes up. Maybe the soil in her pot doesn’t have enough food left in it.”

“She could have my broccoli.”

Ma laughs. “Not that kind of food, plant food.”

“We could ask for it, for Sundaytreat.”

“I’ve got a long list of things to ask for already.”

“Where?”

“Just in my head,” she says. She pulls out a worm of spaghetti and bites it. “I think they like fish.”

“Who do?”

“Plants, they like rotten fish. Or is it fish bones?”

“Yuck.”

“Maybe next time we have fish fingers, we can bury a bit under Plant.”

“Not one of my ones.”

“OK, a bit of one of mine.”

The why I like spaghetti best is the song of the meatball, I sing it when Ma fills our plates.

After dinner something amazing, we make a birthday cake. I bet it’s going to be *delicioso* with candles the same number as me and on fire like I’ve never seen for real.

I’m the best egg blower, I make the goo spill out nonstop. I have to blow three for the cake, I use the pin from the *Impression: Sunrise* picture because I think the crazy horse would get mad if I took down *Guernica,* even though I always put the pin back right after. Ma thinks *Guernica* is the best masterpiece because it’s realest, but actually it’s all mixed up, the horse is screaming with lots of teeth because there’s a spear stabbed in him, plus a bull and a woman holding a floppy kid with his head upside down and a lamp like an eye, and the worst is the big bulgy foot in the corner, I always think it’s going to stamp on me.

30 **spear** *Speer, Lanze* – 33 **bulgy** swollen

I get to lick the spoon, then Ma puts the cake into Stove's hot tummy. I try juggling with the eggshells all up at the same time. Ma catches one. "Little Jacks with faces?"

"Nah," I say.

"Will we make them a nest of flour dough? If we defrost those beets tomorrow, we could use the juice to make it purple ..."

I shake my head. "Let's add them to Eggsnake."

Eggsnake is more longer than all around Room, we've been making him since I was three, he lives in Under Bed all coiled up keeping us safe. Most of his eggs are brown but sometimes there's a white, some have patterns on from pencils or crayons or Pen or bits stuck on with flour glue, a foil crown and a yellow ribbon belt and threads and bits of tissue for hairs. His tongue is a needle, that keeps the red thread going right through him. We don't bring Eggsnake out much anymore because sometimes he tangles and his eggs get cracked around the holes or even fall off, and we have to use the bits for mosaics. Today I put his needle in one of the holes of the new eggs, I have to dangle it till it comes out the other hole all sharp, it's pretty tricky. Now he's three eggs longer, I extra gently wind him up again so all of him fits in Under Bed.

Waiting for my cake takes hours and hours, we breathe in the lovely air. Then when it's cooling we make stuff called icing but not cold like ice, it's sugar melted with water. Ma spreads it all over the cake. "Now you can put on the chocolates while I'm washing up."

"But there aren't any."

"Aha," she says, holding up the little bag and shaking it *shickety shick,* "I saved a few from Sunday treat three weeks ago."

"You sneaky Ma. Where?"

She zips her mouth shut. "What if I need a hiding place another time?"

"Tell me!"

2 **to juggle** *jonglieren* – 5 **flour dough** [doʊ] *Mehlteig* – 6 **beet** *Rote Bete* – 9 **to coil up** *zusammengerollt* – 31 **sneaky** ['sni:ki] clever – 32 **to zip** *schließen wie einen Reißverschluss*

Ma's not smiling anymore. "Shouting hurts my ears."

"Tell me the hidey place."

"Jack—"

"I don't like there to be hidey places."

"What's the big deal?"

"Zombies."

"Ah."

"Or ogres or vampires—"

She opens Cabinet and takes out the box of rice. She points in the dark hole. "It was just in with the rice that I hid them. OK?"

"OK."

"Nothing scary would fit in here. You can check anytime."

There's five chocolates in the bag, pink, blue, green, and two reds. Some of the color comes off on my fingers when I'm putting them on, I get icing on me and suck it every bit.

Then it's time for the candles but there aren't any.

"You're shouting again," says Ma, covering her ears.

"But you said a birthday cake, it's not a birthday cake if there's no five candles on fire."

She puffs her breath. "I should have explained better. That's what the five chocolates say, they say you're five."

"I don't want this cake." I hate it when Ma waits all quiet. "Stinky cake."

"Calm down, Jack."

"You should have asked for candles for Sundaytreat."

"Well, last week we needed painkillers."

"I didn't need any, just you," I shout.

Ma looks at me like I have a new face she's never seen. Then she says, "Anyway, remember, we have to choose things he can get easily."

"But he can get anything."

"Well, yeah," she says, "if he went to the trouble—"

"Why he went to trouble?"

8 **ogre** [ˈoʊgɚ] *Ungeheuer, Riese* – 13 **scary** frightening

"I just mean, he might have to go to two or three stores, and that would make him cranky. And what if he didn't find the impossible thing, then we probably wouldn't get Sunday treat at all."

"But Ma." I laugh. "He doesn't go in stores. Stores are in TV."

She's chewing her lip. Then she looks at the cake. "Well, anyway, I'm sorry, I thought the chocolates would do instead."

"Silly Ma."

"Dumbo." She slaps her head.

"Numbskull," I say, but not in a nasty way. "Next week when I'll be six you better get candles."

"Next year," says Ma, "you mean next year." Her eyes are shut. They always do that sometimes and she doesn't say anything for a minute. When I was small I thought her battery was used up like happened to Watch one time, we had to ask a new battery for him for Sundaytreat.

"Promise?"

"Promise," she says, opening her eyes.

She cuts me a humongous piece and I swipe all the five onto mine when she's not looking, the two reds, the pink, the green, the blue, and she says, "Oh, no, another one's been swiped, how did that happen?"

"You'll never find it now, ha ha ha," I say like Swiper when he swipes a thing from Dora. I pick up one of the reds and zoom it in Ma's mouth, she moves it to her front teeth that are less rotted and she nibbles it smiling.

"Look," I show her, "there's holes in my cake where the chocolates were till just now."

"Like craters," she says. She puts her fingertop in one. "What's craters?"

"Holes where something happened. Like a volcano or an explosion or something."

I put the green chocolate back in its crater and do ten, nine, eight, seven, six, five, four, three, two, one, boom. It flies up into

2 **cranky** bad tempered – 19 **humongous** Jack means "huge" – 23 **Swiper** figure in a children's TV series

Outer Space and around into my mouth. My birthday cake is the best thing I ever ate.

Ma isn't hungry for any right now. Skylight's sucking all the light away, she's nearly black. "It's the spring equinox," says Ma, "I remember it said on TV, the morning you were born. There was still snow that year too."

"What's equinox?"

"It means equal, when there's the same amount of dark and light."

It's too late for any TV because of the cake, Watch says 08:33. My yellow hoody nearly rips my head off when Ma's pulling it. I get into my sleep T-shirt and brush my teeth while Ma ties up the trash bag and puts it beside Door with our list that I wrote, tonight it says

Please, Pasta, Lentils, Tuna, Cheese (if not too $), O.J., Thanks.

"Can we ask for grapes? They're good for us."

At the bottom Ma puts *Grapes if poss (or any fresh fruit or canned).*

"Can I have a story?"

"Just a quick one. What about ... *GingerJack*?"

She does it really fast and funny, Gingerjack jumps out of the stove and runs and rolls and rolls and runs so nobody can catch him, not the old lady or the old man or the threshers or the plowers. But at the end he's an idiot, he lets the fox carry him across the river and gets eat up snap.

If I was made of cake I'd eat myself before somebody else could.

We do a quick quick prayer that's hands clicked together, eyes shut. I pray for John the Baptist and Baby Jesus to come around for a playdate with Dora and Boots. Ma prays for sunshine to melt the snow off Skylight.

"Can I have some?"

"First thing tomorrow," says Ma, pulling her T-shirt back down.

23 **thresher** *Drescher* – 24 **plower** or ploughman ['plaʊɚ] *Pflüger*

"No, tonight."

She points up at Watch that says 08:57, that's only three minutes before nine. So I run into Wardrobe and lie down on my pillow and wrap up in Blanket that's all gray and fleecy with the red piping. I'm just under the drawing of me I forgot was there. Ma puts her head in. "Three kisses?"

"No, five for Mr. Five."

She gives me five then squeaks the doors shut.

There's still light coming in the slats so I can see some of me in the drawing, the bits like Ma and the nose that's only like me. I stroke the paper, it's all silky. I go straight so my head is pressing on Wardrobe and so are my feet. I listen to Ma getting into her sleep T-shirt and taking the killers, always two at night because she says pain is like water, it spreads out as soon as she lies down. She spits toothpaste. "Our friend Zack has an itch on his back," she says.

I think of one. "Our friend Zah says blah blah blah."

"Our friend Ebeneezer lives in a freezer."

"Our friend Dora went to the store-a."

"That's a cheat rhyme," says Ma.

"Oh, man!" I groan like Swiper. "Our friend Baby Jesus … likes to eat cheeses."

"Our friend Spoon sang a song to the moon."

The moon is God's silver face that only comes on special occasions.

I sit and put my face up against the slats, I can see slices of TV that's off, Toilet, Bath, my blue octopus picture going curly, Ma putting our clothes back in Dresser. "Ma?"

"Mmm?"

"Why am I hided away like the chocolates?"

I think she's sitting on Bed. She talks quiet so I can hardly hear. "I just don't want him looking at you. Even when you were a baby, I always wrapped you up in Blanket before he came in."

"Would it hurt?"

"Would what hurt?"

"If he saw me."

"No, no. Go to sleep now," Ma tells me.

"Do the Bugs."

"Night-night, sleep tight, don't let the bugs bite."

The Bugs are invisible but I talk to them and sometimes count, last time I got to 347. I hear the snap of the switch and Lamp goes out all at the same second. Sounds of Ma getting under Duvet.

I've seen Old Nick through the slats some nights but never all of him close up. His hair has some white and it's smaller than his ears. Maybe his eyes would turn me to stone. Zombies bite kids to make them undead, vampires suck them till they're floppy, ogres dangle them by the legs and munch them up. Giants can be just as bad, *be he alive or be he dead I'll grind his bones to make my bread,* but Jack ran away with the golden hen and he was slithering down the Beanstalk quick quick. The Giant was climbing down after him but Jack shouted to his Ma for the ax, that's like our knives but bigger, and his Ma was too scared to chop the Beanstalk on her own but when Jack got to the ground they did it together and the Giant went smash with all his insides coming out, ha ha. Then Jack was Jack the Giant Killer.

I wonder if Ma's switched off already.

In Wardrobe I always try to squeeze my eyes tight and switch off fast so I don't hear Old Nick come, then I'll wake up and it'll be the morning and I'll be in Bed with Ma having some and everything OK. But tonight I'm still on, the cake is fizzing in my tummy. I count my top teeth with my tongue from right to left till ten, then my bottom teeth from left to right, then back the other way, I have to get to ten each time and twice ten equals twenty, that's how many I have.

There's no *beep beep,* it must be a lot after nine. I count my teeth again and get nineteen, I must have done it wrong or else one's disappeared. I nibble my finger just a bit and then another

3 **bug** insect that bites – 16 **to slither** *schlittern* – 16 **beanstalk** *Bohnenstange*

bit. I wait for hours. "Ma?" I whisper. "Is he not coming or yeah?"

"Doesn't look like it. Come on in."

I jump up and shove Wardrobe open, I'm in Bed in two secs. It's extra hot under Duvet, I have to put my feet out so they don't burn. I have lots, the left and then the right. I don't want to be asleep because then it won't be my birthday anymore.

* * *

There's light flashing at me, it stabs my eyes. I look out of Duvet but squinting. Ma standing beside Lamp and everything bright, then *snap* and dark again. Light again, she makes it last three seconds then dark, then light for just a second. Ma's staring up at Skylight. Dark again. She does this in the night, I think it helps her get to sleep again.

I wait till Lamp's off properly. I whisper in the dark, "All done?"

"Sorry I woke you," she says.

"That's OK."

She gets back into Bed colder than me, I tie my arms around her middle.

* * *

Now I'm five and one day.

Silly Penis is always standing up in the morning, I push him down.

When we're scrubbing hands after peeing, I sing "He's Got the Whole World in His Hands," then I can't think of another hands one, but the dickey bird one is about fingers.

"'Fly away Peter,
Fly away Paul.' "

9 **to stab** to strike forcefully

My two fingers zoom all around Room and nearly have a midair collision.

"'Come back Peter,
Come back Paul.' "

"I think they're actually angels," says Ma.

"Huh?"

"Or no, sorry, saints."

"What are saints?"

"Extra-holy people. Like angels with no wings."

I'm confused. "How come they fly off the wall, then?"

"No, that's the dickey birds, they can fly all right. I just mean they're named after Saint Peter and Saint Paul, two of Baby Jesus' friends."

I didn't know he has more friends after John the Baptist. "Actually, Saint Peter was in jail, one time—"

I laugh. "Babies don't go in jail."

"This happened when they were all grown up."

I didn't know Baby Jesus grows up. "Is Saint Peter a bad guy?"

"No, no, he was put in jail by mistake, I mean it was some bad police who put him there. Anyway, he prayed and prayed to get out, and you know what? An angel flew down and smashed the door open."

"Cool," I say. But I prefer when they're babies running around all nakedy together.

There's a funny banging sound and a *scrunch scrunch*. Brightness is coming in Skylight, the dark snow's nearly gone. Ma's looking up too, she's got a small smile on, I think the prayer did magic.

"Is it still the equals thing?"

"Oh, the equinox?" she says. "No, the light's starting to win a little bit."

She lets me have cake for breakfast, I never did that before. It's gone crunchy, but it's still good.

27 **dickey bird** (children's language) a small bird

TV is *Wonder Pets!*, pretty fuzzy, Ma keeps moving Bunny but he doesn't sharpen them up much. I make a bow on his wire ear with the purple ribbon. I wish it was *Backyardigans,* I haven't met them in ages. Sundaytreat's not here yet because Old Nick didn't come last night, actually that was the best bit of my birthday. What we asked is not very exciting anyway, new pants because my black ones have holes instead of knees. I don't mind the holes but Ma says they make me look homeless, she can't explain what that is.

After bath I play with the clothes. Ma's pink skirt is a snake this morning, he's having a quarrel with my white sock. "I'm Jack's best friend."

"No, I'm Jack's best friend."

"I banged you."

"I zapped you."

"I'm going to pow you with my shooter flyer pump."

"Yeah, well, I've got a jumbo megatron transformerblaster—"

"Hey," says Ma, "will we play Catch?"

"We don't have Beach Ball anymore," I remember her. He burst by accident when I kicked him against Cabinet super fast. I wanted to ask for another instead of stupid pants.

But Ma says we can make one, we scrunch up all the pages I've been practicing my writing on and fill a grocery bag and squeeze it till it's kind of ball shape, then we draw a scary face on it with three eyes. Wordy Ball doesn't go as high as Beach Ball did but every time we catch him he makes a loud *scrunch.* Ma's the best at catching, only it pings her bad wrist sometimes, and I'm the best at throwing.

Because of cake for breakfast we have Sunday pancakes for lunch instead. There isn't much mix left so they're thin ones that spread out, I like that. I get to fold them up, some of them crack. There's not much jelly, so we mix water in that too.

1 **fuzzy** not clear – 16 **pow** *Peng* – 27 **ping** *here*: hurt – 27 **wrist** *Handgelenk*

A corner of mine drips, Ma scrubs Floor with Sponge. "The cork's wearing away," she says with her teeth shut, "how are we supposed to keep it clean?"

"Where?"

"Here, where our feet rub."

I get down under Table, there's a hole in Floor with brown stuff underneath that's harder on my nail.

"Don't make it worse, Jack."

"I'm not, I'm just looking with my finger." It's like a tiny crater.

We move Table over to beside Bath so we can sunbathe on Rug right under Skylight where it's extra warm. I sing "Ain't No Sunshine," Ma does "Here Comes the Sun," I pick "You Are My Sunshine." Then I want some, the left is extra creamy this afternoon.

God's yellow face makes red through my lids. When I open it's too bright to look. My fingers do shadows on Rug, little squished ones.

Ma is snoozing.

I hear a sound so I get up not waking her. Over by Stove, a tiny scritchy scratchy sound.

An alive thing, an animal, for really real not TV. It's on Floor, eating something, maybe a crumb of pancake. It's got a tail, I think what it is is, what it is is a mouse.

I go nearer and *whee* it's gone under Stove so I hardly saw it, I never knowed anything could go so fast. "O Mouse," I say in a whisper so he won't be scared. That's how to talk to a mouse, it's in *Alice,* only she talks about her cat Dinah by mistake and the mouse gets nervous and swims away. I put my hands praying now, "O Mouse, come on back, please, please, please …"

I wait for hours but he doesn't come.

Ma's definitely asleep.

I open Refrigerator, she doesn't have much inside. Mice like cheese, but we haven't any left. I get out the bread and crumble

1 **to drip** to fall in drops – 2 **to wear away** to get thin – 17 **to squish** *zermatschen* – 28 **Alice** Jack is refering to his book *Alice in Wonderland*

a bit on a plate and put it down where Mouse was. I crouch down small and wait for more hours and hours.

Then the wonderfulest thing, Mouse puts his mouth out, it's pointy. I nearly jump in the air but I don't, I stay extra still. He comes up to the crumbs and sniffs. I'm only about two feet away, I wish I had Ruler to measure but he's tidied in Box in Under Bed and I don't want to move and scare Mouse. I watch his hands, his whiskers, his tail all curly. He's alive for real, he's the biggest alive thing I ever saw, millions of times bigger than the ants or Spider.

Then something smashes into Stove, *whaaaaaack.* I scream and stand on the plate by accident, Mouse is gone, where's he gone? Did the book break him? She's *Pop-Up Airport,* I look in all her pages but he's not there. The Baggage Claim is all ripped and won't stand up anymore.

Ma's got a weird face. "You made him gone," I shout at her.

She's got BrushPan, she's sweeping up the broken bits of plate. "What was this doing on the floor? Now we're down to two big plates and one small, that's *it*—"

The cook in *Alice* throws plates at the baby and a saucepan that almost takes off his nose.

"Mouse was liking the crumbs."

"Jack!"

"He was real, I saw him."

She drags Stove out, there's a little crack at the bottom of Door Wall, she gets the bundle of aluminum foil and starts pushing balls of it into the crack.

"Don't. Please."

"I'm sorry. But where there's one there's ten."

That's crazy math.

Ma puts down the foil and holds me hard by my shoulders. "If we let him stay, we'd soon be overrun with his babies. Stealing our food, bringing in germs on their filthy paws …"

"They could have my food, I'm not hungry."

8 **whiskers** *Barthaare* – 17 **BrushPan** Jack means "dustpan" *Kehrschaufel* – 33 **paw** an animal's foot

Ma's not listening. She shoves Stove back to Door Wall.

After, we use a little bit of tape to make the Hangar page stand up better in *Pop-Up Airport,* but the Baggage Claim is too torn to fix.

We sit curled up in Rocker and Ma reads me *Dylan the Digger* three times, that means she's sorry. "Let's ask for a new book for Sundaytreat," I say.

She twists her mouth. "I did, a few weeks ago; I wanted you to have one for your birthday. But he said to quit bugging him, don't we have a whole shelf of them already."

I look up past her head at Shelf, she could fit hundreds more books if we put some of the other things in Under Bed beside Eggsnake. Or on top of Wardrobe ... but that's where Fort and Labyrinth live. It's tricky figuring out where everything's home is. Ma sometimes says we have to throw things in the trash but I usually find a spot for them.

"He thinks we should just watch TV all the time."

That sounds fun.

"Then our brains would rot, like his," says Ma. She leans over to pick up *My Big Book of Nursery Rhymes.* She reads me one I choose from every page. My bests are the Jack ones, like *Jack Sprat* or *Little Jack Horner.*

Jack be nimble,
Jack be quick,
Jack jump over the candlestick.

I think he wanted to see if he could not burn his nightshirt. In TV there's pajamas instead, or nighties on girls. My sleep T-shirt is my biggest, it has a hole on the shoulder that I like to put my finger in it and tickle myself when I'm switching off. There's *Jackie Wackie pudding and pie,* but when I figured out to read I

9 **to quit** to stop – 20 **Nursery Rhymes** *old* and well-known songs for children – 23 **nimble** quick and clever

saw it's actually *Georgie Porgie*. Ma changed it to fit me, that's not lying, it's just pretending. Same with

Jack, Jack, the piper's son,
Stole a pig and away he run.

It actually says Tom in the book but Jack sounds better. Stealing is when a boy takes what belongs to some boy else, because in books and TV all persons have things that belong just to them, it's complicated.

It's 05:39 so we can have dinner, it's quick noodles. While they're in the hot water, Ma finds hard words to test me from the milk carton like *nutritional* that means food, and *pasteurized* that means laser guns zapped away the germs. I want more cake but Ma says beets chopped all juicy first. Then I have cake that's pretty crispy now and Ma does too, a little bit.

I get up on Rocker to find Games Box at the end of Shelf, tonight I pick Checkers and I'm going to be red. The pieces are like little chocolates, but I've licked them lots of times and they don't taste like anything. They stick to the board by magnetic magic. Ma likes Chess best but it aches my head.

At TV time she chooses the wildlife planet, there's turtles burying their eggs in sand. When Alice gets long with eating the mushroom, the pigeon's mad because she thinks Alice is a nasty serpent trying to eat her pigeon eggs. Here come the turtle babies out of their shells, but the turtle mothers are gone already, that's weird. I wonder if they meet sometime in the sea, the mothers and the babies, if they know each other or maybe they just swim on by.

The wildlife ends too quick so I switch over to two men only wearing shorts and sneakers and dripping hot. "Uh-oh, hitting's not allowed," I tell them. "Baby Jesus is going to be mad."

The one in yellow shorts bashes the hairy one on the eye. Ma groans as if she's hurting. "Do we have to watch this?"

2 **to pretend** *so tun als ob* – 16 **Checkers** a game *Dame* – 19 **Chess** a game *Schach* – 23 **serpent** a large snake – 25 **weird** [wɪrd] strange – 29 **sneakers** *Turnschuhe*

I tell her, "In a minute the police are going to come *weee-ahhh weee-ahhh weee-ahhh* and lock those bad guys up in jail." "Actually, boxing ... it's nasty but it's a game, it's kind of allowed if they have those special gloves on. Now time's up."

"One game of Parrot, that's good for vocabulary."

"OK." She goes over and switches to the red couch planet where the puffy-hair woman that's the boss asks the other persons questions and hundreds of other persons clap.

I listen extra hard, she's talking to a man with one leg, I think he lost the other in a war.

"Parrot," shouts Ma and she mutes them with the button.

"*Most poignant aspect, I think for all our viewers that's what's most deeply moving about what you endured*—" I run out of words.

"Good pronunciation," says Ma. "*Poignant* means sad." "Again."

"The same show?"

"No, a different."

She finds a news one that's even harder. "Parrot." She mutes it again.

"Ah, with the whole labeling debate coming hard on the heels of health-care reform, and bearing in mind of course the midterms—"

"Any more?" Ma waits. "Good, again. But it was *labor law,* not *labeling.*"

"What's the difference?"

"*Labeling* is stickers on tomatoes, say, and *labor law*—" I do a huge yawn.

"Never mind." Ma grins and switches the TV off.

I hate when the pictures disappear and the screen's just gray again. I always want to cry but just for a second.

I get on Ma's lap in Rocker with our legs all jumbled up. She's the wizard transformed into a giant squid and I'm Prince

5 **Parrot** Papagei; *here*: a TV programme – 7 **puffy-hair woman** *here*: the woman who runs the show – 12 **poignant** ['pɔɪnjənt] sad – 27 **labor law** *Arbeitsgesetz* – 33 **wizard** a man who has magic powers – 33 **squid** *Tintenfisch*

JackerJack and I escape in the end. We do tickles and Bouncy Bouncy and jaggedy shadows on Bed Wall.

Then I ask for JackerJackRabbit, he's always doing cunning tricks on that Brer Fox. He lies down in the road pretending to be dead and Brer Fox sniffs him and says, "I better not take him home, he's too stinky ..." Ma sniffs me all over and makes hideous faces and I try not to laugh so Brer Fox won't know I'm actually alive but I always do.

For a song I want a funny, she starts, " 'The worms crawl in, the worms crawl out—' "

" 'They eat your guts like sauerkraut—,' " I sing.

" 'They eat your eyes, they eat your nose—' "

" 'They eat the dirt between your toes—' "

I have lots on Bed but my mouth is sleepy. Ma carries me into Wardrobe, she tucks Blanket around my neck, I pull her looser again. My fingers go choo-choo along her red line.

Beep beep, that's Door. Ma jumps up and makes a sound, I think she hit her head. She shuts Wardrobe tight.

The air that comes in is freezing, I think it's a bit of Outer Space, it smells yum. Door makes his *thump* that means Old Nick's in now. I'm not sleepy anymore. I get up on my knees and look through the slats, but all I can see is Dresser and Bath and a curve of Table.

"Looks tasty." Old Nick's voice is extra deep.

"Oh, it's just the last of the birthday cake," says Ma.

"Should have reminded me, I could have brought him something. What's he now, four?"

I wait for Ma to say, but she doesn't. "Five." I whisper it.

But she must hear me, because she comes close to Wardrobe and says "Jack" in a mad voice.

Old Nick laughs, I didn't know he could. "It speaks."

Why does he say *it* not *he?*

"Want to come out of there and try on your new jeans?"

2 **jaggedy** Jack means "jagged" *gezackt* – 11 **guts** *Eingeweide* – 20 **yum** *sl lecker*

It's not Ma he's saying that to, it's me. My chest starts to go *dung dung dung.*

"He's nearly asleep," says Ma.

No I'm not. I wish I didn't whisper *five* so he heard me, I wish I didn't anything.

Something else I can't quite hear—

"OK, OK," Old Nick is saying. "Can I've a slice?"

"It's getting stale. If you really want—"

"No, forget it, you're the boss."

Ma doesn't say anything.

"I'm just the grocery boy, take out your trash, trek around the kidswear aisles, up the ladder to deice your skylight, at your service ma'am ..."

I think he's doing sarcasm, when he says the really opposite with a voice that's all twisty.

"Thanks for that." Ma doesn't sound like her. "It makes it much brighter."

"There, that didn't hurt, did it?"

"Sorry. Thanks a lot."

"Like pulling teeth sometimes," says Old Nick.

"And thanks for the groceries, and the jeans."

"You're welcome."

"Here, I'll get you a plate, maybe the middle's not too bad." There's some clinks, I think she's giving him cake. My cake. After a minute he talks blurry. "Yup, pretty stale."

His mouth is full of my cake.

Lamp goes off *snap,* that makes me jump. I don't mind dark but I don't like when it surprises me. I lie down under Blanket and I wait.

When Old Nick creaks Bed, I listen and count fives on my fingers, tonight it's 217 creaks. I always have to count till he makes that gaspy sound and stops. I don't know what would happen if I didn't count, because I always do.

7 **slice** *here*: piece – 8 **stale** *opp of* fresh – 12 **aisle** passage *here*: kidswear aisle: children's clothes department – 12 **to deice** [ˌdiːˈaɪs] to defrost – 15 **twisty** *opp of* straight forward – 25 **blurry** not clear – 30 **to creak** to make a harsh unpleasant sound, Jack means "makes the bed creak" – 32 **to gasp** to take a short, quick breath

What about the nights I'm asleep?

I don't know, maybe Ma does the counting.

After the 217 it's all quiet.

I hear the TV switch on, it's just the news planet, I see bits with tanks through the slats that's not very interesting. I put my head under Blanket. Ma and Old Nick are talking a bit but I don't listen.

* * *

I wake up in Bed and it's raining, that's when Skylight's all blurry. Ma gives me some and she's doing "Singing in the Rain" very quietly.

Right doesn't taste yummy. I sit up remembering. "Why you didn't tell him before that it was my birthday?"

Ma stops smiling. "You're meant to be asleep when he's here."

"But if you told him, he'd brung me something."

"Bring you something," she says. "So he says."

"What kind of something?" I wait. "You should have remembered him."

Ma stretches her arms over her head. "I don't want him bringing you things."

"But Sundaytreat—"

"That's different, Jack, that's stuff we need that I ask him for." She points to Dresser, there's a blue folded up. "There are your new jeans, by the way."

She goes over to pee.

"You could ask him for a present for me. I never got a present in my life."

"Your present was from me, remember? It was the drawing."

"I don't want the dumbo drawing." I'm crying.

Ma dries her hands and comes to hold me. "It's OK."

5 **tank** a military vehicle (*Panzer*) – 10 **blurry** not clear – 19 **to remember** Jack means "to remind" (*jmd erinnern*)

"It might—"

"I can't hear you. Take a big breath."

"It might—"

"Tell me what's the matter."

"It might be a dog."

"What might?"

I can't stop, I have to talk through the crying. "The present. It might be a dog turned to real, and we could call it Lucky."

Ma wipes my eyes with the flat of her hands. "You know we don't have room."

"Yeah we do."

"Dogs need walks."

"We walk."

"But a dog—"

"We run a long long way on Track, Lucky could go beside us. I bet he'd be faster than you."

"Jack. A dog would drive us nuts."

"No he wouldn't."

"He would so. Cooped up, with the barking, the scratching …"

"Lucky wouldn't be scratching."

Ma rolls her eyes. She goes over to Cabinet to get out the cereal, she pours it in our bowls not even counting.

I do a roaring lion face. "In the night when you're asleep, I'm going to be awake, I'll pull the foil out of the holes so Mouse will come back."

"Don't be silly."

"I'm not silly, you're the silly numbskull."

"Listen, I understand—"

"Mouse and Lucky are my friends." I'm crying again.

"There is no Lucky." Ma's talking with her teeth shut.

"Yeah there is and I love him."

"You just made him up."

15 **Track** a narrow path, *here*: *Laufbahn im Raum* – 17 **to drive us nuts** *inf* to make us go crazy – 19 **to be cooped up** to be shut in (enclosed) in a small space – 24 **roaring** making a very loud voice

"Also there's Mouse, he's my real friend and you made him gone—"

"Yeah," shouts Ma, "so he won't run over your face in the night and bite you."

I'm crying so much my breath's all whoopy. I never knowed Mouse would bite my face, I thought that was only vampires.

Ma drops down on Duvet and doesn't move.

After a minute I go beside her and lie down. I lift her T-shirt to have some, I have to keep stopping to wipe my nose. The left is good but there's not much.

Later I try on my new jeans. They keep falling down.

Ma pulls at a sticking-out thread.

"Don't."

"It was loose already. Cheap piece of—" She doesn't say what. "Denim," I tell her, "that's what jeans are made of." I put the thread in Cabinet in Crafts Tub.

Ma gets down Kit to sew some stitches in the waist, after that my jeans stay up.

We have a pretty busy morning. First we undo Pirate Ship that we made last week and turn it into Tank. Balloon is the driver, she used to be as big as Ma's head and pink and fat, now she's small like my fist only red and wrinkly. We only blow up one when it's the first of a month, so we can't make Balloon a sister till it's April. Ma plays with Tank too but not as long. She gets sick of things fast, it's from being an adult.

Monday is a laundry day, we get into Bath with socks, underwears, my gray pants that ketchup squirted on, the sheets and dish towels, and we squish all the dirt out. Ma hots Thermostat way up for the drying, she pulls Clothes Horse out from beside Door and stands him open and I tell him to be strong. I would love to ride him like when I was a baby but I'm so huge now I might break his back. It would be cool to sometimes go smaller again and sometimes bigger like Alice.

5 **whoppy** *keuchend* – 12 **thread** [θred] a long thin piece of cotton (*Faden*) – 16 **Crafts Tub** a container with needles and thread in it – 22 **fist** *Faust* – 27 **pants** *AE* trousers – 27 **to squirt** *spritzen*

When we've twisted the water out of everything and hanged them up, Ma and me have to rip off our T-shirts and take turns pushing ourselves into Refrigerator to cool down.

Lunch is bean salad, my second worst favorite. After nap we do Scream every day but not Saturdays or Sundays. We clear our throats and climb up on Table to be nearer Skylight, holding hands not to fall. We say "On your mark, get set, go," then we open wide our teeth and shout holler howl yowl shriek screech scream the loudest possible. Today I'm the most loudest ever because my lungs are stretching from being five.

Then we shush with fingers on lips. I asked Ma once what we're listening for and she said just in case, you never know.

Then I do rubbings of a fork and Comb and jar lids and the sides of my jeans. Ruled paper is smoothest for rubbings, but toilet paper is good for a drawing that goes on forever, like today I do me with a cat and a parrot and an iguana and a raccoon and Santa and an ant and Lucky and all my TV friends in a procession and I'm King Jack. When I'm all done I roll it again so we can use it for our butts. I take a fresh bit from the next roll for a letter to Dora, I have to sharpen the red pencil with Smooth Knife. I squeeze the pencil hard because it's so short it's nearly gone, I write perfectly only sometimes my letters go back to front. *I am five the day before yesterday, you can have the last bit of cake but there is no candles, bye love Jack.* It only tears a little on the *of*. "When will she get it?"

"Well," says Ma, "I'd imagine it'll take a few hours to reach the sea, then it'll wash up on a beach …"

She sounds funny from sucking an ice cube for Bad Tooth. Beaches and sea are TV but I think when we send a letter it turns them real for a bit. The poos sink and the letters float on the waves. "Who'll find it? Diego?"

2 **to rip off** to take off quickly – 5 **scream** a loud high-pitched cry – 5 **to clear your throat** *räuspern* – 11 **to shush** *inf* child's language for "to be quiet" – 13 **rubbing** a picture that you make by rubbing a wax crayon over a piece of paper which is placed on top of an object (*here*: on top of a fork and a comb) – 14 **ruled paper** paper that has thin, straight lines printed across it – 16 **iguana** *Leguan* – 17 **raccoon** *Waschbär* – 19 **butt** *AE inf* bottom (*Po*) – 30 **poo** Jack's word for feces ("*Kacka*")

"Probably. And he'll take it to his cousin Dora—"

"In his safari jeep. *Zoom zoom* through the jungle."

"So tomorrow morning, I'd say. Lunchtime at the latest."

The ice cube is making less bulge in Ma's face now. "Let's see?" She puts it out on her tongue.

"I think I have a bad tooth too."

Ma wails, "Oh, Jack."

"Really real for real. Ow, ow, ow."

Her face changes. "You can suck an ice cube if you want, you don't have to have a toothache."

"Cool."

"Don't scare me like that."

I didn't know I could scare her. "Maybe it'll hurt when I'm six." She puffs her breath when she's getting the cubes out of Freezer. "Liar, liar, pants on fire."

But I wasn't lying, only pretending.

It's rainy all the afternoon, God doesn't look in at all. We sing "Stormy Weather" and "It's Raining Men" and the one about the desert missing the rain.

Dinner is fish sticks and rice, I get to squirt the lemon that's not an actual but a plastic. We had a real lemon once but it shriveled up too fast. Ma puts a bit of her fish stick under Plant in the soil.

The cartoon planet's not in evenings, maybe because it's dark and they don't have lamps there. I choose a cooking tonight, it's not like real food, they don't have any cans. The she and the he smile at each other and do a meat with a pie on top and green things around other green things in bunches. Then I switch over to the fitness planet where persons in underwear with all machines have to keep doing things over and over, I think they're locked in. That's over soon and it's the knockerdowners, they make houses into different shapes and also millions of

12 **to scare** to frighten – 19 **desert** ['dezɚt] *e.g.* the Sahara – 22 **to shrivel** to become dry and wrinkled – 28 **bunch** *Bund, Büschel* – 31 **to be locked in** to be unable to get out of somewhere (*eingeschlossen*) – 31 **knockerdowners** Jack's language for "to knock down, to demolish"

colors with paint, not just on a picture but all over everything. Houses are like lots of Rooms stuck together, TV persons stay in them mostly but sometimes they go in their outsides and weather happens to them.

"What if we put the bed over there?" says Ma.

I stare at her, then I look where she's pointing. "That's TV Wall."

"That's just what we call it," she says, "but the bed could probably fit there, between the toilet and … we'd have to shift the wardrobe over a bit. Then the dresser would be right here instead of the bed, with the TV on top of it."

I'm shaking my head a lot. "Then we couldn't see."

"We could, we'd be sitting right here in the rocker."

"Bad idea."

"OK, forget it." Ma folds her arms tight.

The TV woman is crying because her house is yellow now. "Did she like it brown better?" I ask.

"No," says Ma, "she's so happy it's making her cry."

That's weird. "Is she happysad, like you get when there's lovely music on TV?"

"No, she's just an idiot. Let's switch the TV off now." "Five more minutes? Please?"

She shakes her head.

"I'll do Parrot, I'm getting even better." I listen hard to the TV woman. I say, " *Dream come to life, I have to tell you Darren it's just beyond my very wildest imaginings, the cornices—*"

Ma hits the off. I want to ask her what a cornices is but I think she's still cranky about moving the furniture, that was a crazy plan.

In Wardrobe I should be going to sleep but I'm counting fights. That's three we had in three days, one about the candles and one about Mouse and one about Lucky. I'd rather be four again if five means fighting all the days.

19 **happysad** Jack means "happy and sad at the same time" – 26 **cornice** border around the top of a wall (just for decoration) (*Kranzleiste*) – 28 **cranky** *inf* in a bad mood

"Good night, Room," I say very quiet. "Good night, Lamp and Balloon."

"Good night, stove," says Ma, "and good night, table."

I'm grinning. "Good night, Wordy Ball. Good night, Fort. Good night, Rug."

"Good night, air," says Ma.

"Good night, noises everywhere."

"Good night, Jack."

"Good night, Ma. And Bugs, don't forget the Bugs." "Night-night," she says, "sleep tight, don't let the bugs bite."

* * *

When I wake up, Skylight's all blue in her glass, there's no snow left even in the corners. Ma's sitting in her chair holding her face, that means hurting. She's looking at something on Table, two things.

I jump up and grab. "It's a jeep. A remote-control jeep!" I'm zooming it in the air, it's red, as big as my hand. The remote is silver and a rectangle, when I wiggle one of the switches with my thumb the jeep's wheels spin *zhhhhung*.

"It's a late birthday present."

I know who brung it, it's Old Nick but she won't say.

I don't want to eat my cereal but Ma says I can play with the jeep again right after. I eat twenty-nine of them, then I'm not hungry anymore. Ma says that's waste, so she eats the rest.

I figure out to move Jeep just with Remote. The thin silver antenna, I can make it really long or really short. One switch makes Jeep go forward and backward, the other does side to side. If I flip both the same time, Jeep gets paralyzed like by a poison dart, he says *arghhhhhh*.

Ma says she'd better start cleaning because it's Tuesday. "Gently," she says, "remember it's breakable."

I know that already, everything's breakable.

18 **rectangle** *Rechteck* – 18 **to wiggle** to move up and down – 28 **poison dart** a small object with a sharp point which is deadly

"And if you keep it turned on for a long time the batteries will get used up, and we don't have any spares."

I can make Jeep go all around Room, it's easy except at the edge of Rug, she gets curled up under his wheels. Remote is the boss, he says, "Off you go now, you slowcoach Jeep. Twice around that Table leg, lickety-split. Keep those wheels turning." Sometimes Jeep is tired, Remote turns his wheels *grrrrrrrr*. That naughty Jeep hides in Wardrobe but Remote finds him by magic and makes him zoom back and forward crashing into the slats.

Tuesdays and Fridays always smell of vinegar. Ma's scrubbing under Table with the rag that used to be one of my diapers I wore till I was one. I bet she's wiping Spider's web away but I don't care much. Then she picks up Vacuum who makes it all noisy dusty *wah wah wah*.

Jeep sneaks way off in Under Bed. "Come back, my little baby Jeepy," says Remote. "If you become a fish in the river, I will be a fisherman and catch you in my net." But that tricksy Jeep stays quiet till Remote is having a nap with his antenna all the way down, then Jeep sneaks up behind him and takes out his batteries ha ha ha.

I play with Jeep and Remote all day except when I'm in Bath they have to park on Table not to get rusty. When we do Scream I push them up really near Skylight and Jeep *vrums* his wheels as loud as he can.

Ma lies down again holding her teeth. Sometimes she does a big breath out out out.

"Why are you hissing so long?"

"Trying to get on top of it."

I go sit by her head and stroke her hair out of her eyes, her forehead is slippy. She grabs my hand and holds it tight. "It's OK."

11 **vinegar** ['vɪnegɚ] sour liquid used to make a salad dressing (*Essig*) – 12 **diaper** *AE* absorbent towel worn by babies abound their bottoms (*Pampers*) – 16 **to sneak** to go somewhere quietly trying not to be seen or heard – 23 **rusty** affected by rust (*rostig*)

It doesn't look OK. "You want to play with Jeep and Remote and me?"

"Maybe later."

"If you play you won't mind and you won't matter."

She smiles a bit but the next breath comes out louder like a moan.

At 05:57 I say, "Ma, it's nearly six," so she gets up to make dinner but she doesn't eat any. Jeep and Remote wait in Bath because it's dry now, it's their secret cave. "Actually Jeep died and went to Heaven," I say, eating my chicken slices really fast.

"Oh, yeah?"

"But then in the night when God was asleep, Jeep snuck out and slid down the Beanstalk to Room to visit me."

"That was cunning of him."

I eat three green beans and have a big drink of milk and another three, they go down a bit faster in threes. Five would be fasterer but I can't manage that, my throat would shut. One time I was four, Ma wrote *Green beans / other froz green veg* on the shopping list and I scribbled out *Green beans* with the orange pencil, she thought it was funny. At the end I have the soft bread because I like to keep it in my mouth like a cushion. "Thanks, Baby Jesus, especially for the chicken slices," I say, "and please no more green beans for a long time. Hey, why do we thank Baby Jesus and not him?"

"Him?"

I nod at Door.

Her face gets flat even though I didn't say his name. "Why should we thank him?"

"You did the other night, for the groceries and the snow offing and the pants."

"You shouldn't listen." Sometimes when she's really mad her mouth doesn't really open. "It was a fake thank."

9 **cave** a large hole (*Höhle*) – 12 **to sneak out** to go somewhere very quietly – 14 **cunning** clever, but in a negative and tricky way; devious – 29 **snow offing** Jack means: "the fact that Old Nick clears the snow off (the skylight?)" – 32 **fake** not genuine (*unecht*)

"Why it—?"

She butts in. "He's only the bringer. He doesn't actually make the wheat grow in the field."

"Which field?"

"He can't make the sun shine on it, or the rain fall, or anything."

"But Ma, bread doesn't come out of fields."

She presses on her mouth.

"Why you said—?"

"It must be time for TV," she says fast.

It's videos, I love them. Ma does the moves with me most times but not tonight. I jump on Bed and teach Jeep and Remote to shake their booties. It's Rihanna and T.I. and Lady Gaga and Kanye West. "Why do rappers wear shades even in the night," I ask Ma, "are their eyeballs sore?"

"No, they just want to look cool. And not have fans staring into their faces all the time because they're so famous."

I'm confused. "Why the fans are famous?"

"No, the stars are."

"And they don't want to be?"

"Well, I guess they do," says Ma, getting up to switch off the TV, "but they want to stay a bit private as well."

When I'm having some, Ma won't let me bring Jeep and Remote into Bed even though they're my friends. And then she says they have to go up on Shelf while I'm sleeping. "Otherwise they'll poke you in the night."

"No they won't, they promise."

"Listen, let's put your jeep away, then you can sleep with the remote because it's smaller, as long as the antenna's right down. Deal?"

"Deal."

When I'm in Wardrobe, we talk through the slats. "God bless Jack," she says.

2 **to butt in** to interrupt rudely – 14 **shades** *inf* sunglasses – 15 **sore** ill, infected – 26 **to poke** to push sb with sth sharp – 30 **deal** *here*: Is that a deal? Is that an agreement?

"God bless Ma and magic her teeth better. God bless Jeep and Remote."

"God bless books."

"God bless everything here and Outer Space and Jeep as well. Ma?"

"Yeah."

"Where are we when we're asleep?"

I can hear her yawn. "Right here."

"But dreams." I wait. "Are they TV?" She still doesn't answer. "Do we go into TV for dreaming?"

"No. We're never anywhere but here." Her voice sounds a long way away.

I lie curled up touching the switches with my fingers. I whisper "Can't you sleep, little switches? It's OK, have some." I put them at my nipples, they take turns. I'm sort of asleep but only nearly.

Beep beep. That's Door.

I listen very hard. In comes the cold air. If I had my head out of Wardrobe, there'd be Door opening, I bet I could see right into the stars and the spaceships and the planets and the aliens zooming around in UFOs. I wish I wish I wish I could see it.

Boom, that's Door shutting and Old Nick is telling Ma how there wasn't any of something and something else was a ridiculous price anyway.

I wonder if he looked up on Shelf and saw Jeep. Yeah he brung him for me, but he never played with him I don't think. He won't know how Jeep suddenly goes when I switch Remote on, *vrummmm.*

Ma and him only talk for a bit tonight. Lamp goes off *click* and Old Nick creaks the bed. I count in ones sometimes instead of fives just for different. But I start losing count so I switch to fives that go faster, I count to 378.

All quiet. I think he must be asleep. Does Ma switch off when he's off or does she stay awake waiting for him to be gone?

1 **(to) magic** Jack means "to make your teeth better by magic" – 33 **to switch off** *here*: to fall asleep

Maybe they're both off and me on, that's weird. I could sit up and crawl out of Wardrobe, they wouldn't even know. I could draw a picture of them in Bed or something. I wonder are they beside each other or opposite sides.

Then I have a terrible idea, what if he's having some? Would Ma let him have some or would she say, *No way Jose, that's only for Jack?*

If he had some he might start getting realer.

I want to jump up and scream.

I find Remote's on switch, I make it green. Wouldn't it be funny if his superpowers started Jeep's wheels spinning up there on Shelf? Old Nick might wake up all surprised ha ha.

I try the forward switch, nothing happens. Doh, I forgot to put up the antenna. I make it all the way long and try again but Remote still doesn't work. I poke his antenna through the slats, it's outside and I'm inside all at the same time. I flick the switch. I hear a tiny sound that must be Jeep's wheels coming alive and then—

SMASHSHSHSHSHSH.

Old Nick roaring like I never heard him, something about Jesus but it wasn't Baby Jesus that did it, it was me. Lamp's on, light's banging in the slats at me, my eyes squeeze shut. I wriggle back and pull Blanket over my face.

He's shouting, "What are you trying to pull?"

Ma sounds all wobbly, she says, "What, what? Did you have a bad dream?"

I'm biting Blanket, soft like gray bread in my mouth.

"Did you try something? Did you?" His voice goes downer. "Because I told you before, it's on your head if—"

"I was asleep." Ma's talking in a squashed tiny voice. "Please—look, look, it was the stupid jeep that rolled off the shelf."

Jeep's not a stupid.

"I'm sorry," Ma's saying, "I'm so sorry, I should have put it somewhere it wouldn't fall. I'm really really totally—"

15 **to poke sth through** to push sth sharply into a hole or gap – 16 **to flick** *schnippen* – 25 **wobbly** *inf* unsteady

"OK."

"Look, let's turn the light off—"

"Nah," says Old Nick, "I'm done."

Nobody says anything, I count one hippopotamus two hippopotamus three hippopotamus—

Beep beep, Door opens and shuts *boom*. He's gone.

Lamp clicks off again.

I feel around on the floor of Wardrobe for Remote, I find a terrible thing. His antenna all short and sharp, it must have snapped in the slats.

"Ma," I whisper.

No answer.

"Remote got broke."

"Go to sleep." Her voice is so hoarse and scary I think it's not her.

I count my teeth five times, I get twenty every time but I still have to do it again. None of them hurt yet but they might when I'm six. I must be asleep but I don't know it, because then I wake up.

I'm still in Wardrobe, it's all dark. Ma didn't bring me into Bed yet. Why she didn't bring me in?

I push the doors and listen for her breath. She's asleep, she can't be mad in her sleep, can she?

I crawl under Duvet. I lie near Ma not touching, there's all heat around her.

4 **hippopotamus** *Nilpferd* (Jack is counting "hippopotamus" for each second, out of habit) – 14 **hoarse** [hɔːrs] rough and unclear

Unlying

In the morning we're eating oatmeal and I see marks. "You're dirty on your neck." Ma just drinks some water, the skin moves when she swallows. Actually that's not dirt, I don't think.

I have a bit of oatmeal but it's too hot, I spit it back in Meltedy Spoon. I think Old Nick put those marks on her neck. I try saying but nothing comes out. I try again. "Sorry I made Jeep fall down in the night."

I get off my chair, Ma lets me onto her lap. "What were you trying to do?" she asks, her voice is still hoarse.

"Show him."

"What's that?"

"I was, I was, I was—"

"It's OK, Jack. Slow down."

"But Remote got snapped and you're all mad at me."

"Listen," says Ma, "I couldn't care less about the jeep." I blink at her. "He was my present."

"What I'm mad about"—her voice is getting bigger and scratchier—"is that you woke him up."

"Jeep?"

"Old Nick."

It makes me jump that she says him out loud.

"You scared him."

"He got scared at *me?*"

"He didn't know it was you," says Ma. "He thought I was attacking him, dropping something heavy on his head."

I hold my mouth and my nose but the giggles fizz out.

"It's not funny, it's the opposite of funny."

I see her neck again, the marks that he put on her, I'm all done giggling.

The oatmeal's still too hot so we go back to Bed for a cuddle.

This morning it's *Dora*, yippee. She's on a boat that nearly crashes into a ship, we have to wave our arms and shout,

31 **cuddle** putting your arms around sb and holding them close

"Watch out," but Ma doesn't. Ships are just TV and so is the sea except when our poos and letters arrive. Or maybe they actually stop being real the minute they get there? Alice says if she's in the sea she can go home by the railway, that's old-fashioned for trains. Forests are TV and also jungles and deserts and streets and skyscrapers and cars. Animals are TV except ants and Spider and Mouse, but he's gone back now. Germs are real, and blood. Boys are TV but they kind of look like me, the me in Mirror that isn't real either, just a picture. Sometimes I like to undo my ponytail and put all my hair over and worm my tongue through, then stick my face out to say boo.

It's Wednesday so we wash hair, we make turbans of bubbles out of Dish Soap. I look all around Ma's neck but not at it.

She does me a mustache, it's too tickly so I rub it off. "What about a beard, then?" she says. She puts all bubbles on my chin for a beard.

"Ho ho ho. Is Santa a giant?"

"Ah, I guess he's pretty big," says Ma.

I think he must be real because he brung us the million chocolates in the box with the purple ribbon.

"I'm going to be Jack the Giant Giant Killer. I'll be a good giant, I'll find all the evil ones and knock their heads off *smush splat.*"

We make drums different from filling up the glass jars more or waterfalling some out. I make one into a jumbo megatron transformermarine with an antigravity blaster that's actually Wooden Spoon.

I twist around to look at the *Impression: Sunrise*. There's a black boat with two tiny persons and God's yellow face above and blurry orange light on the water and blue stuff that's other boats I think, it's hard to know because it's art.

For Phys Ed Ma chooses Islands, that's I stand on Bed and Ma puts the pillows and Rocker and chairs and Rug all folded up and Table and Trash in surprising places. I have to visit every

14 **mustache** *AmE* hair that grows on a man's upper lip – 26 **antigravity blaster** science-fiction type, nonsense words

island not twice. Rocker's the trickiest, she's always trying to catapult me down. Ma swims around being the Loch Ness Monster trying to eat my feet.

My go, I choose Pillowfight, but Ma says actually the foam's starting to come out of my pillow so better do Karate instead. We always bow to respect our opponent. We go *Huh* and *Hi-yah* really fierce. One time I chop too hard and hurt Ma's bad wrist but by accident.

She's tired so she chooses Eye Stretch because that's lying down side by side on Rug with arms by sides so we both fit. We look at far things like Skylight then near like noses, we have to see between them quick quick.

While Ma's hotting up lunch I zoom poor Jeep everywhere because he can't go on his own anymore. Remote pauses things, he freezes Ma like a robot. "Now on," I say.

She stirs the pot again, she says, "Grub's up."

Vegetable soup, *bluhhhhh*. I blow bubbles to make it funner.

I'm not tired for nap yet so I get some books down. Ma does the voice, "*Heeeeeeeeere's Dylan!*" Then she stops. "I can't stand Dylan."

I stare at her. "He's my friend."

"Oh, Jack—I just can't stand the book, OK, I don't—it's not that I can't stand Dylan himself."

"Why you can't stand *Dylan* the book?"

"I've read it too many times."

But when I want something I want it always, like chocolates, I never ate a chocolate too many times.

"You could read it yourself," she says.

That's silly, I could read all them myself, even *Alice* with her old-fashioned words. "I prefer when you read them."

Her eyes are all hard and shiny. Then she opens the book again.

"'*Heeeeeeeeere's Dylan!*'"

16 **to stir** to move a spoon around (*rühren*) – 16 **Grub's up!** *inf* "Food is ready to eat!" – 17 **funner** Jack means "funnier"

Because she's cranky I let her do *The Runaway Bunny*, then some *Alice*. My best of the songs is "Soup of the Evening," I bet it's not vegetable. Alice keeps being in a hall with lots of doors, one is teeny tiny, when she gets it open with the golden key there's a garden with bright flowers and cool fountains but she's always the wrong size. Then when she finally gets into the garden, it turns out the roses are just painted not real and she has to play croquet with flamingos and hedgehogs.

We lie down on top of Duvet. I have lots. I think Mouse just might come back if we're really quiet but he doesn't, Ma must have stuffed up every single hole. She's not mean but sometimes she does mean things.

When we get up we do Scream, I crash the pan lids like cymbals. Scream goes on for ages because every time I'm starting to stop Ma screeches some more, her voice is nearly disappearing. The marks on her neck are like when I'm painting with beet juice. I think the marks are Old Nick's fingerprints.

After, I play Telephone with toilet rolls, I like how the words boom when I talk through a fat one. Usually Ma does all the voices but this afternoon she needs to lie down and read. It's *The Da Vinci Code* with the eyes of a woman peeking out, she looks like Baby Jesus's Ma.

I call Boots and Patrick and Baby Jesus, I tell them all about my new powers now I'm five. "I can be invisible," I whisper at my phone, "I can turn my tongue inside out and go blasting like a rocket into Outer Space."

Ma's eyelids are shut, how can she be reading through them?

I play Keypad, that's I stand on my chair by Door and usually Ma says the numbers but today I have to make them up. I press them on Keypad quick quick no mistakes. The numbers don't make Door beep open but I like the little clicks when I push them.

8 **croquet** ['kroʊkeɪ] a game played on a lawn with a large hammer, balls and hoops, mainly in Britain – 8 **hedgehog** *Igel* – 11 **mean** *inf* unkind – 14 **cymbals** musical instrument (*Becken*) – 25 **to blast** to destroy or damage with an explosion – 28 **keypad** an electronic lock that opens when a set of figures are pressed

Dress-up is a quiet game. I put on the royal crown that's some bits gold foil and some bits silver foil and milk carton underneath. I invent Ma a bracelet out of two socks of her tied together, one white one green.

I get down Games Box from Shelf. I measure with Ruler, each domino is nearly one inch and the checkers are a half. I make my fingers into Saint Peter and Saint Paul, they bow to each other before and do flying after each turn.

Ma's eyes are open again. I bring her the sock bracelet, she says it's beautiful, she puts it on right away.

"Can we play Beggar My Neighbor?"

"Give me a second," she says. She goes to Sink and washes her face, I don't know why because it wasn't dirty but maybe there were germs.

I beggar her twice and she beggars me once, I hate losing. Then Gin Rummy and Go Fish, I win mostly. Then we just play with the cards, dancing and fighting and stuff. Jack of Diamonds is my favorite and his friends the other Jacks.

"Look." I point to Watch. "05:01, we can have dinner." It's a hot dog each, yum.

For TV I go in Rocker but Ma sits on Bed with Kit, she's putting the hem back up on her brown dress with pink bits. We watch the medical planet where doctors and nurses cut holes in persons to pull the germs out. The persons are asleep not dead. The doctors don't bite the thread like Ma, they use super sharp daggers and after, they sew the persons up like Frankenstein.

When the commercials come on Ma asks me to go over and press mute. There's a man in a yellow helmet drilling a hole in a street, he holds his forehead and makes a face. "Is he hurting?" I ask.

She looks up from sewing. "He must have a headache from that noisy drill."

1 **crown** kings or queens wear a crown at official ceremonies – 3 **bracelet** a band around one's wrist (*Armband*) – 11 **Beggar My Neighbor** a card game – 22 **hem** the bottom edge of a dress or skirt (*Saum*) – 26 **to sew** [soʊ] to stitch together using a needle and thread (*nähen*) – 29 **Is he hurting?** Jack means: "Is he in pain?"

We can't hear the drill because it's on mute. The TV man's at a sink taking a pill from a bottle, next he's smiling and throwing a ball on a boy. "Ma, Ma."

"What?" She's doing a knot.

"That's our bottle. Were you looking? Were you looking at the man with the headache?"

"No."

"The bottle where he took the pill, that's the exact one we've got, the killers."

Ma stares at the TV, but it's showing a car speeding around a mountain now.

"No, before," I say. "He actually had our bottle of killers." "Well, maybe it was the same kind as ours, but it's not our one." "Yeah it is."

"No, there's lots of them."

"Where?"

Ma looks at me, then back at her dress, she pulls at the hem. "Well, our bottle is right here on Shelf, and the rest are ..."

"In TV?" I ask.

She's staring at the threads and winding them around the little cards to fit back in Kit.

"You know what?" I'm bouncing. "You know what that means? He must go in TV." The medical planet's come back on but I'm not even watching. "Old Nick," I say, so she won't think I mean the man in the yellow helmet. "When he's not here, in the daytime, you know what? He actually goes in TV. That's where he got our killers in a store and brung them here."

"Brought," says Ma, standing up. "Brought, not brung. It's time for bed." She starts singing "Indicate the Way to My Abode" but I don't join in.

I don't think she understands how amazing this is. I think about it right through putting on my sleep T-shirt and brushing my teeth and even when I'm having some on Bed. I take my mouth back, I say, "How come we never see him in TV?"

29 **abode** *old* a place where one lives; home

Ma yawns and sits up.

"All the times we're watching, we never see him, how come?"

"He's not there."

"But the bottle, how did he get it?"

"I don't know."

The way she says it, it's strange. I think she's pretending. "You have to know. You know everything."

"Look, it really doesn't matter."

"It does matter and I do mind." I'm nearly shouting.

"Jack—"

Jack what? What does *Jack* mean?

Ma leans back on the pillows. "It's very hard to explain."

I think she can explain, she just won't. "You can, because I'm five now."

Her face is turned toward Door. "Where our bottle of pills used to be, right, is a store, that's where he got them, then he brought them here for Sunday treat."

"A store in TV?" I look up at Shelf to check the bottle's there. "But the killers are real—"

"It's a real store." Ma rubs her eye.

"How—?"

"OK, OK, OK."

Why is she shouting?

"Listen. What we see on TV is … it's pictures of real things."

That's the most astonishing I ever heard.

Ma's got her hand over her mouth.

"Dora's real for real?"

She takes her hand away. "No, sorry. Lots of TV is made-up pictures—like, Dora's just a drawing—but the other people, the ones with faces that look like you and me, they're real."

"Actual humans?"

She nods. "And the places are real too, like farms and forests and airplanes and cities …"

27 **Dora** "the Explorer": a children's program on TV

"Nah." Why is she tricking me? "Where would they fit?" "Out there," says Ma. "Outside." She jerks her head back. "Outside Bed Wall?" I stare at it.

"Outside Room." She points the other way now, at Stove Wall, her finger goes around in a circle.

"The stores and forests zoom around in Outer Space?" "No. Forget it, Jack, I shouldn't have—"

"Yes you should." I shake her knee hard, I say, "Tell me." "Not tonight, I can't think of the right words to explain." Alice says she can't explain herself because she's not herself, she knows who she was this morning but she's changed several times since then.

Ma suddenly stands up and gets the killers down off Shelf, I think she's checking are they the same as the ones in TV but she opens the bottle and eats one then another one.

"Will you find the words tomorrow?"

"It's eight forty-nine, Jack, would you just go to bed?" She ties the trash bag and puts it beside Door.

I lie down in Wardrobe but I'm wide awake.

* * *

Today is one of the days when Ma is Gone.

She won't wake up properly. She's here but not really. She stays in Bed with the pillows on her head.

Silly Penis is standing up, I squish him down.

I eat my hundred cereal and I stand on my chair to wash the bowl and Meltedy Spoon. It's very quiet when I switch off the water. I wonder did Old Nick come in the night. I don't think he did because the trash bag is still by Door, but maybe he did only he didn't take the trash? Maybe Ma's not just Gone. Maybe he squished her neck even harder and now she's—

2 **to jerk** to pull sth suddenly – 20 **gone** Ma is extremely depressed and withdraws completely from Jack and the world on some days, because of her situation. – 23 **to squish** *inf* to push while making a squelching sound

I go up really close and listen till I hear breath. I'm just one inch away, my hair touches Ma's nose and she puts her hand up over her face so I step back.

I don't have a bath on my own, I just get dressed.

There's hours and hours, hundreds of them.

Ma gets up to pee but no talking, with her face all blank. I already put a glass of water beside Bed but she just gets back under Duvet.

I hate when she's Gone, but I like that I get to watch TV all day. I put it on really quiet at first and make it a bit louder at a time. Too much TV might turn me into a zombie but Ma's like a zombie today and she's not watching even. There's *Bob the Builder* and *Wonder Pets!* and *Barney*. For each I go up to touch hello. Barney and his friends do lots of hugs, I run to get in the middle but sometimes I'm too late. Today it's about a fairy that sneaks in at night and turns old teeth into money. I want Dora but she doesn't come.

Thursday means laundry, but I can't do it all myself and Ma's still lying on the sheets anyway.

When I'm hungry again I check Watch but he only says 09:47. Cartoons are over so I watch football and the planet where people win prizes. The puffy-hair woman is on her red couch talking to a man who used to be a golf star. There's another planet where women hold up necklaces and say how exquisite they are. "Suckers," Ma always says when she sees that planet. She doesn't say anything today, she doesn't notice I'm watching and watching and my brain is starting to be stinky.

How can TV be pictures of real things?

I think about them all floating around in Outside Space outside the walls, the couch and the necklaces and the bread and the killers and the airplanes and all the shes and hes, the boxers and the man with one leg and the puffy-hair woman, they're floating past Skylight. I wave to them, but there's

16 **to sneak** to go quietly and secretly – 24 **necklace** a band worn around the neck (*Halskette*) – 25 **sucker** *inf* here: sb who falls for a trick or (*here*) wants to buy sth that is low quality rubbish

skyscrapers as well and cows and ships and trucks, it's crammed out there, I count all the stuff that might crash into Room. I can't breathe right, I have to count my teeth instead, left to right on the top then right to left on the bottom, then backwards, twenty every time but I still think maybe I'm counting wrong.

When it's 12:04 it can be lunch so I cut a can of baked beans open, I'm careful. I wonder would Ma wake up if I cutted my hand and screamed help? I never had beans cold before. I eat nine, then I'm not hungry. I put the rest in a tub for not waste. Some are stuck to the can at the bottom, I pour water in. Maybe Ma will get up and scrub it later. Maybe she'll be hungry, she'll say, "Oh Jack, how thoughtful of you to save me beans in a tub."

I measure more things with Ruler but it's hard to add up the numbers on my own. I do him end over end and he's an acrobat of a circus. I play with Remote, I point him at Ma and whisper, "Wake up," but she doesn't. Balloon is all squishy, she goes for a ride on Prune Juice Bottle up near Skylight, they make the light all brownly sparkly. They're scared of Remote because of his sharp end, so I put him in Wardrobe and fold the doors shut. I tell all the things it's OK because Ma will be back tomorrow. I read the five books all myself only just bits of *Alice*. Mostly I just sit.

I don't do Scream because of disturbing Ma. I think it's probably OK to skip one day.

Then I switch the TV on again and wiggle Bunny, he makes the planets a bit less fuzzy but only a bit. It's racing cars, I like to see them go super fast but it's not very interesting after they do the oval about a hundred times. I want to wake Ma up and ask about Outside with the actual humans and things all zooming around, but she'd be mad. Or maybe she wouldn't switch on at all even if I shake her. So I don't. I go up very close, half her face is showing and her neck. The marks are purple now.

1 **crammed** crowded, too full – 11 **to scrub** to rub sth with a brush to clean it – 24 **to skip** *inf* to leave out

I'm going to kick Old Nick till I break his butt. I'll zap Door open with Remote and whiz into Outside Space and get everything at the real stores and bring it back to Ma.

I cry a bit but no noise.

I watch a show of weather and one of enemies are besieging a castle, the good guys are building a barricade so the door won't open. I nibble my finger, Ma can't tell me to stop. I wonder how much of my brain is gooey yet and how much is still OK. I think I might throw up like when I was three and had diarrhea too. What if I throw up all over Rug, how will I wash her on my own?

I look at her stain from when I got born. I kneel down and stroke, it feels sort of warm and scratchy like the rest of Rug, no different.

Ma's never Gone more than one day. I don't know what I do if I wake up tomorrow and she's still Gone.

Then I'm hungry, I have a banana even though it's a bit green.

Dora is a drawing in TV but she's my real friend, that's confusing. Jeep is actually real, I can feel him with my fingers. Superman is just TV. Trees are TV but Plant is real, oh, I forgot to water her. I carry her from Dresser to Sink and do that right away. I wonder did she eat Ma's bit of fish.

Skateboards are TV and so are girls and boys except Ma says they're actual, how can they be when they're so flat? Ma and me could make a barricade, we could shove Bed against Door so it doesn't open, won't he get a shock, ha ha. *Let me in*, he's shouting, *or I'll huff and I'll puff and I'll blow your house down.* Grass is TV and so is fire, but it could come in Room for real if I hot the beans and the red jumps onto my sleeve and burns me up. I'd like to see that but not it happen. Air's real and water only in Bath and Sink, rivers and lakes are TV, I don't know

1 **to break his butt** *inf* to hurt sb very badly – 5 **to besiege** *belagern* – 8 **gooey** *inf* here: soft, no longer working properly – 27 **to huff and puff** *einen Aufstand machen.* This line is from a fairytale that is very well-known in English speaking countries: "The Three Little Pigs", in which the big bad wolf threatens to blow the pigs' houses down when he says (chants): "Let me in, let me in, or I'll huff, and I'll puff, and I'll BLOW your house down!"

about the sea because if it whizzed around Outside it would make everything wet. I want to shake Ma and ask her if the sea is real. Room is real for real, but maybe Outside is too only it's got a cloak of invisibility on like Prince JackerJack in the story? Baby Jesus is TV I think except in the painting with his Ma and his cousin and his Grandma, but God is real looking in Skylight with his yellow face, only not today, there's only gray.

I want to be in Bed with Ma. Instead I sit on Rug with my hand just on the bump of her foot under Duvet. My arm gets tired so I drop it down for a while then put it back. I roll up the end of Rug and let her flop open again, I do that hundreds of times.

When it gets dark I try and eat more baked beans but they're disgusting. I have some bread and peanut butter instead. I open Freezer and put my face in beside the bags of peas and spinach and horrible green beans, I keep it there till I'm numb even my eyelids. Then I jump out and shut the door and rub my cheeks to warm them up. I can feel them with my hands but I can't feel them feeling my hands on them, it's weird.

It's dark in Skylight now, I hope God will put his silver face in.

I get into my sleep T-shirt. I wonder am I dirty because I didn't have a bath, I try to smell myself. In Wardrobe I lie down in Blanket but I'm cold. I forgot to put up Thermostat today, that's why, I only just remembered, but I can't do it now it's night.

I want some very much, I didn't have any all day. The right even, but I'd rather the left. If I could get in with Ma and have some—but she might push me away and that would be worse.

What if I'm in Bed with her and Old Nick comes? I don't know if it's nine yet, it's too dark for seeing Watch.

I sneak into Bed, extra slow so Ma won't notice. I just lie near. If I hear the *beep beep* I can jump back in Wardrobe quick quick.

1 **to whizz** *inf* to move very fast – 14 **disgusting** very bad, awful – 16 **numb** [nʌm] unable to feel anything

What if he comes and Ma won't wake up, will he be even more madder? Will he make worse marks on her?

I stay awake so I can hear him come.

He doesn't come but I stay awake.

* * *

The trash bag is still beside Door. Ma got up before me this morning and unknotted it and put in the beans she scraped out of the can. If the bag's still here, I guess that means he didn't come, that's two nights he didn't, yippee.

Friday means Mattress time. We flip her over front to back and sideways as well so she doesn't get bumpy, she's so heavy I have to use all my muscles and when she flomps down she knocks me onto Rug. I see the brown mark on Mattress from when I came out of Ma's tummy the first time. Next we have a dusting race, dust is tiny invisible pieces of our skins that we don't need anymore because we grow new ones like snakes. Ma sneezes really high like an opera star we heard one time in TV.

We do our grocery list, we can't decide about Sundaytreat. "Let's ask for candy," I say. "Not even chocolate. Some kind of candy we never had before."

"Some really sticky kind, so you'll end up with teeth like mine?" I don't like when Ma does sarcasm.

Now we're reading sentences out of no-pictures books, this one's *The Shack* with a spooky house and all white snow. " 'Since then,' " I read, " 'he and I have been, as the kids say these days, hangin' out, sharing a coffee—or for me a chai tea, extra hot with soy.' "

"Excellent," says Ma, "only *soy* should rhyme with *boy*."

Persons in books and TV are always thirsty, they have beer and juice and champagne and lattes and all sorts of liquids, sometimes they click their glasses on each other's glasses when

11 **to flomp** Jack's language for "to fall with a bang" – 16 **to sneeze** *niesen* – 23 **spooky** *inf* frightening

they're happy but they don't break them. I read the line again, it's still confusing. "Who's the *he* and the *I,* are they the kids?"

"Hmm," says Ma, reading over my shoulder, "I think *the kids* means kids in general."

"What's *in general*?"

"Lots of kids."

I try and see them, the lots, all playing together. "Actual human ones?"

Ma doesn't say anything for a minute, and then, "Yeah," very quiet. So it was true, everything she said.

The marks are still there on her neck, I wonder if they'll ever go away.

* * *

In the night she's flashing, it wakes me in Bed. Lamp on, I count five. Lamp off, I count one. Lamp on, I count two. Lamp off, I count two. I do a groan.

"Just a bit more." She's still staring up at Skylight that's all black.

There's no trash bag beside Door, that means he must have been here when I was asleep. "Please, Ma."

"In a minute."

"It hurts my eyes."

She leans over Bed and kisses me beside my mouth, she puts Duvet over my face. The light's still flashing but darker.

After a while she comes back into Bed and gives me some for getting back to sleep.

* * *

On Saturday Ma makes me three braids for a change, they feel funny. I wave my face to whack myself with them.

29 **to whack** *inf* to hit

I don't watch the cartoon planet this morning, I choose a bit of a gardening and a fitness and a news, and everything I see I say, "Ma, is that real?" and she says yeah, except one bit about a movie with werewolves and a woman bursting like a balloon is just special effects, that's drawing on computers.

Lunch is a can of chickpea curry and rice as well.

I'd like to do an extra big Scream but we can't on weekends.

Most of the afternoon we play Cat's Cradle, we can do the Candles and the Diamonds and the Manger and the Knitting Needles and we keep practicing the Scorpion except Ma's fingers always end up stuck.

Dinner is mini pizzas, one each plus one to share. Then we watch a planet where persons are wearing lots of frilly clothes and huge white hair. Ma says they're real but they're pretending to be people who died hundreds of years ago. It's a sort of game but it doesn't sound much fun.

She switches the TV off and sniffs. "I can still smell that curry from lunch."

"Me too."

"It tasted good but it's nasty the way it lingers."

"Mine tasted nasty too," I tell her.

She laughs. The marks on her neck are getting less, they're greenish and yellowish.

"Can I have a story?"

"Which one?"

"One you never told me before.

Ma smiles at me. "I think at this point you know everything I know. *The Count of Monte Cristo*?"

"I've heard that millions of times."

"*GulliJack in Lilliput*?"

6 **chickpea** a large pea (*Kichererbse*) – 8 **Cat's Cradle** game played by wrapping string or wool around your hands and making shapes – 13 **frilly** *mit Rüschen besetzt* – 28 **The Count of Monte Cristo** an adventure novel by Alexander Dumas about a successful merchant and sailor, Edmond Dantès, who spends 14 years imprisoned, manages to escape and then recovers some treasure on the island of Monte Cristo. – 30 **GulliJack in Lilliput** Jack's language for the novel **Gulliver's Travel** by Jonathan Swift. Gulliver is washed ashore after a shipwreck and finds himself a prisoner of a race of people, the members of which are less than 6 inches (15 cm) high.

"Zillions."

"*Nelson on Robben Island*?"

"Then he got out after twenty-seven years and became the government."

"*Goldilocks*?"

"Too scary."

"The bears only growl at her," says Ma. "Still."

"*Princess Diana*?"

"Should have worn her seat belt."

"See, you know them all." Ma puffs her breath. "Hang on, there's one about a mermaid ..."

"The Little Mermaid."

"No, a different one. This mermaid is sitting on the rocks one evening, combing her hair, when a fisherman creeps up and catches her in his net."

"To fry her for his dinner?"

"No, no, he brings her home to his cottage and she has to marry him," says Ma. "He takes away her magic comb so she can't ever go back into the sea. So after a while the mermaid has a baby—"

"—called JackerJack," I tell her.

"That's right. But whenever the fisherman's out fishing she looks around the cottage, and one day she finds where he's hidden her comb—"

"Ha ha."

"And she runs away to the rocks, and slips down into the sea."
"No."

Ma looks at me close. "You don't like this story?"

"She shouldn't be gone."

"It's OK." She takes the tear out of my eye with her finger. "I forgot to say, of course she takes her baby, JackerJack, with her, he's all knotted up in her hair. And when the fisherman comes back, the cottage is empty, and he never sees them again."

1 **zillions** *inf* an extremely large number – 11 **mermaid** a woman from the head to the waist but with a fish's tail instead of legs

"Does he drown?"

"The fisherman?"

"No, JackerJack, under the water."

"Oh, don't worry," says Ma, "he's half merman, remember? He can breathe air or water, whichever." She goes to look at Watch, it's 08:27.

I'm lying in Wardrobe for ages, but I don't get sleepy. We do songs and prayers. "Just one nursery rhyme," I say, "please?" I pick "The House That Jack Built" because it's the longest.

Ma's voice is yawny. " 'This is the man all tattered and torn—' " " 'That kissed the maiden all forlorn—' "

" 'That milked the cow with the crumpled horn—' "

I steal a few lines in a hurry. " 'That tossed the dog that worried the cat that killed the rat that—' "

Beep beep.

I shut my mouth tight.

The first thing Old Nick says I don't hear.

"Mmm, sorry about that," says Ma, "we had curry. I was wondering, actually, if there was any chance—" Her voice is all high. "If it might be possible sometime to put in an extractor fan or something?" He doesn't say anything. I think they're sitting on Bed.

"Just a little one," she says.

"Huh, there's an idea," says Old Nick. "Let's start all the neighbors wondering why I'm cooking up something spicy in my workshop."

I think that's sarcasm again.

"Oh. Sorry," says Ma, "I didn't think—"

"Why don't I stick a flashing neon arrow on the roof while I'm at it?"

I wonder how an arrow flashes.

"I'm really sorry," says Ma, "I didn't realize that the smell, that it, that a fan would—"

1 **to drown** to die by being underwater and unable to breathe – 10 **yawny** Jack's language for "tired as if yawning" (*gähnen*) – 12 **crumpled** uneven – 13 **to steal a few lines** to leave a few lines out – 20 **extractor** a fan which takes out stale or unpleasant air from a kitchen

"I don't think you appreciate how good you've got it here," says Old Nick. "Do you?"

Ma doesn't say anything.

"Above ground, natural light, central air, it's a cut above some places, I can tell you. Fresh fruit, toiletries, what have you, click your fingers and it's there. Plenty girls would thank their lucky stars for a setup like this, safe as houses. Specially with the kid—"

Is that me?

"No drunk drivers to worry about," he says, "drug pushers, perverts …"

Ma butts in very fast. "I shouldn't have asked for a fan, it was dumb of me, everything's fine."

"OK, then."

Nobody says anything for a little bit.

I count my teeth, I keep getting it wrong, nineteen then twenty then nineteen again. I bite my tongue till it hurts.

"Of course there's wear and tear, that's par for the course." His voice is moved, I think he's over near Bath now. "This seam's buckling, I'll have to sand and reseal. And see here, the underlayment's showing through."

"We are careful," says Ma, very quietly.

"Not careful enough. Cork's not meant for high traffic, I was planning on one sedentary user."

"Are you coming to bed?" asks Ma in that funny high voice.

"Let me get my shoes off." There's a sort of grunt, I hear something drop on Floor. "You're the one hassling me about renovations before I'm here two minutes …"

Lamp goes out.

1 **to appreciate** to recognize – 4 **a cut above** *inf* a lot better than – 7 **setup** an arrangement – 12 **to butt in** *inf* to interrupt – 18 **wear and tear** [ˌwer.n.ˈter] the damaging effect of use over a long period (*Verschleiß*) – 18 **that is par for the course** that is only natural and to be expected – 19 **seam** *Fuge, Spalt* – 20 **to buckle** to become bent – 20 **to reseal** to seal again, to fix again – 24 **sedentary** [ˈsedənteri] sitting and not moving – 27 **to hassle** to annoy, to get on sb's nerves

Old Nick squeaks Bed, I count to ninety-seven then I think I missed one so I lose count.

I stay awake listening even when there's nothing to hear.

* * *

On Sunday we're having bagels for dinner, very chewy, with jelly and peanut butter as well. Ma takes her bagel out of her mouth and there's a pointy thing stuck in it. "At last," she says.

I pick it up, it's all yellowy with dark brown bits. "Bad tooth?" Ma nods. She's feeling in the back of her mouth.

That's so weird. "We could stick him back in, with flour glue, maybe."

She shakes her head, grinning. "I'm glad it's out, now it can't hurt anymore."

He was part of her a minute ago but now he's not. Just a thing. "Hey, you know what, if you put him under your pillow a fairy will come in the night invisibly and turn him into money."

"Not in here, sorry," says Ma.

"Why not?"

"The tooth fairy doesn't know about Room." Her eyes are looking through the walls.

Outside has everything. Whenever I think of a thing now like skis or fireworks or islands or elevators or yo-yos, I have to remember they're real, they're actually happening in Outside all together. It makes my head tired. And people too, firefighters teachers burglars babies saints soccer players and all sorts, they're all really in Outside. I'm not there, though, me and Ma, we're the only ones not there. Are we still real?

After dinner Ma tells me *Hansel and Gretel* and *How the Berlin Wall Fell Down* and *Rumpelstiltskin.* I like when the queen has to guess the little man's name or else he'll take her baby away. "Are stories true?"

"Which ones?"

15 **fairy** a small figure with magical powers (*Fee*) – 25 **burglar** ['bɜːglɚ] thief

"The mermaid mother and Hansel and Gretel and all them."

"Well," says Ma, "not literally."

"What's—"

"They're magic, they're not about real people walking around today."

"So they're fake?"

"No, no. Stories are a different kind of true."

My face is all scrunched up from trying to understand. "Is the Berlin Wall true?"

"Well, there was a wall, but it's not there anymore."

I'm so tired I'm going to rip in two like Rumpelstiltskin did at the end.

"Night-night," says Ma, shutting the doors of Wardrobe, "sleep tight, don't let the bugs bite."

* * *

I didn't think I was switched off but then Old Nick's here all loud. "But vitamins—" Ma is saying.

"Highway robbery."

"You want us getting sick?"

"It's a giant rip-off," says Old Nick. "I saw this exposé one time, they all end up in the toilet."

Who ends up in Toilet?

"It's just that, if we had a better diet—"

"Oh, here we go. Whine, whine, whine ..." I can see him through the slats, he's sitting on the edge of Bath.

Ma's voice gets mad. "I bet we're cheaper to keep than a dog. We don't even need shoes."

"You have no idea about the world of today. I mean, where do you think the money's going to keep coming from?"

Nobody says anything. Then Ma. "What do you mean? Money in general, or—?"

2 **literally** really – 6 **fake** sth that is not what it looks like or pretends to be (*Fälschung*) – 8 **scrunched** twisted – 22 **diet** ['daɪət] food and drink which is consumed by a person (*Ernährung*) – 23 **to whine** to complain

"Six months." His arms are folded, they're huge. "Six months I've been laid off, and have you had to worry your pretty little head?"

I can see Ma too, through the slats, she's nearly beside him.

"What happened?"

"Like it matters."

"Are you looking for another job?"

They stare at each other.

"Are you in debt?" she asks. "How're you going to—?"

"Shut your mouth."

I don't mean to but I'm so scared he's going to hurt her again the sound just bursts out of my head.

Old Nick's looking right at me, he takes a step and another and another and he knocks on the slats. I see his hand shadow. "Hey in there."

He's talking to me. My chest's going *clang clang*. I hug my knees and press my teeth together. I want to get under Blanket but I can't, I can't do anything.

"He's asleep." That's Ma.

"She keep you in the closet all day as well as all night?" The *you* is me. I wait for Ma to say *no,* but she doesn't. "Doesn't seem natural." I can see in his eyes, they're all pale. Can he see me, am I turning to stone? What if he opens the door? I think I might—

"I figure there must be something wrong," he's saying to Ma, "you've never let me get a good look since the day he was born. Poor little freak's got two heads or something?"

Why he said that? I nearly want to put my one head out of Wardrobe, just to show him.

Ma's there in front of the slats, I can see the knobs of her shoulder blades through her T-shirt. "He's just shy."

"He's got no reason to be shy of me," says Old Nick. "Never laid a hand on him."

Why would he laid his hand on me?

1 **I've been laid off** I have lost my job – 9 **in debt** [det] *Schulden haben* – 27 **freak** [fri:k] *inf* a strange creature

"Bought him that fancy jeep, didn't I? I know boys, I was one once. C'mon, Jack—"

He said my name.

"C'mon out and get your lollipop."

A lollipop!

"Let's just go to bed." Ma's voice is strange.

Old Nick does a kind of laugh. "I know what you need, missy." What Ma needs? Is it something on the list?

"Come on," she says again.

"Didn't your mother ever teach you manners?"

Lamp goes out.

But Ma doesn't have a mother.

Bed's loud, that's him getting in.

I put Blanket over my head and press my ears so not to hear. I don't want to count the creaks but I do.

* * *

When I wake up I'm still in Wardrobe and it's totally dark. I wonder if Old Nick is still here. And the lollipop?

The rule is, stay in Wardrobe till Ma comes for me.

I wonder what color the lollipop is. Are there colors in the dark? I try to switch off again but I'm all on.

I could put my head out just to—

I push open the doors, real slow and quiet. All I can hear is the hum of Refrigerator. I stand up, I go one step, two step, three. I stub my toe on something *owwwwwww.* I pick it up and it's a shoe, a giant shoe. I'm looking at Bed, there he is, Old Nick, his face is made of rock I think. I put my finger out, not to touch it, just nearly.

His eyes flash all white. I jump back, I drop the shoe. I think he might shout but he's grinning with big shiny teeth, he says, "Hey, sonny."

4 **lollipop** a hard sweet fixed on a stick (*Lutscher*) – 25 **to stub** to hurt by hitting against sth

I don't know what that—

Then Ma is louder than I ever heard her even doing Scream. "Get away, get away from him!"

I race back to Wardrobe, I bang my head, *arghhhhh,* she keeps screeching, "Get away from him."

"Shut up," Old Nick is saying, "shut up." He calls her words I can't hear through the screaming. Then her voice gets blurry. "Stop that noise," he's saying.

Ma is going *mmmmmmm* instead of words. I hold my head where it banged, I wrap it up in my two hands.

"You're a basket case, you know that?"

"I can be quiet," she says, she's nearly whispering, I hear her breath all scratchy. "You know how quiet I can be, so long as you leave him alone. It's all I've ever asked."

Old Nick snorts. "You ask for stuff every time I open the door."

"It's all for Jack."

"Yeah, well, don't forget where you got him."

I'm listening very hard but Ma doesn't say anything.

Sounds. Him getting his clothes? His shoes, I think he's doing on his shoes.

I don't sleep after he's gone. I'm on all the night in Wardrobe. I wait hundreds of hours but Ma doesn't come for me.

* * *

I'm looking up at Roof when suddenly it lifts off and the sky rushes in and the rockets and the cows and the trees are crashing down on my head—

No, I'm in Bed, Skylight's starting to drip down light, it must be morning.

"Just a bad dream," says Ma, stroking my cheek.

I have some but not much, the yummy left.

10 **to wrap** [ræp] to cover – 11 **basket case** *inf* a crazy person (*Spinner*) – 13 **scratchy** hot, rough – 29 **to stroke** to pass your hand gently over sth (*streicheln*)

Then I remember, and I wriggle up in Bed to check her for new marks on her but I don't see any. "I'm sorry I came out of Wardrobe in the night."

"I know," she says.

Is that the same as forgiving? I'm remembering more. "What's a little freak?"

"Oh, Jack."

"Why he said something's wrong with me?"

Ma groans. "There's not a thing wrong with you, you're right all the way through." She kisses my nose.

"But why he said it?"

"He's just trying to drive me crazy."

"Why he's—?"

"You know how you like to play with cars and balloons and stuff? Well, he likes to play with my head." She taps it.

I don't know to play with heads. "Is *laid off* like lying down?"

"No, it means he lost his job," says Ma.

I thought only things could get lost, like one of our pins from the six. Everything must be different in Outside. "Why he said don't forget where you got me?"

"Oh, give it a rest for one minute, will you?"

I'm counting on mute, one hippopotamus two hippopotamus, all the sixty seconds the questions are bouncing up and down in my head.

Ma is filling a glass of milk for her, she doesn't do one for me. She stares into Refrigerator, the light's not coming on, that's weird. She shuts the door again.

The minute's up. "Why he said don't forget where you got me? Wasn't it Heaven?"

Ma is clicking Lamp but he won't wake up either. "He meant—who you belong to."

"I belong to you."

She gives me a small grin.

"Is Lamp's bulb used up?"

34 **bulb** the part of a lamp that gives out light

"I don't think that's it." She shivers, she goes over to look at Thermostat.

"Why he told you not to forget?"

"Well actually, he's got it all wrong, he thinks you belong to him." Ha! "He's a numbskull."

Ma's staring at Thermostat. "Power cut."

"What's that?"

"There's no power in anything just now."

It's a strange kind of day.

We have our cereal and brush teeth and get dressed and water Plant. We try and fill Bath but after the first bit the water comes out all icy so we just wash with cloths. It gets brighter through Skylight only not very. TV doesn't work too, I miss my friends. I pretend they're coming on the screen, I pat them with my fingers. Ma says let's put on another shirt and pants each to be warm, even two socks each foot. We run Track for miles and miles and miles to warm us up, then Ma lets me take off the outside socks because my toes are all squished. "My ears hurt," I tell her.

Her eyebrows go up.

"It's too quiet in them."

"Ah, that's because we're not hearing all the little sounds we're used to, like the heat coming on or the refrigerator hum."

I play with Bad Tooth, I hide him in different places like under Dresser and in the rice and behind Dish Soap. I try and forget where he is, then I'm all surprised. Ma's chopping all the green beans from Freezer, why is she chopping so many?

That's when I remember the one good bit of last night. "Oh, Ma, the lollipop."

She keeps chopping. "It's in the trash."

Why he left it there? I run over, I step on the pedal and the lid goes *ping* but I don't see the lollipop. I'm feeling around the orange peels and rice and stew and plastic.

6 **power cut** a failure in the supply of electricity (*Stromausfall*) – 13 **too** Jack's language; he means: "TV doesn't work either." – 18 **squished** *inf* here: wet, slippery – 26 **to chop** to cut into small pieces

Ma takes me by the shoulders. “Leave it.”

“It’s my candy for Sundaytreat,” I tell her.

“It’s garbage.”

“No it’s not.”

“It cost him maybe fifty cents. He’s laughing at you.”

“I never had a lollipop.” I pull out of her hands.

Nothing can hot on Stove because the power’s cut. So lunch is slippery freezy green beans which are even nastier than green beans cooked. We have to eat them up because otherwise they’ll melt and rot. I wouldn’t mind that but it’s waste.

“Would you like *The Runaway Bunny*?” Ma asks when we’ve washed up in all cold.

I shake my head. “When the power’s getting uncut?”

“I don’t know, I’m sorry.”

We get into Bed to warm up. Ma pulls up all her clothes and I have lots, the left then the right.

“What if Room gets colder and colderer?”

“Oh, it won’t. It’s April in three days,” she says, spooning me. “It can’t be that cold out.”

We snooze, but me only a bit. I wait till Ma’s all heavy, then I wriggle out and go look in Trash again.

I find the lollipop nearly in the bottom, it’s a red ball shape. I wash my arms and my lollipop too because there’s yucky stew on it. I get the plastic right off and I suck it and suck it, it’s the sweetest thing I ever had. I wonder if this is what Outside tastes like.

If I ran away I’d become a chair and Ma wouldn’t know which one. Or I’d make myself invisible and stick to Skylight and she’d look right through me. Or a tiny speck of dust and go up her nose and she’d sneeze me right out.

Her eyes are open.

I put the lollipop behind my back.

She shuts them again.

18 **spooning** *inf* to sleep like two spoons fitting into each other (*Löffelchen liegen*) – 23 **yucky** *inf* disgusting (*eklig*) – 23 **stew** [stu:] dish consisting of meat and vegetables cooked together – 29 **speck** a very small piece

I keep sucking for hours even though I feel a bit sick. Then it's only a stick and I put it in Trash.

When Ma gets up she doesn't say about the lollipop, maybe she was still asleep with her eyes open. She tries Lamp again but he stays off. She says she'll leave him switched on so we'll know the minute the power cut is over.

"What if he comes on in the middle of the night and wakes us up?"

"I don't think it'll be the middle of the night."

We do Bowling with Bouncy Ball and Wordy Ball, and knock down vitamin bottles that we put different heads on when I was four, like Dragon and Alien and Princess and Crocodile, I win the most. I practice my adding and subtracting and sequences and multiplying and dividing and writing down the biggest numbers there are. Ma sews me two new puppets out of little socks from when I was a baby, they've got smiles of stitches and all different button eyes. I know to sew but it's not much fun. I wish I could remember my baby me, what I was like.

I write a letter to SpongeBob with a picture of me and Ma on the back dancing to keep warm. We play Snap and Memory and Go Fish, Ma wants Chess but it makes my brain floppy so she says OK to Checkers instead.

My fingers get so stiff I put them in my mouth. Ma says that spreads germs, she makes me go wash them again in the freezy water.

We do lots of beads of flour dough for a necklace but we can't string it till they're all dry and hard. We make a spaceship out of boxes and tubs, the tape's nearly gone but Ma says "Oh why not" and uses the last bit.

Skylight's going dark.

Dinner is cheese that's all sweaty and melting broccoli. Ma says I have to eat or I'll feel even colder.

13 **to subtract** *opp of* to add – 13 **sequence** *here*: numbers that come one after another in a fixed order – 15 **to sew** to fasten by stiches made with thread (*nähen*) – 28 **tape** *Klebeband*

She takes two killers and a big gulp to make them go down. "Why you're still hurting even though Bad Tooth's out?"

"I guess I'm noticing the others more now."

We get in our sleep T-shirts but put more clothes back on top. Ma starts a song. " 'The other side of the mountain—' "

" 'The other side of the mountain—, ' " I sing.

" 'The other side of the mountain—' "

" 'Was all that he could see.' "

I do "Ninety-nine Bottles of Beer on the Wall" all the way down to seventy.

Ma puts her hands over her ears and says please can we do the rest tomorrow. "The power will probably be back then."

"Good-o," I say.

"And even if it isn't, he can't stop the sun coming up." Old Nick? "Why would he stop the sun?"

"He can't, I said." Ma gives me a hug hard and says, "I'm sorry." "Why are you sorry?"

She puffs her breath. "It's my fault, I made him mad." I stare at her face but I can hardly see it.

"He can't stand it when I start screaming, I haven't done it in years. He wants to punish us."

My chest is thumping really loud. "How he's going to punish us?"

"No, he is already, I mean. By cutting the power."

"Oh, that's all right."

Ma laughs. "What do you mean? We're freezing, we're eating slimy vegetables ..."

"Yeah, but I thought he was going to punish us too." I try to imagine. "Like if there were two Rooms, if he put me in one and you in the other one."

"Jack, you're wonderful."

"Why I'm wonderful?"

"I don't know," says Ma, "that's just the way you popped out." We spoon even tighter in Bed. "I don't like it dark," I tell her. "Well, it's time to sleep now, so it would be dark anyway."

21 **to punish** to make sb suffer (*bestrafen*) – 33 **popped out** *sl* here: were born

"I guess."

"We know each other without looking, don't we?"

"Yeah."

"Night-night, sleep tight, don't let the bugs bite."

"Don't I have to go in Wardrobe?"

"Not tonight," says Ma.

* * *

We wake up and the air's shiverier. Watch says 07:09, he has a battery, that's his own little power hidden inside.

Ma keeps yawning because she was awake in the night.

I've got a tummy ache, she says maybe it was all the raw vegetables. I want a killer from the bottle, she gives me just a half. I wait and wait but my tummy doesn't feel different.

Skylight's getting brighter.

"I'm glad he didn't come last night," I tell Ma. "I bet he never comes back, that would be super cool."

"Jack." She kind of frowns. "Think about it."

"I am."

"I mean, what would happen. Where does our food come from?"

I know this one. "From Baby Jesus in the fields in Outside."
"No, but—who's the bringer?"

Oh.

Ma gets up, she says it's a good sign the faucets are still working. "He could have turned the water off too, but he hasn't."

I don't know what that's a sign for.

There's bagel for breakfast but it's cold and mushy.

"What happens if he doesn't switch the power on again?" I ask. "I'm sure he will. Maybe later today."

8 **shiverier** Jack means "colder, makes you shiver" – 17 **to frown** [fraʊn] to draw one's eyebrows together, to be annoyed – 24 **faucet** *AE* tap (*Wasserhahn*) – 28 **mushy** soft, full of liquid

I try the buttons on TV sometimes. Just a dumb gray box, I can see my face but not as good like in Mirror.

We do all the Phys Eds we can think to warm up. Karate and Islands and Simon Says and Trampoline. Hopscotch, where we have to hop from one cork tile to another one and never go on the lines or fall over. Ma picks Blindman's Buff, she ties my camouflage pants around her eyes. I hide in Under Bed beside Eggsnake not breathing even, flat like a page in a book, and it takes her hundreds of hours to find me. Next I choose Rappelling, Ma holds my hands and I walk up her legs till my feet are higher than my head, then I dangle upside down, my braids go in my face and make me laugh. I do a flip and I'm right side up again. I want it lots times more but her bad wrist is hurting.

Then we're tired.

We make a mobile from a long spaghetti and threads tied with things pasted on, tiny pictures of me all orange and Ma all green and twisty foil and tufts of toilet paper. Ma fixes the top thread on Roof with the last pin from Kit, and the spaghetti dangles with all the little things flying from it when we stand under and blow hard.

I'm hungry so Ma says I can have the last apple.

What if Old Nick doesn't bring more apples?

"Why he's still punishing us?" I ask.

Ma twists her mouth. "He thinks we're things that belong to him, because Room does."

"How come?"

"Well, he made it."

That's weird, I thought Room just is. "Didn't God make everything?"

Ma doesn't say anything for a minute and then she rubs my neck. "All the good stuff, anyway."

11 **to dangle** to swing loosely – 12 **braid** *AE* hair which has been twisted together and tied (*Zopf*) – 18 **tuft** [tʌft] bunch, clump

We play Noah's Ark on Table, all the things like Comb and Little Plate and Spatula and the books and Jeep have to line up and get into Box quick quick before there's the giant flood. Ma's not really playing anymore, she's got her face in her hands like it's heavy.

I crunch the apple. "Are your other teeth hurting?"

She looks through her fingers at me, her eyes are huger. "Which ones?"

Ma stands up so sudden I'm nearly scared. She sits into Rocker and holds out her hands. "Come here. I have a story for you."

"A new one?"

"Yeah."

"Excellent."

She waits till I'm all folded into her arms. I'm nibbling the second side of the apple to make it last. "You know how Alice wasn't always in Wonderland?"

That was a trick, I know this one already. "Yeah, she goes in White Rabbit's house and grows so big she has to put her arm out the window and her foot up the chimney and she kicks Bill the Lizard out *kaboom,* that bit's funny."

"No, but before. Remember she was lying in the grass?"

"Then she fell down the hole four thousand miles but she didn't hurt herself."

"Well, I'm like Alice," says Ma.

I laugh. "Nah. She's a little girl with a huge head, bigger than Dora's even."

Ma's chewing her lip, there's a dark bit. "Yeah, but I'm from somewhere else, like her. A long time ago, I was—"

"Up in Heaven."

She puts her finger on my mouth to hush me. "I came down and I was a kid like you, I lived with my mother and father."

1 **Noah's Ark** Noah is an Old Testament patriarch whom God commands to build an ark and take his family and one pair of every species of living creature to be saved (*Genesis, chapter 6*). God then destroys all living things in a flood. They are playing a game that is based on this story. – 2 **spatula** an object like a knife with a wide, flat blade (*Spachtel*) – 21 **lizard** *Eidechse* – 31 **to hush** to make silent

I shake my head. "*You're* the mother."

"But I had one of my own I called Mom," she says. "I still have."

Why she's pretending like this, is it a game I don't know?

"She's … I guess you'd call her Grandma."

Like Dora's *abuela*. St. Anne in the picture that the Virgin Mary's sitting in her lap. I'm eating the core, it's nearly nothing now. I put it on Table. "You grew in her tummy?"

"Well—actually no, I was adopted. She and my dad—you'd call him Grandpa. And also I had—I have—a big brother called Paul."

I shake my head. "He's a saint."

"No, a different Paul."

How can there be two Pauls?

"You'd call him Uncle Paul."

That's too many names, my head's full. My tummy's still empty like the apple isn't there. "What's for lunch?"

Ma's not smiling. "I'm telling you about your family." I shake my head.

"Just because you've never met them doesn't mean they're not real. There's more things on earth than you ever dreamed about." "Is there any cheese left that's not sweaty?"

"Jack, this is important. I lived in a house with my mom and dad and Paul."

I have to play the game so she won't be mad. "A house in TV?"

"No, outside."

That's ridiculous, Ma was never in Outside.

"But it looked like a house you'd see on TV, yeah. A house on the edge of a city, with a yard behind it, and a hammock."

"What's a hammock?"

Ma gets the pencil from Shelf and does a drawing of two trees, there's ropes between them all knotted together with a person lying on the ropes.

"Is that a pirate?"

6 **abuela** Spanish for grandmother – 7 **core** central part of a fruit – 32 **rope** a strong, thick cord – 32 **to knot** [nɑ:t] *knoten*

"That's me, swinging in the hammock." She does the paper side to side, she's all excited. "And I used to go to the playground with Paul and swing on the swings as well, and eat ice cream. Your grandma and grandpa took us on trips in the car, to the zoo and to the beach. I was their little girl."

"Nah."

Ma scrunches up the picture. There's wet on Table, it makes her white all shiny.

"Don't be crying," I say.

"I can't help it." She rubs the tears over her face.

"Why you can't help it?"

"I wish I could describe it better. I miss it."

"You miss the hammock?"

"All of it. Being outside."

I hold on to her hand. She wants me to believe so I'm trying to but it hurts my head. "You actually lived in TV one time?"

"I told you, it's not TV. It's the real world, you wouldn't believe how big it is." Her arms shoot out, she's pointing at all the walls. "Room's only a tiny stinky piece of it."

"Room's not stinky." I'm nearly growling. "It's only stinky sometimes when you do a fart."

Ma wipes her eyes again.

"Your farts are much stinkier than mine. You're just trying to trick me and you better stop right this minute."

"OK," she says, all her breath hisses out like a balloon. "Let's have a sandwich."

"Why?"

"You said you were hungry."

"No I'm not."

Her face is fierce again. "I'll make a sandwich," she says, "and you'll eat it. OK?"

It's peanut butter just, because the cheese is all gooey. When I'm eating it, Ma sits beside me, but she doesn't have one. She says, "I know it's a lot to take in."

21 **fart** an escape of air from the bowels (*Furz*) – 30 **fierce** angry, aggressive – 32 **gooey** *sl* soft

The sandwich?

For dessert we have a tub of mandarins between us, I get the big bits because she prefers the little ones.

"I wouldn't lie to you about this," Ma says while I'm slurping the juice. "I couldn't tell you before, because you were too small to understand, so I guess I was sort of lying to you then. But now you're five, I think you can understand."

I shake my head.

"What I'm doing is the opposite of lying. It's, like, unlying." We have a long nap.

Ma's already awake, looking down at me about two inches away. I wriggle down to have some from the left.

"Why you don't like it here?" I ask her.

She sits up and pulls her T-shirt down.

"I wasn't done."

"Yes you were," she says, "you were talking."

I sit up too. "Why you don't like it in Room with me?" Ma holds me tight. "I always like being with you."

"But you said it was tiny and stinky."

"Oh, Jack." She says nothing for a minute. "Yeah, I'd rather be outside. But with you."

"I like it here with you."

"OK."

"How did he make it?"

She knows who I mean. I think she's not going to tell me, and then she says, "Actually it was a garden shed to begin with. Just a basic twelve-by-twelve, vinyl-coated steel. But he added a soundproofed skylight, and lots of insulating foam inside the walls, plus a layer of sheet lead, because lead kills all sound. Oh, and a security door with a code. He boasts about what a neat job he made of it."

The afternoon goes slow.

4 **to slurp** [slɜrp] to drink with the sound of noisy sucking (*schlürfen*) – 26 **shed** small hut, usually made of wood – 27 **vinyl-coated** covered with a kind of plastic – 28 **foam** *Schaum* – 29 **lead** a soft but heavy, greyish-blue metal which melts easily (*Blei*) – 30 **to boast** to show off

We read all our books with pictures in the freezing kind of bright. Skylight's different today. She's got a black bit like an eye. "Look, Ma."

She stares up and grins. "It's a leaf."

"Why?"

"The wind must have blown it off a tree onto the glass."

"An actual tree in Outside?"

"Yeah. See? That proves it. The whole world is out there."

"Let's play Beanstalk. We put my chair here on top of Table ..." She helps me do that. "Then Trash on top of my chair," I tell her. "Then I climb all the way up—"

"That's not safe."

"Yeah it is if you stand on Table holding Trash so I don't wobble."

"Hmm," says Ma, which is nearly no.

"Let's just try, please, please?"

It works perfect, I don't fall at all. When I'm standing on Trash I can actually hold the cork edges of Roof where they go in slanty at Skylight. There's something over her glass I never saw before. "Honeycomb," *I tell Ma, stroking it.*

"It's a polycarbonate mesh," she says, "unbreakable. I used to stand up here looking out a lot, before you were born."

"The leaf's all black with holes in it."

"Yeah, I think it's a dead one, from last winter."

I can see blue around it, that's the sky, with some white in it that Ma says are clouds. I stare through the honeycomb, I'm staring and staring but all I see is sky. There's nothing in it like ships or trains or horses or girls or skyscrapers zooming by.

When I climb back down off Trash and my chair I shove Ma's arm away.

"Jack—"

I jump onto Floor all on my own. "Liar, liar, pants on fire, there's no Outside."

18 **slanty** ['slænti] Jack's language for "at an angle" – 20 **honeycomb** a container made by bees out of wax (*Bienenwabe*) – 21 **polycarbonate mesh** *Netzgewebe, Maschendraht aus Kunststoff*

She starts explaining more but I put my fingers in my ears and shout, “Blah blah blah blah blah.”

I play just me with Jeep. I’m nearly crying but I pretend not.

Ma looks through Cabinet, she’s banging cans, I think I hear her counting. She’s counting what we’ve got left.

I’m extra cold now, my hands are all numb under the socks on them.

For dinner I keep asking can we have the last of the cereal so in the end Ma says yeah. I spill some because of not feeling my fingers.

The dark’s coming back, but Ma has all the rhymes in her head from the Big Book of Nursery Rhymes. I ask for “Oranges and Lemons,” my best line is “I do not know, says the great bell of Bow” because it’s all deep like a lion. Also about the chopper coming to chop off your head. “What’s a chopper?”

“A big knife, I guess.”

“I don’t think so,” I tell her. “It’s a helicopter that its blades spin real fast and chop off heads.”

“Yuck.”

We’re not sleepy but there’s not much to do without seeing. We sit on Bed and do our own rhymes. “Our friend Wickles has the tickles.”

“Our friends the Backyardigans have to try hard again.” “Good one,” I tell Ma. “Our friend Grace winned the race.” “Won it,” says Ma. “Our friend Jools likes swimming pools.” “Our friend Barney lives on a farm-y.”

“Cheat.”

“OK,” I say. “Our friend Uncle Paul had a bad fall.”

“He came off his motorbike once.”

I was forgetting he was real. “Why he came off his motorbike?” “By accident. But the ambulance took him to the hospital and the doctors made him all better.”

“Did they cut him open?”

“No, no, they just put a cast on his arm to stop it hurting.”

17 **blade** long flat piece of metal, part of a propeller – 34 **cast** a broken leg is put in a cast (*Gipsverband*)

So hospitals are real too, and motorbikes. My head's going to burst from all the new things I have to believe.

It's all black now except Skylight has a dark kind of brightness. Ma says in a city there's always some light from the streetlights and the lamps in the buildings and stuff.

"Where's the city?"

"Just out there," she says, pointing at Bed Wall.

"I looked through Skylight and I never saw it."

"Yeah, that's why you got mad at me."

"I'm not mad at you."

She gives me back my kiss. "Skylight looks straight up in the air. Most of the things I've been telling you about are on the ground, so to see them we'd need a window that faces out sideways."

"We could ask for a sideways window for Sundaytreat." Ma sort of laughs.

I was forgetting that Old Nick's not coming anymore. Maybe my lollipop was the last Sundaytreat ever.

I think I'm going to cry but what comes out is a huge yawn. "Good night, Room," I say.

"Is that the time? OK. Good night," says Ma.

"Good night, Lamp and Balloon." I wait for Ma but she's not saying any more of them. "Good night, Jeep, and Good night, Remote. Good night, Rug, and Good night, Blanket, and Good night, the Bugs, and don't bite."

* * *

What wakes me up is a noise over and over. Ma's not in Bed. There's a bit of light, the air's still icy. I look over the edge, she's in the middle of Floor going *thump thump thump* with her hand. "What did Floor do?"

Ma stops, she puffs out a long breath. "I need to hit something," she says, "but I don't want to break anything."

"Why not?"

"Actually, I'd love to break something. I'd love to break everything."

I don't like her like this. "What's for breakfast?"

Ma stares at me. Then she stands up and goes over to Cabinet and gets out a bagel, I think it's the last one.

She only has a quarter of it, she's not very hungry.

When we let our breaths out they're foggy. "That's because it's colder today," says Ma.

"You said it wouldn't get any colder."

"Sorry, I was wrong."

I finish the bagel. "Do I still have a Grandma and Grandpa and Uncle Paul?"

"Yeah," says Ma, she smiles a bit.

"Are they in Heaven?"

"No, no." She twists her mouth. "I don't think so, anyway. Paul's only three years older than me, he's—wow, he must be twenty-nine."

"Actually they're here," I whisper. "Hiding."

Ma looks around. "Where?"

"In Under Bed."

"Oh, that must be a tight squeeze. There's three of them, and they're pretty big."

"As big as hippopotami?"

"Not that big."

"Maybe they're … in Wardrobe."

"With my dresses?"

"Yeah. When we hear a clatter that's them knocking down the hangers."

Ma's face is flat.

"I'm only kidding," I tell her.

She nods.

"Can they come here sometime for real?"

"I wish they could," she says. "I pray for it so hard, every night." "I don't hear you."

21 **squeeze** not much room – 27 **clatter** a loud noise – 28 **hanger** an object on which you hang clothes (*Kleiderbügel*)

"Just in my head," says Ma.

I didn't know she prays things in her head where I can't hear. "They're wishing it too," she says, "but they don't know where I am."

"You're in Room with me."

"But they don't know where it is, and they don't know about you at all."

That's weird. "They could look on Dora's Map, and when they come I could pop out at them for a surprise."

Ma nearly laughs but not quite. "Room's not on any map."

"We could tell them on a telephone, Bob the Builder has one."

"But we don't."

"We could ask for one for Sundaytreat." I remember. "If Old Nick stops being mad."

"Jack. He'd never give us a phone, or a window." Ma takes my thumbs and squeezes them. "We're like people in a book, and he won't let anybody else read it."

For Phys Ed we run on Track. It's hard moving Table and the chairs with hands that feel not here. I run ten there-and-backs but I'm still not warmed up, my toes are stumbly. We do Trampoline and Karate, *Hi-yah,* then I choose Beanstalk again. Ma says OK if I promise not to freak out when I can't see anything. I climb up Table onto my chair onto Trash and I don't even wobble. I hold on to the edges where Roof slants into Skylight, I stare hard through the honeycomb at the blue so it makes me blink. After a while Ma says she wants to get down and make lunch.

"No vegetables, please, my tummy can't manage them." "We have to use them up before they rot."

"We could have pasta."

"We're nearly out."

"Then rice. What if—?" Then I forget to talk because I see it through the honeycomb, the thing so small I think it's just one

24 **to wobble** to move unsteadily from side to side

of those floaters in my eye, but it's not. It's a little line making a thick white streak on the sky. "Ma—"

"What?"

"An airplane!"

"Really?"

"Really real for real. Oh—"

Then I'm falling on Ma then on Rug, Trash is banging on us and my chair too. Ma's saying *ow ow ow* and rubbing her wrist. "Sorry, sorry," I say, I'm kissing it better. "I saw it, it was a real airplane only tiny."

"That's just because it's far away," she says all smiling. "I bet if you saw it up close it would actually be huge."

"The most amazing thing, it was writing a letter *I* on the sky."

"That's called a …" She slaps her head. "Can't remember. It's a sort of streak, it's the smoke of the plane or something."

For lunch we have all the seven rest of the crackers with the gloopy cheese, we hold our breaths not to taste it.

Ma gives me some under Duvet. There's shine from God's yellow face but not enough for sunbathing. I can't switch off. I stare up at Skylight so hard my eyes get itchy but I don't see any more airplanes. I really did see that one though when I was up Beanstalk, it wasn't a dream. I saw it flying in Outside, so there really is Outside where Ma was a little girl.

We get up and play Cat's Cradle and Dominoes and Submarine and Puppets and lots of other things but only a little while each. We do Hum, the songs are too easy to guess. We go back in Bed to warm up.

"Let's go in Outside tomorrow," I say.

"Oh, Jack."

I'm lying on Ma's arm that's all thick in two sweaters. "I like how it smells there."

She moves her head to stare at me.

1 **floater** Jack's language for "a tiny object that swims in the eye" – 15 **streak** [stri:k] a thin line – 17 **gloopy** *inf* soft, old, stale – 20 **itchy** woollen socks are sometimes itchy (*jucken*)

"When Door opens after nine and the air whooshes in that's not like our air."

"You noticed," she says.

"I notice all the things."

"Yeah, it's fresher. In the summer, it smells of cut grass, because we're in his backyard. Sometimes I get a glimpse of shrubs and hedges."

"Whose backyard?"

"Old Nick's. Room is made out of his shed, remember?"

It's hard to remember all the bits, none of them sound very true. "He's the only one who knows the code numbers to tap into the outside keypad."

I stare at Keypad, I didn't know there was another. "I tap numbers."

"Yeah, but not the secret ones that open the door—like an invisible key," says Ma. "Then when he's going back to the house he taps in the code again, on this one"—she points at Keypad.

"The house with the hammock?"

"No." Ma's voice is loud. "Old Nick lives in a different one."
"Can we go to his one someday?"

She presses her mouth with her hand. "I'd rather go to your grandma and grandpa's house."

"We could swing in the hammock."

"We could do what we liked, we'd be free."

"When I'm six?"

"Definitely someday."

There's wet running down Ma's face onto mine. I jump, it's salty. "I'm OK," she says, rubbing her cheek, "it's OK. I'm just—I'm a bit scared."

"You can't be scared." I'm nearly shouting. "Bad idea." "Just a little bit. We're OK, we've got the basics."

Now I'm even scareder. "But what if Old Nick doesn't uncut the power and he doesn't bring more food, not ever ever ever?"

7 **shrub** a low bush – 7 **hedge** a row of bushes planted close together (*Hecke*) – 33 **scareder** Jack's language for "more scared, more frightened"

"He will," she says, she's still breathing gulpy. "I'm nearly a hundred percent sure he will."

Nearly a hundred, that's ninety-nine. Is ninety-nine enough? Ma sits up, she scrubs her face with the arm of her sweater.

My tummy rumbles, I wonder what we've got left. It's getting dark again already. I don't think the light is winning.

"Listen, Jack, I need to tell you another story."

"A true one?"

"Totally true. You know how I used to be all sad?"

I like this one. "Then I came down from Heaven and grew in your tummy."

"Yeah, but see, why I was sad—it was *because* of Room," says Ma. "Old Nick—I didn't even know him, I was nineteen. He stole me."

I'm trying to understand. Swiper no swiping. But I never heard of swiping people.

Ma's holding me too tight. "I was a student. It was early in the morning, I was crossing a parking lot to get to the college library, listening to—it's a tiny machine that holds a thousand songs and plays them in your ear, I was the first of my friends to get one."

I wish I had that machine.

"Anyway—this man ran up asking for help, his dog was having a fit and he thought it might be dying."

"What's he called?"

"The man?"

I shake my head. "The dog."

"No, the dog was just a trick to get me into his pickup truck, Old Nick's truck."

"What color is it?"

"The truck? Brown, he's still got the same one, he's always griping about it."

"How many wheels?"

"I need you to concentrate on what matters," says Ma.

24 **fit** a short attack of an illness (*Anfall*) – 32 **to gripe** [graɪp] *inf* to complain

I nod. Her hands are too tight, I loosen them.

"He put a blindfold on me—"

"Like Blindman's Buff?"

"Yeah, but not fun. He drove and drove, I was terrified."

"Where was I?"

"You hadn't happened yet, remember?"

I forgot. "Was the dog in the truck too?"

"There was no dog." Ma's sounding cranky again. "You have to let me tell this story."

"Can I pick another?"

"It's what happened."

"Can I have *Jack the Giant Killer*?"

"Listen," says Ma, putting her hand over my mouth. "He made me take some bad medicine so I'd fall asleep. Then when I woke up I was here."

It's nearly black and I can't see Ma's face at all now, it's turned away so I can only hear.

"The first time he opened the door I screamed for help and he knocked me down, I never tried that again."

My tummy's all knotted.

"I used to be scared to go to sleep, in case he came back," says Ma, "but when I was asleep was the only time I wasn't crying, so I slept about sixteen hours a day."

"Did you make a pool?"

"What?"

"Alice cries a pool because she can't remember all her poems and numbers, then she's drowning."

"No," says Ma, "but my head ached all the time, my eyes were scratchy. The smell of the cork tiles made me sick."

What smell?

"I drove myself crazy looking at my watch and counting the seconds. Things spooked me, they seemed to get bigger or smaller while I was watching them, but if I looked away they started sliding. When he finally brought the TV, I left it on

2 **blindfold** a strip of material that covers the eyes (makes you "blind") – 20 **knotted** ['nɑːt̬ɪd] Jack's language for "tense" (*verkrampft*)

twenty-four/seven, stupid stuff, commercials for food I remembered, my mouth hurt wanting it all. Sometimes I heard voices from the TV telling me things."

"Like Dora?"

She shakes her head. "When he was at work I tried to get out, I tried everything. I stood on tiptoe on the table for days scraping around the skylight, I broke all my nails. I threw everything I could think of at it but the mesh is so strong, I never even managed to crack the glass."

Skylight's just a square of not quite so dark. "What everything?" "The big saucepan, chairs, the trash can …"

Wow, I wish I saw her throw Trash.

"And another time I dug a hole."

I'm confused. "Where?"

"You can feel it, would you like that? We'll have to wriggle …" Ma throws Duvet back and pulls Box out from Under Bed, she makes a little grunt going in. I slide in beside her, we're near Eggsnake but not to squish him. "I got the idea from *The Great Escape*." Her voice is all boomy beside my head.

I remember that story about the Nazi camp, not a summer one with marshmallows but in winter with millions of persons drinking maggot soup. The Allies burst open the gates and everybody ran out, I think Allies are angels like Saint Peter's one.

"Give me your fingers …" Ma pulls on them. I feel the cork of Floor. "Just here." Suddenly there's a bit that's down with rough edges. My chest's going *boom boom,* I never knowed there was a hole. "Careful, don't cut yourself. I made it with the zigzag knife," she says. "I pried up the cork, but the wood took me a while. Then the lead foil and the foam were easy enough, but you know what I found then?"

"Wonderland?"

1 **twenty-four/seven** 24 hours, seven days a week (so: "all the time") – 19 **to boom** to make a deep hollow sound, boomy *here*: *dröhnen* – 22 **maggot** a small wormlike creature that usually lives in very dirty places (*Made*) – 29 **to pry** [praɪ] *here*: to open with an effort (usually: with a sharp object)

Ma makes a mad sound so loud I bang my head on Bed.

"Sorry."

"What I found was a chain-link fence."

"Where?"

"Right there in the hole."

A fence in a hole? I put my hand down and downer.

"Something metal, are you there?"

"Yeah." Gold, all smooth, I grab it in my fingers.

"When he was turning the shed into Room," says Ma, "he hid a layer of fence under the floor joists, and in all the walls and even the roof, so I could never ever cut through."

We've wriggled out now. We're sitting with our backs against Bed. I'm all out of breath.

"When he found the hole," says Ma, "he howled."

"Like a wolf?"

"No, laughing. I was afraid he'd hurt me but that time, he thought it was just hilarious."

My teeth are hard together.

"He laughed more back then," says Ma.

Old Nick's a stinking swiping zombie robber. "We could have a mutiny at him," I tell her. "I'll smash him all to bits with my jumbo megatron transformerblaster."

She puts a kiss on the side of my eye. "Hurting him doesn't work. I tried that once, when I'd been here about a year and a half."

That is the most amazing. "You hurted Old Nick?"

"What I did was, I took the lid off the toilet, and I had the smooth knife as well, and just before nine one evening, I stood against the wall beside the door—"

I'm confused. "Toilet doesn't have a lid."

"There used to be one, on top of the tank. It was the heaviest thing in Room."

"Bed's super heavy."

3 **chain-link** *Geflecht aus Metall* – 10 **joist** *Fußbodenbalken* – 21 **mutiny** ['mju:təni] a revolt (usually on a ship) (*Meuterei*) – 27 **lid** top

"But I couldn't pick the bed up, could I?" asks Ma. "So when I heard him coming in—"

"The *beep beep.*"

"Exactly. I smashed the toilet lid down on his head."

I've got my thumb in my mouth and I'm biting and biting.

"But I didn't do it hard enough, the lid fell on the floor and broke in two, and he—Old Nick—he managed to shove the door shut."

I taste something weird.

Ma's voice is all gulpy. "I knew my only chance was to make him give me the code. So I pressed the knife against his throat, like this." She puts her fingernail under my chin, I don't like it. "I said, 'Tell me the code.' "

"Did he?"

She puffs her breath. "He said some numbers, and I went to tap them in."

"Which numbers?"

"I don't think they were the real ones. He jumped up and twisted my wrist and got the knife."

"Your bad wrist?"

"Well, it wasn't bad before that. Don't cry," Ma says into my hair, "that was a long time ago."

I try to talk but it doesn't come out.

"So, Jack, we mustn't try and hurt him again. When he came back the next night, he said, number one, nothing would ever make him tell me the code. And number two, if I ever tried a stunt like that again, he'd go away and I'd get hungrier and hungrier till I died."

She's stopped I think.

My tummy creaks really loud and I figure it out, why Ma's telling me the terrible story. She's telling me that we're going—

Then I'm blinking and covering my eyes, everything's all dazzling because Lamp's come back on.

7 **to shove** [ʃʌv] to push – 27 **stunt** an act of skill that is dangerous – 32 **to blink** to open and shut your eyes quickly – 33 **dazzling** so bright that one can't see properly

Dying

It's all warm. Ma's up already. On Table there's a new box of cereal and four bananas, yippee. Old Nick must have come in the night. I jump out of Bed. There's macaroni too, and hot dogs and mandarins and—

Ma's not eating any of it, she's standing at Dresser looking at Plant. There's three leaves off. Ma touches Plant's stalk and—

"No!"

"She was dead already."

"You broke her."

Ma shakes her head. "Alive things bend, Jack. I think it was the cold, it made Plant go all stiff inside."

I'm trying to fit her stem back together. "She needs some tape." I remember we don't have any left, Ma put the last bit on Spaceship, stupid Ma. I run over to pull Box out from Under Bed, I find Spaceship and rip the bits of tape off.

Ma just watches.

I'm pressing the tape on Plant but it just slips off and she's in pieces.

"I'm so sorry."

"Make her be alive again," I tell Ma.

"I would if I could."

She waits till I stop crying, she wipes my eyes. I'm too hot now, I pull off my extra clothes.

"I guess we better put her in the trash," says Ma.

"No," I say, "down Toilet."

"That could block the pipes."

"We can break her up in tiny pieces ..."

I kiss a few leaves of Plant and flush them, then another few and flush again, then the stalk in bits. "Good-bye, Plant," I whisper. Maybe in the sea she'll stick all back together again and grow up to Heaven.

7 **stalk** [stɑːk] stem – 29 **to flush** to clean out with a sudden flow of water

The sea's real, I'm just remembering. It's all real in Outside, everything there is, because I saw the airplane in the blue between the clouds. Ma and me can't go there because we don't know the secret code, but it's real all the same.

Before I didn't even know to be mad that we can't open Door, my head was too small to have Outside in it. When I was a little kid I thought like a little kid, but now I'm five I know everything.

We have a bath right after breakfast, the water's all steamy, yum. We fill Bath so high it nearly makes a flood. Ma lies back and goes nearly asleep, I wake her up to wash her hair and she does mine. We do laundry too, but then there's long hairs on the sheets so we have to pick them off, we have a race to see who gets more fasterer.

The cartoons are over already, kids are coloring eggs for the Runaway Bunny. I look at each different kid and I say in my head: *You're real.*

"The Easter Bunny, not the Runaway Bunny," says Ma. "Me and Paul used to—when we were kids, the Easter Bunny brought chocolate eggs in the night and hid them all around our backyard, under bushes and in holes in the trees, even in the hammock."

"Did he take your teeth?" I ask.

"No, it was all for free." Her face is flat.

I don't think the Easter Bunny knows where Room is, anyway we don't have bushes and trees, they're outside Door.

This is a pretty happy day because of the heat and the food, but Ma's not happy. Probably she misses Plant.

I choose Phys Ed, it's Hiking, where we walk hand in hand on Track and call out what we can see. "Look, Ma, a waterfall."

After a minute I say, "Look, a wildebeest."

"Wow."

"Your turn."

13 **race** competition (*Wettkampf*) – 16 **Runaway Bunny** figure from a children's book – 18 **Easter Bunny** *Osterhase* – 31 **wildebeest** another word for gnu (large animal related to the antelope)

"Oh, look," says Ma, "a snail."

I bend down to see it. "Look, a giant bulldozer knocking down a skyscraper."

"Look," she says, "a flamingo flying by."

"Look, a zombie all drooling."

"Jack!" That makes her smile for half a second.

Then we march faster and sing "This Land Is Your Land." Then we put Rug down again and she's our flying carpet, we zoom over the North Pole.

Ma picks Corpse, where we lie extra still, I forget and scratch my nose so she wins. Next I choose Trampoline but she says she doesn't want to do any more Phys Ed.

"You just do the commentary and I do the boinging."

"No, sorry, I'm going back to Bed for a bit."

She's not much fun today.

I pull Eggsnake out from Under Bed real slow, I think I can hear him hiss with his needle tongue, *Greetingssssss*. I stroke him especially his eggs that are cracked or dented. One crumbles off in my fingers, I go make glue with a pinch of flour and stick the pieces on a ruled paper for a jaggedy mountain. I want to show Ma but her eyes are closed.

I go in Wardrobe and play I'm a coal miner. I find a gold nugget under my pillow, he's actually Tooth. He's not alive and he didn't bend, he broke, but we don't have to put him down Toilet. He's made of Ma, her dead spit.

I stick my head out and Ma's eyes open. "What are you doing?" I ask her.

"Just thinking."

I can think and do interesting stuff at the same time. Can't she? She gets up to make lunch, it's a box of macaroni all orangey *delicioso*.

5 **to drool** to let water drip from the mouth – 10 **corpse** dead body – 13 **boinging** Jack's language for "jumping" – 20 **jaggedy** Jack's language for "jagged" (*gezackt*)

Afterwards I play Icarus with his wings melting. Ma's washing up real slow. I wait for her to be done so she can play but she doesn't want to play, she sits in Rocker and just rocks.

"What are you doing?"

"Still thinking." After a minute, she asks, "What's in the pillowcase?"

"It's my backpack." I've tied two corners of it around my neck. "It's for going in Outside when we get rescued." I've put in Tooth and Jeep and Remote and an underwear for me and one for Ma and socks too and Scissors and the four apples for if we get hungry. "Is there water?" I ask her.

Ma nods. "Rivers, lakes …"

"No, but for drinking, is there a faucet?"

"Lots of faucets."

I'm glad I don't have to bring a bottle of water because my backpack's pretty heavy now, I have to hold it at my neck so it doesn't squish my talking.

Ma's rocking and rocking. "I used to dream about being rescued," she says. "I wrote notes and hid them in the trash bags, but nobody ever found them."

"You should have sent them down Toilet."

"And when we scream, nobody hears us," she says. "I was flashing the light on and off half the night last night, then I thought, nobody's looking."

"But—"

"Nobody's going to rescue us."

I don't say anything. And then I say, "You don't know everything there is."

Her face is the strangest I ever saw.

I'd rather she was Gone for the day than all not-Ma like this.

I get all my books down from Shelf and read them, *Pop-Up Airport* and *Nursery Rhymes* and *Dylan the Digger* who's my

1 **Icarus** a figure from Greek mythology: Icarus and his father Daedalus were held prisoners by King Minos. They tried to escape by fastening wings to their bodies with wax. As they were escaping Icarus flew too close to the sun, the wax melted and the boy fell into the sea. – 17 **squish** *inf* here: *erdrücken*

favorite and *The Runaway Bunny* but I stop halfway and save that for Ma, I read some *Alice* instead, I skip the scary Duchess.

Ma finally stops rocking.

"Can I have some?"

"Sure," she says, "come here."

I sit in her lap and lift up her T-shirt and I have lots for a long time.

"All done?" she says in my ear.

"Yeah."

"Listen, Jack. Are you listening?"

"I'm always listening."

"We have to get out of here."

I stare at her.

"And we have to do it all by ourselves."

But she said we were like in a book, how do people in a book escape from it?

"We need to figure out a plan." Her voice is all high.

"Like what?"

"I don't know, do I? I've been trying to think of one for seven years."

"We could smash down the walls." But we don't have a jeep to smash them down or a bulldozer even. "We could … blow up Door."

"With what?"

"The cat did it on *Tom and Jerry*—"

"It's great that you're brainstorming," says Ma, "but we need an idea that'll actually work."

"A *really* big explosion," I tell her.

"If it's really big, it'll blow us up too."

I hadn't thought of that. I do another brainstorm.

"Oh, Ma! We could … wait till Old Nick comes one night and you could say, 'Oh, look at this yummy cake we made, have a big slice of our yummy Easter cake,' and actually it would be poison."

2 **to skip** to leave out

Ma shakes her head. "If we make him sick, he still won't give us the code."

I think so hard it hurts.

"Any other ideas?"

"You say no to all of them."

"Sorry. Sorry. I'm just trying to be realistic."

"Which ideas are realistic?"

"I don't know. I don't know." Ma licks her lips. "I keep obsessing about the moment the door opens, if we timed it exactly right for that split second, could we rush past him?"

"Oh yeah, that's a cool idea."

"If you could slip out, even, while I go for his eyes—" Ma shakes her head. "No way."

"Yes way."

"He'd grab you, Jack, he'd grab you before you got halfway up the yard and—" She stops talking.

After a minute I say, "Any other ideas?"

"Just the same ones going around and around like rats on a wheel," says Ma through her teeth.

Why rats go on a wheel? Is it like a Ferris at a fair?

"We should do a cunning trick," I tell her.

"Like what?"

"Like, maybe like when you were a student and he tricked you into his truck with his dog that wasn't a real dog."

Ma lets out her breath. "I know you're trying to help, but maybe you could hush for a while now so I can think?"

But we were thinking, we were thinking hard together. I get up and go eat the banana with the big brown bit, the brown is the sweetest

"Jack!" Ma's eyes are all huge and she's talking extra fast. "What you said about the dog—actually that was a brilliant idea. What if we pretend you're ill?"

I'm confused, then I see. "Like the dog that wasn't?"

9 **to obsess** to be obsessed (*besessen sein*) – 20 **Ferris** ferris wheel; big wheel at a fair (*Riesenrad*)

"Exactly. When he comes in—I could tell him you're really sick."

"What kind of sick?"

"Maybe a really, really bad cold," says Ma. "Try coughing a lot."

I cough and cough and she listens. "Hmm," she says.

I don't think I'm very good at it. I cough louder, it feels like my throat's going to rip.

Ma shakes her head. "Forget the cough."

"I can do it even bigger—"

"You're doing a great job, but it still sounds pretend."

I let out the biggest horriblest cough ever.

"I don't know," says Ma, "maybe coughing is just too hard to fake. Anyway—" She slaps her head. "I'm so dumb."

"No you're not." I rub where she hit.

"It has to be something you picked up from Old Nick, d'you see? He's the only one who brings in the germs, and he hasn't had a cold. No, we need … something in the food?" She looks all fierce at the bananas. "E. coli? Would that give you a fever?"

Ma's not meant to ask me things, she's meant to know.

"A really bad fever, so you can't talk or wake up properly …"

"Why I can't talk?"

"It'll make the pretending easier if you don't. Yeah," says Ma, her eyes all shiny, "I'll tell him, 'You've got to take Jack to the hospital in your truck so the doctors can give him the right medicine.' "

"Me riding in the brown truck?"

Ma nods. "To the hospital."

I can't believe it. But then I think about the medical planet. "I don't want to be cutted open."

"Oh, the doctors won't do anything to you for real, because you won't actually have anything wrong with you, remember?" She strokes my shoulder. "It's just a trick for our Great Escape.

12 **horriblest** Jack's language for "most horrible" – 13 **to fake** to pretend – 19 **E. coli** bacteria in the intestine that make you really sick

Old Nick will carry you into the hospital, and the first doctor you see—or nurse, whatever—you shout, 'Help!' "

"You can shout it."

I think maybe Ma didn't hear me. Then she says, "I won't be at the hospital."

"Where will you be?"

"Right here in Room."

I have a better idea. "You could be pretend-sick too, like that time we had diarrhea both at the same time, then he'd bring both of us in his truck."

Ma chews her lip. "He won't buy it. I know it'll be really weird to go on your own, but I'll be talking to you in your head every minute, I promise. Remember when Alice was falling down, down, down, she was talking to Dinah her cat in her head all the time?"

Ma won't be in my head really. My tummy hurts just thinking about it. "I don't like this plan."

"Jack—"

"It's a bad idea."

"Actually—"

"I'm not going in Outside without you."

"Jack—"

"No way Jose no way Jose no way Jose."

"OK, calm down. Forget it."

"Really?"

"Yeah, there's no point trying this if you're not ready." She still sounds cranky.

It's April today so I get to blow up a balloon. There's three left, red, yellow, and another yellow, I choose yellow so there'll still be one of each red or yellow for next month. I blow it up and let it zoom around Room lots of times, I like the spluttery noise. It's hard to decide when to tie the knot because after, the balloon won't zoom anymore, just slow flying. But I need to tie the knot to play Balloon Tennis. So I let it go *splutterzoom* a lot and blow

27 **cranky** very strange, odd – 31 **spluttery** *stotternd*

it up three times more, then I tie the knot, with my finger in it by accident. When it's tied right, Ma and me play Balloon Tennis, I win five times of seven.

She says, "Would you like some?"

"The left, please," I say, getting onto Bed.

There isn't very much but it's yummy.

I think I snooze for a while but then Ma's talking in my ear. "Remember how they crawled through the dark tunnel away from the Nazis? One at a time."

"Yeah."

"That's how we'll do it, when you're ready."

"What tunnel?" I look all around.

"*Like* the tunnel, not an actual one. What I'm saying is, the prisoners had to be really brave and go one at a time."

I shake my head.

"It's the only workable plan." Ma's eyes are too shiny. "You're my brave Prince JackerJack. You'll go to the hospital first, see, then you'll come back with the police—"

"Will they arrest me?"

"No no, they'll help. You'll bring them back here to rescue me and we'll be together again always."

"I can't rescue," I tell her, "I'm only five."

"But you've got superpowers," Ma tells me. "You're the only one who can do this. Will you?"

I don't know what to say but she's waiting and waiting. "OK."

"Is that a yes?"

"Yes."

She gives me an enormous kiss.

We get out of Bed and have a tub of mandarins each.

Our plan has problem bits, Ma keeps thinking of them and saying oh no, but then she figures out a way.

"The police won't know the secret code to get you out," I tell her.

"They'll think of something."

14 **brave** courageous – 31 **to figure out** to discover by thinking

"What?"

She rubs her eye. "I don't know, a blowtorch?"

"What's—?"

"It's a tool with flame coming out, it could burn the door right open."

"We could make one," I tell her, jumping up and down. "We could, we could take the vitamin bottle with the Dragon head and put him on Stove with the power on till he's on fire, and—"

"And burn ourselves to death," says Ma, not friendly.

"But—"

"Jack, this is not a game. Let's go over the plan again ..."

I remember all the parts but I keep getting them the wrong way around.

"Look, it's like on *Dora*," says Ma, "when she goes to one place and then a second place to get to the third place. For us it's *Truck, hospital, Police.* Say it?"

"Truck, Hospital, Police."

"Or maybe it's five steps, actually. *Sick, Truck, Hospital, Police, Save Ma.*" She waits.

"Truck—"

"Sick."

"Sick," I say.

"*Hospital*—no, sorry, *Truck. Sick, Truck—*"

"Sick, Truck, Hospital, Save Ma."

"You forgot *Police,*" she says. "Count on your fingers. *Sick, Truck, Hospital, Police, Save Ma.*"

We do it over and over. We make a map of it on ruled paper with pictures, the sick one has me with my eyes closed and my tongue all hanging out, then there's a brown pickup truck, then a person in a long white coat that means doctors, then a police car with a flashing siren, then Ma waving and smiling because of being free, with the blowtorch all fiery like a dragon. My head is tired but Ma says we have to practice the being sick bit, that's the most important. "Because if he doesn't believe it, none of

2 **blowtorch** *Lötlampe* – 32 **fiery** ['faɪə·i] as if on fire

the rest will happen. I've had an idea, I'm going to make your forehead really hot and let him touch it …"

"No."

"It's OK, I won't burn you—"

She doesn't understand. "No him touching me."

"Ah," says Ma. "Just one time, I promise, and I'll be right beside you."

I keep shaking my head.

"Yeah, this could work," she says, "maybe you could lie against the vent …" She kneels down and puts her hand in Under Bed near Bed Wall, then she frowns and says, "Not hot enough. Maybe … a bag of really hot water on your forehead, just before he comes? You'll be in bed, and when we hear the door going *beep beep* I'll hide the bag of water."

"Where?"

"It doesn't matter."

"It does matter."

Ma looks at me. "You're right, we have to figure out all the details so nothing messes up our plan. I'll drop the bag of water under the bed, OK? Then when Old Nick feels your forehead it'll be super hot. Will we try that?"

"With the bag of water?"

"No, just get into bed for now and practice being all floppy, like when we play Corpse."

I'm very good at that, my mouth hangs open. She pretends to be him, with a really deep voice. She puts her hand over my eyebrows and says all gruff, "Wow, that's hot."

I giggle.

"Jack."

"Sorry." I lie extra still.

We practice a lot more, then I'm sick of being pretend-sick, so Ma lets me stop.

Dinner's hot dogs. Ma's hardly eating hers. "So do you remember the plan?" she asks.

2 **forehead** *Stirn* – 10 **vent** pipe of the heating system (*Ventil*) – 11 **to frown** to bring your eyebrows together (in concentration) – 27 **gruff** (of a person's voice) deep and rough

I nod.

"Tell me."

I swallow my end of roll. *"Sick, Truck, Hospital, Police, Save Ma."*

"Wonderful. Are you ready, then?"

"For what?"

"Our Great Escape. Tonight."

I didn't know it's tonight. I'm not ready. "Why is it tonight?" "I don't want to wait any longer. After he cut the power—" "But he switched it back on last night."

"Yeah, after three days. And Plant was dead from the cold. And who knows what he'll do tomorrow?" Ma stands up with her plate, she's nearly shouting. "He looks human, but there's nothing inside."

I'm confused. "Like a robot?"

"Worse."

"One time there was this robot on *Bob the Builder*—" Ma butts in. "You know your heart, Jack?"

"Bam bam." I show her on my chest.

"No, but your feeling bit, where you're sad or scared or laughing or stuff?"

That's lower down, I think it's in my tummy.

"Well, he hasn't got one."

"A tummy?"

"A feeling bit," says Ma.

I'm looking at my tummy. "What does he have instead?" She shrugs. "Just a gap."

Like a crater? But that's a hole where something happened. What happened?

I still don't understand why Old Nick being a robot means we have to do the cunning plan tonight. "Let's do it another night." "OK," says Ma, she flops down in her chair.

"OK?"

18 **to butt in** *sl* to interrupt – 27 **gap** an empty space

"Yeah." She rubs her forehead. "I'm sorry, Jack, I know I'm rushing you. I've had a long time to think this through, but it's all new to you."

I nod and nod.

"I guess another couple of days can't make much difference. So long as I don't let him pick another fight." She smiles at me. "Maybe in a couple of days?"

"Maybe when I'm six."

Ma's staring at me.

"Yeah, I'll be ready to trick him and go in Outside when I'm six."

She puts her face down on her arms.

I pull at her. "Don't."

When it comes up it's a scary face. "You said you were going to be my superhero."

I don't remember saying that.

"Don't you want to escape?"

"Yeah. Only not really."

"Jack!"

I look at my last piece of hot dog but I don't want it. "Let's just stay."

Ma's shaking her head. "It's getting too small."

"What is?"

"Room."

"Room's not small. Look." I climb up on my chair and jump with my arms out and spin, I don't bang into anything.

"You don't even know what it's doing to you." Her voice is shaky. "You need to see things, touch things—"

"I do already."

"More things, other things. You need more room. Grass. I thought you wanted to meet Grandma and Grandpa and Uncle Paul, go on the swings at the playground, eat ice cream …"

"No, thanks."

"OK, forget it."

4 **to nod** *nicken* – 26 **to spin** to turn around fast

Ma pulls her clothes off and puts on her sleeping T-shirt. I do mine. She doesn't say anything she's so furious at me. She ties up the trash bag and puts it beside Door. There's no list on it tonight.

We brush teeth. She spits. There's white on her mouth. Her eyes look in mine in Mirror. "I'd give you more time if I could," she says. "I swear, I'd wait as long as you needed if I thought we were safe. But we're not."

I turn around quick to the real her, I hide my face in her tummy. I get some toothpaste on her T-shirt but she doesn't mind.

We lie on Bed and Ma gives me some, the left, we don't talk. In Wardrobe I can't get to sleep. I sing quietly, " 'John Jacob Jingleheimer Schmidt.' " I wait. I sing it again.

Finally Ma answers, " 'His name is my name, too.' "

" 'Whenever I go out—' "

" 'The people always shout—' "

" 'There goes John Jacob Jingleheimer Schmidt—' "

Usually she joins in for the "na na na na na na na," it's the funnest bit, but not this time.

* * *

Ma wakes me but it's still night. She's leaning in Wardrobe, I bang my shoulder sitting up. "Come see," she whispers.

We stand beside Table and look up, there's the most hugest round silver face of God. So bright, shining all of Room, the faucets and Mirror and the pots and Door and Ma's cheeks even. "You know," she whispers, "sometimes the moon is a semicircle, and sometimes a crescent, and sometimes just a little curve like a fingernail clipping."

"Nah." Only in TV.

She points up at Skylight. "You've just seen it when it's full and right overhead. But when we get out, we'll be able to spot it

28 **crescent** the shape of the moon when it forms less than a semi-circle

lower down in the sky, when it's all kind of shapes. And even in the daytime."

"No way Jose."

"I'm telling you the truth. You're going to enjoy the world so much. Wait till you see the sun when it's going down, all pink and purple ..."

I yawn.

"Sorry," she says, whispering again, "come on into bed."

I look to see if the trash bag is gone, it is. "Was Old Nick here?"

"Yeah. I told him you were coming down with something. Cramps, diarrhea." Ma's voice is nearly laughing.

"Why you—?"

"That way he'll start believing our trick. Tomorrow night, that's when we'll do it."

I yank my hand out of hers. "You shouldn't told him that."

"Jack—"

"Bad idea."

"It's a good plan."

"It's a stupid dumbo plan."

"It's the only one we've got," says Ma very loud.

"But I said no."

"Yeah, and before that you said maybe, and before that you said yes."

"You're a cheater."

"I'm your mother." Ma's nearly roaring. "That means sometimes I have to choose for both of us."

We get into Bed. I curl up tight, with her behind me.

I wish we got those special boxing gloves for Sundaytreat so I'd be allowed hit her.

* * *

I wake up scared and I stay scared.

6 **purple** a dark colour made by mixing red and blue – 15 **to yank** *inf* to pull suddenly – 24 **cheater** a dishonest person – 25 **to roar** to shout – 27 **to curl up** to lie comfortably on your side with your arms and legs drawn close to your body

Ma doesn't let us flush after poo, she breaks it all up with the handle of Wooden Spoon so it'll look like poo soup, it smells the worst.

We don't play anything, we just practice me being floppy and not saying one single word. I feel a bit sick for real, Ma says that's just the power of suggestion. "You're so good at pretending, you're even tricking yourself."

I pack my backpack again that's really a pillowcase, I put Remote in and my yellow balloon, but Ma says no. "If you have anything with you, Old Nick will guess you're running away."

"I could hide Remote in my pants pocket."

She shakes her head. "You'll just be in your sleep T-shirt and underwear, because that's what you'd be wearing if you were really scorching hot with a fever."

I think about Old Nick carrying me into the truck, I'm dizzy like I'm going to fall down.

"Scared is what you're feeling," says Ma, "but brave is what you're doing."

"Huh?"

"Scaredybrave."

"Scave."

Word sandwiches always make her laugh but I wasn't being funny.

Lunch is beef soup, I just suck the crackers.

"Which bit are you worrying about right now?" asks Ma. "The hospital. What if I don't say the right words?"

"All you have to do is tell them your mother's locked up and the man who brought you in did it."

"But the words—"

"What?" She waits.

"What if they don't come out at all?"

Ma leans her mouth on her fingers. "I keep forgetting you've never talked to anybody but me."

I wait.

14 **scorching** burning – 20 **scaredybrave** an invented word meaning a combination of scared and brave – 21 **scave** a short version of scaredybrave

Ma lets her breath out long and noisy. "Tell you what, I have an idea. I'll write you a note for you to keep hidden, a note that explains everything."

"Good-o."

"You just give it to the first person—not a patient, I mean, the first person in a uniform."

"What'll the person do with it?"

"Read it, of course."

"TV persons can read?"

She stares at me. "They're real people, remember, just like us." I still don't believe that but I don't say.

Ma does the note on a bit of ruled paper. It's a story all about us and Room and *Please send help a.s.a.p.*, that means super fast. Near the start, there's two words I never saw before, Ma says they're her names like TV persons have, what everybody in Outside used to call her, it's only me who says Ma.

My tummy hurts, I don't like her to have other names that I never even knowed. "Do I have other names?"

"No, you're always Jack. Oh, but—I guess you'd have my last name too." She points at the second one.

"What for?"

"Well, to show you're not the same as all the other Jacks in the world."

"Which other Jacks? Like in the magic stories?"

"No, real boys," says Ma. "There are millions of people out there, and there aren't enough names for everyone, they have to share."

I don't want to share my name. My tummy hurts harder. I don't have a pocket so I put the note inside my underwear, it's scratchy.

The light's all leaking away. I wish the day stayed longer so it wouldn't be night.

13 **a.s.a.p.** *abb* for "as soon as possible" – 30 **scratchy** rough and uncomfortable – 31 **to leak away** Jack means "to fade"

It's 08:41 and I'm in Bed practicing. Ma's filled a plastic bag with really hot water and tied it tight so none spills out, she puts it in another bag and ties that too. "Ouch." I try to get away.

"Is it your eyes?" She puts it back on my face. "It's got to be hot, or it won't work."

"But it hurts."

She tries it on herself. "One more minute."I put up my fists between.

"You have to be as brave as Prince JackerJack," says Ma, "or this won't work. Maybe I should just tell Old Nick you got better?"

"No."

"I bet Jack the Giant Killer would put a hot bag on his face if he had to. Come on, just a bit longer."

"Let me." I put the bag down on the pillow, I scrunch up my face and put it on the hotness. Sometimes I come up for a break and Ma feels my forehead or my cheeks and says, "Sizzling," then she makes me put my face back. I'm crying a bit, not about the hot but because of Old Nick coming, if he's coming tonight, I don't want him to, I think I'm going to be sick for actual. I'm always listening for the *beep beep*. I hope he doesn't come, I'm not scave I'm just regular scared.

I run to Toilet and do more poo and Ma stirs it up. I want to flush but she says no, Room has to stink like I've had diarrhea all day.

When I get back into Bed she kisses the back of my neck and says, "You're doing great, crying is a big help."

"Why's—?"

"Because it makes you look sicker. Let's do something about your hair. … I should have thought of that before." She puts some dish soap on her hands and rubs it hard all on my head. "That looks good and greasy. Oh but it smells too nice, you need to smell worse." She runs over to look at Watch again. "We're

15 **to scrunch** *inf* to press and twist – 17 **sizzling** a sound like food cooking in hot fat – 20 **for actual** Jack means "for real"

running out of time," she says, all shaky. "I'm an idiot, you have to smell bad, you really—Hang on."

She leans over Bed, she makes a weird cough and puts her hand in her mouth. She keeps making the weird sound. Then stuff falls out of her mouth like spit but much thicker. I can see the fish sticks we had for dinner.

She's rubbing it on the pillow, on my hair. "Stop," I shriek, I'm trying to wriggle away.

"Sorry, I have to." Ma's eyes are weird and shiny. She's wiping her vomit on my T-shirt, even my mouth. It smells the worst ever, all sharp and poisonous. "Put your face on the hot bag again."

"But—"

"Do it, Jack, hurry."

"I want to stop now."

"We're not playing, we can't stop. Do it."

I'm crying because the stink and my face in the hot bag so I think it's going to melt off. "You're mean."

"I've got a good reason," says Ma.

Beep beep. Beep beep.

Ma grabs the bag of water away, it's ripping off my face. "Shh." She presses my eyes shut, pushes my face down into the awful pillow, she pulls Duvet right up over my back.

The colder air comes in with him. Ma calls out right away, "There you are."

"Keep your voice down." Old Nick says it quietly like a growl. "I just—"

"Shh." Another *beep beep,* then the *boom.* "You know the drill," he says, "not a peep out of you till the door's shut."

"Sorry, sorry. It's just, Jack's really bad." Ma's voice is shaking and for a minute I nearly believe it, she's even better pretending than me. "It reeks in here."

"That's because he's had it coming out both ends."

"Probably just a twenty-four-hour bug," says Old Nick.

3 **weird** strange – 26 **growl** the deep, rough sound of an animal giving a warning – 32 **to reek** to stink – 34 **bug** *inf* germ (*Virus*)

"It's been more like thirty hours already. He's got chills, he's burning up—"

"Give him one of those headache pills."

"What do you think I've been trying all day? He just pukes them up again. He can't even keep water down."

Old Nick puffs his breath. "Let's have a look at him."

"No," says Ma.

"Come on, get out of the way—"

"No, I said no—"

I keep my face in the pillow, it's sticky. My eyes are shut. Old Nick's there, right by Bed, he can see me. I feel his hand on my cheek, I make a sound because I'm so scared, Ma said it would be my forehead but it isn't, it's my cheek he's touching and his hand isn't like Ma's, it's cold and heavy—

Then it's gone. "I'll get him something stronger from the allnight drugstore."

"Something stronger? He's barely five years old, he's totally dehydrated, with a fever of God knows what." Ma's shouting, she shouldn't shout, Old Nick's going to get mad.

"Just shut up for a second and let me think."

"He needs to go to the ER right now, that's what he needs and you know it."

Old Nick makes a sound, I don't know what it means.

Ma's voice is like she's crying. "If you don't bring him in now, he'll, he could—"

"Enough with the hysterics," he says.

"Please. I'm begging you."

"No way."

I nearly say *Jose*. I think it but I don't say it, I'm not saying anything, I'm just being limp all Gone.

"Just tell them he's an illegal alien with no papers," says Ma, "he's in no state to say a word, you can drive him right back

4 **to puke** *sl* to throw up, to be sick – 16 **drugstore** *AE* pharmacy, a store which sells not only medicine but beauty products etc. – 18 **to dehydrate** [ˌdiːhaɪˈdreɪt] to lose water from the body – 21 **ER** Emergency Room (*Notaufnahme*)

here as soon as they've got some fluids into him …" Her voice is moving after him. "Please. I'll do anything."

"There's no talking to you." He sounds like he's over by Door.

"Don't go. Please, please …"

Something falls down. I'm so scared I'm never opening my eyes. Ma's wailing. The *beep beep. Boom,* Door's shut, we're on our own.

It's all quiet. I count my teeth five times, always twenty except one time it's nineteen but I count again till it's twenty. I peek sideways. Then I lift my head off the stinky pillow.

Ma's sitting on Rug with her back against Door Wall. She's staring at nothing. I whisper, "Ma?"

She does the strangest thing, she sort of smiles.

"Did I mess up the pretending?"

"Oh, no. You were a star."

"But he didn't take me to the hospital."

"That's OK." Ma gets up and wets a cloth in Sink, she comes to wipe my face.

"But you said." All that burning face and vomit and him touching me. "*Sick, Truck, Hospital, Police, Save Ma.*"

Ma's nodding, she lifts my T-shirt off and wipes my chest. "That was Plan A, it was worth a try. But like I figured, he was too scared."

She's got it wrong. "*He* was scared?"

"Just in case you'd tell the doctors about Room and the police would put him in jail. I hoped he'd risk it, if he thought you were in serious danger—but I never really thought he would."

I get it. "You tricked me," I roar. "I didn't get to ride in the brown truck."

"Jack," she says, she's pressing me against her, her bones hurt my face. I push away. "You said no more lying and you were unlying now, but then you lied again."

"I'm doing my best," says Ma.

1 **fluid** liquid (*Flüssigkeit*) – 6 **to wail** to cry out as if in pain – 9 **to peek** *inf* to take a quick look at sb – 14 **to mess up** to ruin – 22 **to figure** *AE* to believe – 28 **to roar** *inf* to laugh long and loudly

I suck on my lip.

"Listen. Will you listen to me for a minute?"

"I'm sick of listening to you."

She nods. "I know. But listen anyway. There's a Plan B. Plan A was really the first part of Plan B."

"You never said."

"It's pretty complicated. I've been puzzling over it for a few days now."

"Yeah, well I've got millions of brains for puzzling."

"You do," says Ma.

"Way more than you."

"That's true. But I didn't want you to have to hold both plans in your head at the same time, you might get confused."

"I'm confused already, I'm one hundred percent confused."

She kisses me through my hair that's all sticky. "Let me tell you about Plan B."

"I don't want to hear your stinky dumb plans."

"OK."

I'm shivering from having no T-shirt on. I find a clean one in Dresser, a blue.

We get into Bed, the smell is awful. Ma shows me to breathe through my mouth only because mouths don't smell anything. "Can we lie with our heads the other way?"

"Brilliant idea," says Ma.

She's being nice but I'm not going to forgive her.

We put our feet at the stinky wall end and our faces at the other. I think I'm never going to switch off.

* * *

It's 08:21 already, I slept for long and now I'm having some, the left is so creamy. Old Nick didn't come back I don't think.

"Is it Saturday?" I ask.

"That's right."

"Cool, we wash our hair."

Ma shakes her head. "You can't smell clean."

I was forgetting for a minute. "What is it?"

"What?"

"Plan B."

"Are you ready to hear it now?"

I don't say anything.

"Well. Here goes." Ma clears her throat. "I've been going over it and over it every which way, I think it just might work. I don't know, I can't be sure, it sounds crazy and I know it's incredibly dangerous but—"

"Just tell me," I say.

"OK, OK." She takes a loud breath. "Do you remember the Count of Monte Cristo?"

"He was locked up in a dungeon on an island."

"Yeah, but remember how he got out? He pretended to be his dead friend, he hid in the shroud and the guards threw him into the sea but the Count didn't drown, he wriggled out and swam away."

"Tell the rest of the story."

Ma waves her hand. "It doesn't matter. The point is, Jack, that's what you're going to do."

"Get thrown in the sea?"

"No, escape like the Count of Monte Cristo."

I'm confused again. "I don't have a dead friend."

"I just mean you'll be disguised as dead."

I stare at her.

"Actually it's more like a play I saw in high school. This girl Juliet, to run away with the boy she loved, she pretended she was dead by drinking medicine, then a few days later she woke up, ta-da."

"No, that's Baby Jesus."

"Ah—not really." Ma rubs her forehead. "He was actually dead for three days, then he came back to life. You're not going to be dead at all, just pretending like the girl in the play."

14 **dungeon** ['dʌndʒn] a dark underground prison, esp beneath a castle – 16 **shroud** [ʃraʊd] a cloth for covering a dead body for burial – 17 **to wriggle out** *sich loswinden*

"I don't know to pretend I'm a girl."

"No, pretending you're dead." Ma's voicc is a bit cranky. "We don't have a shroud."

"Aha, we're going to use the rug."

I stare down at Rug, all her red and black and brown zigzag pattern.

"When Old Nick comes back—tonight, or tomorrow night, or whenever—I'm going to tell him you died, I'm going to show him the rug all rolled up with you inside it."

That's the craziest thing I ever heard. "Why?"

"Because your body didn't have enough water left, and I guess the fever stopped your heart."

"No, why in Rug?"

"Ah," says Ma, "smart question. It's your disguise, so he doesn't guess you're actually alive. See, you did a super job of pretending to be sick last night, but dead is much harder. If he notices you breathing even one time, he'll know it's a trick. Besides, dead people are really cold."

"We could use a bag of cold water …"

She shakes her head. "Cold all over, not just your face. Oh, and they go stiff as well, you'll need to lie like you're a robot."

"Not floppy?"

"The opposite of floppy."

But it's him that's the robot, Old Nick, I have a heart.

"So I think wrapping you up in the rug is the only way to keep him from guessing you're actually alive. Then I'll tell him he has to take you somewhere and bury you, see?"

My mouth's starting to shake. "Why he has to bury me?" "Because dead bodies start to get stinky fast."

Room's pretty stinky already today from not flushing and the vomity pillow and all. " 'The worms crawl in, the worms crawl out …' " "Exactly."

"I don't want to get buried and gooey with the worms crawling."

Ma strokes my head. "It's just a trick, remember?"

33 **gooey** *inf* sticky (*klebrig*)

"Like a game."

"But no laughing. A serious game."

I nod. I think I'm going to cry.

"Believe me," says Ma. "If there was anything else I thought had a chance in hell ..."

I don't know what a chance in hell is.

"OK." Ma gets out of Bed. "Let me tell you how it's going to be and then you won't be so scared. Old Nick will tap in the numbers to open the door, then he'll carry you out of Room all rolled up in the rug."

"Will you be in Rug too?" I know the answer but I ask just in case.

"I'll be right here, waiting," says Ma. "He'll carry you to his pickup truck, he'll put you in the back of it, the open bit—"

"I want to wait here too."

She puts her finger on my mouth to shush me. "And that's your chance."

"What is?"

"The truck! The first time it slows down at a stop sign, you're going to wriggle out of the rug, jump down onto the street, run away, and bring the police to rescue me."

I stare at her.

"So this time the plan is *Dead, Truck, Run, Police, Save Ma.* Say it?"

"Dead, Truck, Run, Police, Save Ma."

We have our breakfast, 125 cereal each because we need extra strength. I'm not hungry but Ma says I should eat them all up.

Then we get dressed and practice the dead bit. It's like the strangest Phys Ed we ever played. I lie down on the edge of Rug and Ma wraps her over me and tells me to go on my front, then my back, then my front, then my back again, till I'm all rolled up tight. It smells funny in Rug, dusty and something, different from if I lie just on her.

5 **a chance in hell** *inf* any chance at all – 16 **to shush sb** [ʃʌʃ] to keep sb quiet

Ma picks me up, I'm squished. She says I'm like a long, heavy package, but Old Nick will lift me easily because he has more muscles. "He'll carry you up the backyard, probably into his garage, like this—" I feel us going around Room. I'm scrunched in my neck but I don't move one bit. "Or maybe over his shoulder like this—" She heaves me, she grunts, I'm being pressed in half.

"Is it a long long ways?"

"What's that?"

My words are getting lost in Rug.

"Hang on," says Ma, "I just thought, he might put you down a couple of times, to open doors." She sets me down, my head end first. "Ow."

"But you won't make a sound, will you?"

"Sorry." Rug's on my face, she's itching my nose but I can't reach it.

"He'll drop you into the flatbed of his truck, like this." She drops me *thump,* I bite my mouth to not shout.

"Stay stiff, stiff, stiff, like a robot, OK, no matter what happens?"

"OK."

"Because if you go soft or move or make a single sound, Jack, if you do any of that by mistake, he'll know you're really alive, and he'll be so mad he—"

"What?" I wait. "Ma. What'll he do?"

"Don't worry, he's going to believe you're dead."

How does she know for sure?

"Then he'll get in the front of his truck and start driving."

"Where?"

"Ah, out of the city, probably. Somewhere there's no people to see him digging a hole, like a forest or something. But the thing is, as soon as the engine starts—it'll feel loud and buzzy and shaky like this"—she blows a raspberry on me through Rug,

6 **to heave** to lift with great effort (*wuchten*) – 15 **to itch** *jucken* – 17 **flatbed** *AE offener Laderaum* – 33 **to blow a raspberry** *prusten*

raspberries usually make me laugh but not now—"that's your signal to start getting out of the rug. Try it?"

I wriggle, but I can't, it's too tight. "I'm stuck. I'm stuck, Ma." She unrolls me right away. I breathe lots of air.

"OK?"

"OK."

She smiles at me but it's a weird smile like she's pretending. Then she rolls me up again a bit looser.

"Still squishes."

"Sorry, I didn't think it would be so stiff. Hang on—" Ma undoes me again. "Hey, try folding your arms with your elbows stuck out a bit to make some room."

This time after she rolls me up with folded arms, I can get them over my head, I wave my fingers out the end of Rug.

"Great. Try wriggling up now, like it's a tunnel."

"It's too tight." I don't know how the Count did it while he was drowning. "Let me out."

"Hang on a minute."

"Let me out now!"

"If you keep panicking," says Ma, "our plan's not going to work."

I'm crying again, Rug's wet on my face. "Out!"

Rug unrolls, I'm breathing again.

Ma puts her hand on my face but I throw it off.

"Jack—"

"No."

"Listen."

"Numbskull Plan B."

"I know it's scary. You think I don't know? But we have to try it."

"No we don't. Not till I'm six."

"There's a thing called foreclosure."

"What?" I'm staring at Ma.

"It's hard to explain." She lets out her breath. "Old Nick doesn't really own his house, the bank does. And if he's lost his job and he doesn't have any money left and he stops paying them, the bank—they'll get mad and they might try and take his house away."

I wonder how a bank would do it. Maybe with a giant digger? "With Old Nick inside it," I ask, "like Dorothy when the tornado picked her house up?"

"Listen to me." Ma holds my elbows hard so they nearly hurt. "What I'm trying to tell you is that he'd never let anybody come in his house or his backyard because then they'd find Room, wouldn't they?"

"And rescue us!"

"No, he'd never let that happen."

"What would he do?"

Ma's sucking in her lips so she doesn't have any. "The point is, we need to escape before that. You're going to get back in the rug now and practice some more till you get the knack of the wriggling out."

"No."

"Jack, please—"

"I'm too scared," I shout. "I won't do it not ever and I hate you."

Ma's breathing funny, she sits down on Floor. "That's all right." How is it all right if I hate her?

Her hands are on her tummy. "I brought you into Room, I didn't mean to but I did it and I've never once been sorry."

I stare at her and she stares back.

"I brought you here, and tonight I'm going to get you out."

"OK."

I say it very small but she hears. She nods.

"And you, with the blowtorch. One at a time but both."

Ma's still nodding. "You're the one who matters, though. Just you."

I shake my head till it's wobbling because there's no just me. We look at each other not smiling.

16 **to get the knack of sth** *inf*: to be able to do it after practicing a lot – 30 **blowtorch** *Lötlampe*

"Ready to get back in the rug?"

I nod. I lie down, Ma rolls me up extra tight. "I can't—" "Sure you can." I feel her patting me through Rug.

"I can't, I can't."

"Could you count to one hundred for me?"

I do, easy, very fast.

"You sound calmer already. We're going to figure this out in a minute," says Ma. "Hmm. I wonder—if the wriggling's not working, could you sort of … unwrap yourself instead?"

"But I'm on the inside."

"I know, but you can reach out the top with your hands and find the corner. Let's try that."

I feel around till I get something that's pointy.

"That's it," says Ma. "Great, now pull. Not that way, the other way, so you feel it coming loose. Like peeling a banana."

I do just a bit.

"You're lying on the edge, you're weighing it down."

"Sorry." The tears are coming back.

"You don't have to be sorry, you're doing great. What if you rolled?"

"Which way?"

"Whichever way feels looser. On your tummy, maybe, then find the edge of the rug again and pull it."

"I can't."

I do it. I get one elbow out.

"Excellent," says Ma. "You've really loosened it at the top. Hey, what about sitting up, do you think you could sit up?"

It hurts and it's impossible.

I get sitting up and both my elbows are out and Rug's coming undone around my face. I can pull her all off. "I did it," I shout, "I'm the banana."

"You're the banana," says Ma. She kisses me on my face that's all wet. "Now let's try that again."

When I'm so tired I have to stop, Ma tells me how it'll be in Outside. "Old Nick will be driving down the street. You're in the

13 **pointy** *spitz*

back, the open bit of the truck, so he can't see you, OK? Grab hold of the edge of the truck so you don't fall over, because it'll be moving fast, like this." She pulls me and wobbles me side to side. "Then when he puts the brakes on, you'll feel sort of—yanked the other way, as the truck slows down. That means a stop sign, where drivers have to stop for a second."

"Even him?"

"Oh, yeah. So as soon as you feel like the truck's hardly moving anymore, then it's safe for you to jump over the side."

Into Outer Space. I don't say it, I know that's wrong.

"You'll land on the pavement, it'll be hard like—" She looks around. "Like ceramic, but rougher. And then you run, run, run, like GingerJack."

"The fox ate GingerJack."

"OK, bad example," says Ma. "But this time it's us who're the tricksy trickers. 'Jack be nimble, Jack be quick—' "

" 'Jack jump over the candlestick.' "

"You have to run along the street, away from the truck, super fast, like—remember that cartoon we saw once, *Road Runner*?"

"Tom and Jerry, they run as well."

Ma is nodding. "All that matters is, don't let Old Nick catch you. Oh, but try and get onto the sidewalk if you can, the bit that's higher, then a car won't knock you down. And you need to be screaming as well, so somebody will help you."

"Who?"

"I don't know, anybody."

"Who's anybody?"

"Just run up to the first person you see. Or—it'll be pretty late. Maybe there'll be nobody out walking." She's biting her thumb, the nail of it, I don't tell her to stop. "If you don't see anybody, you'll have to wave at a car to make it stop, and tell the people in it that you and your ma have been kidnapped. Or if there's no cars—oh, man—I guess you'll have to run up to a house—any house that's got lights on—and bang on the door as hard as you

3 **to wobble** *here*: to shake – 5 **to yank** *inf* to pull suddenly and sharply – 15 **tricksy tricker** (children's / Jack's language for:) clever person who cheats people (*Schwindler*)

can with your fists. But only a house with lights on, not an empty one. It has to be the front door, will you know which that is?"

"The one at the front."

"Try it now?" Ma waits. "Talk to them just like you talk to me. Pretend I'm them. What do you say?"

"Me and you have—"

"No, pretend I'm the people in the house, or in the car, or on the sidewalk, tell them you and your Ma ..."

I try again. "You and your ma—"

"No, you say, 'My Ma and I ...' "

"You and me—"

She puffs her breath. "OK, never mind, just give them the note—is the note still safe?"

I look in my underwear. "It's disappeared!" Then I feel it where it slid around in between my butt. I take it out and show her.

"Keep it at the front. If by any chance you drop it, you can just tell them, 'I've been kidnapped.' Say it, just like that."

"I've been kidnapped."

"Say it good and loud so they can hear."

"I've been kidnapped," I shout.

"Fantastic. And they'll call the police," says Ma, "and—I guess the police will look in the backyards all around till they find Room." Her face isn't very certain.

"With the blowtorch," I remember her.

We practice and practice. *Dead, Truck, Wriggle Out, Jump, Run, Somebody, Note, Police, Blowtorch*. That's nine things. I don't think I can keep them in my head all at the same time. Ma says of course I can, I'm her superhero, Mr. Five.

I wish I was still four.

For lunch I get to choose because it's a special day, it's our last one in Room. That's what Ma says but I don't actually

16 **butt** *AE, inf* the part of the body on which a person sits – 26 **to remember** Jack means "to remind"

believe it. I'm suddenly starving hungry, I choose macaroni and hot dogs and crackers, that's like three lunches together.

All the time we're playing Checkers, I'm being scared of our Great Escape, so I lose twice, then I don't want to play anymore.

We try a nap but we can't switch off. I have some, the left then the right then the left again till there's nearly none left.

We don't want any dinner neither of us. I have to put the vomity T-shirt back on. Ma says I can keep my socks. "Otherwise the street might be sore on your feet." She wipes her eye, then the other one. "Wear your thickest pair."

I don't know why she's crying about socks. I go in Wardrobe to find Tooth under my pillow. "I'm going to tuck him down my sock."

Ma shakes her head. "What if you stand on it and hurt your foot?"

"I won't, he'll stay right here at the side."

It's 06:13, that's getting nearly to be the evening. Ma says I really should be wrapped up in Rug already, Old Nick might possibly come in early because of me being sick.

"Not yet."

"Well . . ."

"Please not."

"Sit right here, OK, so I can wrap you up in a rush if we need to."

We say the plan over and over to practice me of the nine. *Dead, Truck, Wriggle Out, Jump, Run, Somebody, Note, Police, Blowtorch.*

I keep twitching every time I hear the *beep beep* but it's not real, just imagining. I'm staring at Door, he's all shiny like a dagger. "Ma?"

"Yeah?"

"Let's do it tomorrow night instead."

She leans over and hugs me tight. That means no.

1 **starving hungry** very hungry – 6 **nap** a short sleep during the day – 31 **dagger** a short knife used as a weapon

I'm hating her again a bit.

"If I could do it for you, I would."

"Why can't you?"

She's shaking her head. "I'm so sorry it has to be you and it has to be now. But I'll be there in your head, remember? I'll be talking to you every minute."

We go over Plan B lots more times. "What if he opens Rug?" I ask. "Just to look at me dead?"

Ma doesn't say anything for a minute. "You know how hitting is bad?"

"Yeah."

"Well, tonight is a special case. I really don't think he will, he'll be in a hurry to, to get the whole thing over with, but if by any chance—what you do is, hit him as hard as you can."

Wow.

"Kick him, bite him, poke him in the eyes—" Her fingers stab the air. "Anything at all so you can get away."

I can't believe this hardly. "Am I allowed kill him even?"

Ma runs over to Cabinet where the things dry after washing up. She picks up Smooth Knife.

I look at his shine, I think about the story of Ma putting him on Old Nick's throat.

"Do you think you could hold this tight, inside the rug, and if—" She stares at Smooth Knife. Then she puts him back with the forks on Dish Rack. "What was I thinking?"

How would I know if she doesn't?

"You'll stab yourself," says Ma.

"No I won't."

"You will, Jack, how could you not, you'll cut yourself to ribbons, lashing around inside a rug with a bare blade—I think I'm losing my mind."

I shake my head. "It's right here." I tap on her hair.

Ma strokes my back.

16 **to poke** *here*: to hit (using his fingers) – 29 **to cut oneself to ribbons** to cut oneself to pieces

I check Tooth is in my sock, the note is in my underwear at the front. We sing to make the time go, but quietly. "Lose Yourself" and "Tubthumping" and "Home on the Range."

" 'Where the deer and the antelope play—,' " I sing.

" 'Where seldom is heard a discouraging word—' "

" 'And the skies are not cloudy all day.' "

"It's time," says Ma, holding Rug open.

I don't want to. I lie down and put my hands on my shoulders and my elbows sticking out. I wait for Ma to roll me up.

Instead she just looks at me. My feet my legs my arms my head, her eyes keep sliding over my whole me like she's counting. "What?" I say.

She doesn't say a word. She leans over, she doesn't even kiss me, she just touches her face to mine till I can't tell whose is whose. My chest is going *dangadangadang*. I won't let go of her.

"OK," says Ma, her voice all scratchy. "We're scave, aren't we? We're totally scave. See you outside." She puts my arms the special way with my elbows sticking out. She folds Rug over me and the light's gone.

I'm rolled up in the itchy dark.

"Not too tight?"

I try if I can get my arms up above my head and back, scraping a bit.

"OK?"

"OK," I say.

Then we just wait. Something comes in the top of Rug and rubs my hair, it's her hand, I know without seeing even. I can hear my breathing that's noisy. I think about the Count in the bag with the worms crawling in. The fall down down down crash into the sea. Can worms swim?

Dead, Truck, Run, Somebody—no, *Wriggle Out*, then *Jump, Run, Somebody, Note, Blowtorch*. I forgot *Police* before

17 **scave** a short version of scaredybrave: scared and brave – 23 **to scrape** *here*: to rub roughly against the rug

Blowtorch, it's too complicated, I'm going to mess it all up and Old Nick will bury me for real and Ma will be waiting always.

After a long while I whisper, "Is he coming or no?"

"I don't know," says Ma. "How could he not? If he's the least bit human …"

I thought humans were or weren't, I didn't know someone could be a bit human. Then what are his other bits?

I wait and wait. I can't feel my arms. Rug's lying against my nose, I want to scratch. I try and try and I reach it. "Ma?"

"Right here."

"Me too."

Beep beep.

I jump, I'm supposed to be dead but I can't help it, I want to get out of Rug right now but I'm stuck and I can't even try or he'll see—

Something pressing on me, that must be Ma's hand. She needs me to be Super Prince JackerJack, so I stay extra still. No more moving, I'm Corpse, I'm the Count, no, I'm his friend even deader, I'm all stiff like a broken robot with a power cut.

"Here you go." That's Old Nick's voice. He sounds like always. He doesn't even know what's happened about me dying. "Antibiotics, only just past the sell-by. For a kid you break them in half, the guy said."

Ma doesn't answer.

"Where is he, in the wardrobe?"

That's me, the *he.*

"Is he in the rug? Are you crazy, wrapping a sick kid up like that?"

"You didn't come back," Ma says and her voice is really weird. "He got worse in the night and this morning he wouldn't wake up."

Nothing. Then Old Nick makes a funny sound. "Are you sure?"

"Am I sure?" Ma shrieks it, but I don't move, I don't move, I'm all stiff no hearing no seeing no nothing.

"Ah, no." I hear his breath all long. "That's just terrible. You poor girl, you—"

Nobody says anything for a minute.

"Guess it must have been something really serious," says Old Nick, "the pills wouldn't have worked anyway."

"You killed him." Ma's howling.

"Come on now, calm down."

"How can I calm down when Jack's—" She's breathing strange, her words come out like gulping. She's pretending so really I nearly believe it.

"Let me." His voice is very near, I go tight and stiff stiff stiff.

"Don't touch him."

"OK, OK." Then Old Nick says, "You can't keep him here."

"My baby!"

"I know, it's a terrible thing. But I've got to take him away now."

"No."

"How long's it been?" he asks. "This morning, you said? Maybe in the night? He must be starting to—it's not healthy, keeping him here. I better take him and, and find a place."

"Not in the backyard." Ma's talking is nearly a growl.

"OK."

"If you put him in the backyard—You never should have done that, it's too close. If you bury him there I'll hear him crying."

"I said OK."

"You have to drive him a long way away, all right?"

"All right. Let me—"

"Not yet." She's crying and crying. "You mustn't disturb him."

"I'll keep him all wrapped up."

"Don't you dare lay a finger—"

"All right."

"Swear you won't even look at him with your filthy eyes."

"OK."

"Swear."

"I swear, OK?"

9 **to gulp** to swallow hastily

I'm dead dead dead.

"I'll know," says Ma, "I'll know if you put him in the backyard, and I'll scream every time that door opens, I'll tear the place apart, I swear I'll never be quiet again. You'll have to kill me too to shut me up, I just don't care anymore."

Why is she telling him to kill her?

"Take it easy." Old Nick sounds like he's talking to a dog. "I'm going to pick him up now and carry him to the truck, OK?"

"Gently. Find somewhere nice," says Ma, she's crying so much I can hardly hear what she's saying. "Somewhere with trees or something."

"Sure. Time to go now."

I'm grabbed through Rug, I'm squeezed, it's Ma, she says, "Jack, Jack, Jack."

Then I'm lifted. I think it's her and then I know it's him. Don't move don't move don't move JackerJack stay stiff stiff stiff. I'm squished in Rug, I can't breathe right, but dead don't breathe anyway. *Don't let him unwrap me.* I wish I had Smooth Knife.

The *beep beep* again, then the *click,* that means Door is open. The ogre's got me, fee fie foe fum. Hot on my legs, oh no, Penis let some pee out. And also a bit of poo squirted out my bum, Ma never said this would happen. Stinky. *Sorry, Rug.* A grunt near my ear, Old Nick's got me tight. I'm so scared I can't be brave, stop stop stop but I can't make a sound or he'll guess the trick and he'll eat me headfirst, he'll rip off my legs …

I count my teeth but I keep losing count, nineteen, twenty-one, twenty-two. I am Prince Robot Super JackerJack Mr. Five, I don't move. *Are you there, Tooth? I can't feel you but you must be in my sock, at the side. You're a bit of Ma, a little bit of Ma's dead spit riding along with me.*

I can't feel my arms.

The air's different. Still the dustiness of Rug but when I lift my nose a tiny bit I get this air that's …

Outside.

20 **ogre** a creature in children's stories (*Ungeheuer*) – 22 **grunt** a short deep sound like that made by a pig – 25 **headfirst** *here*: starting with his head

Could I be?

Not moving. Old Nick's just standing. Why is he standing still in the backyard? What's he going to—?

Moving again. I stay stiff stiff stiff.

Owwww, down onto something hard. I don't think I made a sound, I didn't hear one. I think I bit my mouth, it's got that taste that's blood.

There's another beep but a different. A rattling like all metals. Up again, then crash down, on my face, ow ow ow. *Bang.* Then everything starts to shake and throb and roar under my front, it's an earthquake …

No, it's the truck, it must be. It's not a bit like a raspberry, it's a million times more. *Ma!* I'm shouting in my head. *Dead, Truck,* that's two of the nine. I'm in the back of the brown pickup truck just like in the story.

I'm not in Room. Am I still me?

Moving now. I'm zooming along in the truck for real for really real.

Oh, I have to *Wriggle Out,* I was forgetting. I start to do like a snake, but Rug's got tighter I don't know how, I'm stuck I'm stuck. *Ma Ma Ma* … I can't get out like we practiced even though we practiced and practiced, it's all gone wrong, *sorry.* Old Nick's going to take me to a place and bury me and *the worms crawl in the worms crawl out* … I'm crying again, my nose is running, my arms are knotted under my chest, I'm fighting Rug because she's not my friend anymore, I'm kicking like Karate but she's got me, she's the shroud for the corpses to fall in the sea …

Sound's quieter. Not moving. The truck's stopped.

It's a stop, it's a stop sign stop, that means I'm meant to be doing *Jump* that's five on the list but I didn't do three yet, if I can't wriggle out how can I jump? I can't get to four five six seven eight or nine, I'm stuck on three, he's going to bury me with the worms … Moving again, *vrum vrum.*

8 **to rattle** to make a number of quick sharp noises – 10 **to throb** (of the heart or a machine) to beat heavily and regularly – 27 **shroud** a cloth for covering a dead body (*Leichentuch*)

I get one hand up over my face that's all snotty, my hand scrapes out the top and I drag my other arm up. My fingers grab the new air, something cold, something metal, a thing else that's not metal with bumps on it. I grab and pull pull pull and kick and my knee, ow ow ow. No good, no use. *Find the corner,* is that Ma talking in my head like she said or am I just remembering? I feel all the way around Rug and there's no corner on her, then I find it and pull, it comes loose just a bit I think. I roll on my back but that's even tighter and I can't find the corner anymore.

Stopped, the truck's stopped again, I'm not out already, I was meant to jump at the first. I pull Rug down until she's going to break my elbow and I can see a huge dazzling, then it's gone because the truck's moving again *vrummmmm.*

I think that was Outside I saw, Outside is real and so bright but I can't—

Ma's not here, no time to cry, I'm Prince JackerJack, I have to be JackerJack or the worms crawl in. I'm on my front again, I bend my knees and stick my butt up, I'm going to burst right through Rug and she's looser now, she's coming off my face—

I can breathe all the lovely black air. I'm sitting up and unwrapping Rug like I'm a smushed kind of banana. My ponytail's come out, there's all hair in my eyes. I'm finding my legs one and two, I get my whole self out, I did it, I did it, I wish Dora could see me, she'd sing the "We Did It" song.

Another light whizzing by over. Things sliding in the sky that I think they're trees. And houses and lights on giant poles and some cars everything zooming. It's like a cartoon I'm inside but messier. I'm holding on to the edge of the truck, it's all hard and cold. The sky is the most enormous, over there there's a pink orange bit but the rest is gray. When I look down, the street is black and a long long way. I know to jump good but not when everything's roaring and bumping and the lights all blurry and

2 **to scrape** *here*: to push out against the rug – 3 **a thing else** Jack means "something else" – 22 **to smush** Jack means "mushed" (*zerquetscht*) – 26 **to whizz** to move very fast – 26 **to slide** to pass or move quietly

the air so strange smells like apple or something. My eyes aren't working right, I'm too scared to be scave.

The truck's stopped again. I can't jump, I just can't move. I manage to stand up and I look over but—

I'm slipping and crashing across the truck, my head hits on something sore, I shout by accident *arghhhhhh*—

Stopped again.

A metal sound. Old Nick's face. He's out of the truck with the maddest face I ever saw and—

Jump.

The ground breaks my feet smash my knee hits me in the face but I'm running running running, where's *Somebody,* Ma said to scream to a somebody or a car or a lighted house, I see a car but dark inside and anyway nothing comes out of my mouth that's full of my hair but I keep running *GingerJack be nimble be quick.* Ma's not here but she promised she's in my head going *run run run.* A roaring behind me that's him, it's Old Nick coming to tear me in half *fee fie foe fum,* I have to find *Somebody* to shout *help help* but there isn't a somebody, there's no somebody, I'm going to have to keep running forever but my breath is used up and I can't see and—

A bear.

A wolf?

A dog, is a dog a somebody?

Somebody coming behind the dog but it's a very small person, a baby walking, it's pushing something that has wheels with a smaller baby inside. I can't remember what to shout, I'm on mute, I just keep running at them. The baby laughs, it has nearly no hair. The tiny one in the push-thing isn't a real one, I think, it's a doll. The dog is small but a real one, it's doing a poo on the ground, I never saw TV dogs do that. A person comes up behind the baby and picks up the poo in a bag like it's a treasure, I think it's a he, the somebody with short hair like Old Nick but curlier and he's browner than the baby. I go, "Help," but it

28 **on mute** *here*: not saying a word (usually a music player is on mute (*"Ton aus"*)

doesn't come out very loud. I'm running till I'm nearly at them and the dog barks and jumps up and *eats me—*

I open my mouth for the widest scream but no sound comes out. "Raja!"

Red on my finger all spots.

"Raja, down." The man person's got the dog by the neck. My blood's falling out of my hand.

Then *bam* grabbed from behind, it's Old Nick, his giant hands on my ribs. I messed up, he catched me, *sorry sorry sorry Ma.* He's lifting me up. I scream then, I scream no words even. He's got me under his arm, he's carrying me back to the truck, Ma said I could hit, I could kill him, I hit and hit but I can't reach, it's only me I'm hitting—

"Excuse me," calls the person holding the poo bag. "Hey, mister?" His voice isn't deep, it's softer.

Old Nick turns us around. I'm forgetting to scream.

"I'm so sorry, is your little girl OK?"

What little girl?

Old Nick clears his throat, he's still carrying me to the truck but walking backwards. "Fine."

"Raja's usually really gentle, but she came at him out of nowhere …"

"Just a tantrum," says Old Nick.

"Hey. Wait up, I think her hand's bleeding."

I look at my eaten finger, the blood's making drops.

Then he has picked the baby person up now, he's holding it on his arm and the poo bag in the other hand and he's looking really confused.

Old Nick stands me down, he's got his fingers on my shoulders so they're burning. "It's under control."

"And her knee too, that looks bad. Raja didn't do that. Has she had a fall?" asks the man.

"I'm not a her," I say but only inside my throat.

"Why don't you mind your own business and I'll mind mine?" Old Nick's nearly growling.

23 **tantrum** a child's fit of bad temper (*Wutanfall*)

Ma, Ma, I need you for talking. She's not in my head anymore, she's not anywhere. She wrote the note, I was forgetting, I put my not eaten hand in my underwear and I can't find the note but then I do, it's all peed. I can't talk but I wave it at the somebody man.

Old Nick rips it out of my hand and makes it disappear.

"OK, I don't—I don't like this," says the man. He's got a little phone in his hand, where did it come from? He's saying, "Yes, police, please."

It's happening just like Ma said, we're at eight that's *Police* already and I haven't even showed the *Note* or said about Room, I'm doing it backwards. I'm meant to talk to the somebody just like they're human. I start to say, "I've been kidnapped," but it only comes out whispery because Old Nick's picked me up again, he's heading for the truck, he's running, I'm all shaking to pieces, I can't find to hit, he's going to—

"I've got your plates, mister!"

That's the man person screaming, is he shouting at me? What plates?

"K nine three—" He's shouting numbers, why is he shouting numbers?

Suddenly *arghhhhhh* the street bangs me in the tummy hands face, Old Nick's running away but without me. He dropped me. He's farther off every second. Those must be magic numbers to make him drop me.

I try to get up but I can't remember how.

A noise like a monster, the truck's *vrummmming* and coming at me *rrrrrrrrrr,* it's going to crush me down to smithereens on the pavement, I don't know how where what—the baby crying, I never heard a real baby cry before—

The truck's gone. It just drove past, around the corner without stopping. I hear it for a bit, then I don't hear it anymore.

17 **plate** numberplate on a car – 28 **to smithereens** [ˌsmɪðəˈriːnz] *inf* into very small pieces

The higher bit, the sidewalk, Ma said to get on the sidewalk. I have to crawl but with my bad knee not putting down. The sidewalk's all in big squares, scrapy.

A terrible smell. The dog's nose is right beside me, it's come back to chew me up, I scream.

"Raja." The man pulls the dog away. The man's squatting down, he's got the baby on one of his knees, it's wriggling. He doesn't have the poo bag anymore. Looks like a TV person but nearer and wider and with smells, a bit like Dish Soap and mint and curry all together. His hand that's not holding the dog tries to get on me but I roll away just in time. "It's OK, sweetie. It's OK."

Who's sweetie? His eyes are looking at my eyes, it's me that's the sweetie. I can't look, it's too weird having him seeing me and talking at me.

"What's your name?"

TV people never ask things except Dora and she knows my name already.

"Can you tell me what you're called?"

Ma said to talk to the somebody, that's my job. I try and nothing comes out. I lick my mouth. "Jack."

"What's that?" He bends nearer, I curl up with my head in my arms. "It's OK, no one's going to hurt you. Tell me your name a little louder?"

It's easier to say if I don't look at him. "Jack."

"Jackie?"

"Jack."

"Oh. Right, sorry. Your dad's gone now, Jack."

What's he saying about?

The baby starts pulling at his, the thing over his shirt, it's a jacket. "I'm Ajeet, by the way," the man person says, "and this is my daughter—hang on, Naisha. Jack needs a Band-Aid for that

3 **scrapy** "scratchy", "rough": Jack means that he is scraping himself on it because it is so rough – 6 **to squat down** to sit with the knees bent – 32 **Band-Aid** a trademark for a type of sticky plaster used to cover small cuts (*Pflaster*)

ouchy on his knee, let's see if …" He's feeling in all the bits of his bag. "Raja's really sorry he bit you."

The dog doesn't look sorry, he's got all pointy dirty teeth. Did he drink my blood like a vampire?

"You don't look too good, Jack, have you been sick lately?" I shake my head. "Ma."

"What's that?"

"Ma throwed up on my T-shirt."

The baby's talking more but not in language. She's grabbing the Raja dog's ears, why isn't she scared of him?

"Sorry, I didn't catch that," says the Ajeet man.

I don't say anything else.

"The police should be here any minute, OK?" He's turned to look up the street, the Naisha baby's crying a bit now. He bounces her on his knee. "Home to Ammi in a minute, home to bed."

I think about Bed. The warm.

He's pressing the little buttons on his phone and talking more but I don't listen.

I want to get away. But I think if I move, the Raja dog will bite me and drink more of my blood. I'm sitting on a line so there's some of me in one square and some in another. My eaten finger hurts and hurts and so does my knee, the right one, there's blood coming out of it where the skin broke, it was red but it's going black. There's a pointy oval beside my foot, I try to pick it up but it's stuck, then it comes in my fingers, it's a leaf. It's a leaf from a real tree like the one that was on Skylight that day. I look up, there's a tree over me that must have dropped the leaf. The huge light pole is blinding me. The whole bigness of the sky behind it is black now, the pink and orange bits are gone where? The air's moving in my face, I'm shaking by accident.

"You must be cold. Are you cold?"

1 **ouchy** Jack's language for a wound or cut – 29 **pole** a long thin piece of metal – 31 **by accident** Jack means "without wanting to"

I think it's the baby Naisha that the Ajeet man is asking but it's me, I know because he's taking off his jacket and holding it out to me. "Here."

I shake my head because it's a person jacket, I never had a jacket.

"How did you lose your shoes?"

What shoes?

The Ajeet man stops talking after that.

A car stops, I know what kind it is, it's a cop car from TV. Persons get out, two of them, short hair, one black hair one yellowy hair, and all moving quick. Ajeet talks to them. The baby Naisha is trying to get away but he keeps her in his arms, not hurting I don't think. Raja is lying down on some brownish stuff, it's grass, I thought it would be green, there's some squares of it all along the sidewalk. I wish I had the note still but Old Nick disappeared it. I don't know the words, they got bumped out of my head.

Ma's in Room still, I want her here so much much much. Old Nick ran off driving fast in his truck but where's he going, not the lake or the trees anymore because he saw me not be dead, I was allowed kill him but I didn't manage it.

I have a suddenly terrible idea. Maybe he went back to Room, maybe he's there right now making Door *beep beep* open and he's mad, it's my fault for not being dead—

"Jack?"

I look for the mouth moving. It's the police, the one that's a she I think but it's hard to tell, the black hair not the yellow. She says, "Jack," again. How does she know? "I'm Officer Oh. Can you tell me how old you are?"

I have to *Save Ma,* I have to talk to the police to get the *Blowtorch,* but my mouth isn't working. She's got a thing on her belt, it's a gun, just like a police on TV. What if they're bad police like locked up Saint Peter, I never thought of that. I look at the belt not the face, it's a cool belt with a buckle.

"Do you know your age?"

Easy-peasy. I hold up five fingers.

"Five years old, great." Officer Oh says something I don't hear. Then about a dress. She says it twice.

I talk as loud as I can but not looking. "I don't have a dress."

"No? Where do you sleep at night?"

"In Wardrobe."

"In a wardrobe?"

Try, Ma's saying in my head, but Old Nick's beside her, he's the maddest ever and—

"Did you say, in a wardrobe?"

"You've got three dresses," I say. "I mean Ma. One is pink and one is green with stripes and one is brown but you—she prefers jeans."

"Your ma, is that what you said?" asks Officer Oh. "Is that who's got the dresses?"

Nodding's easier.

"Where's your ma tonight?"

"In Room."

"In a room, OK," she says. "Which room?"

"Room."

"Can you tell us where it is?"

I remember something. "Not on any map."

She does a breath out, I don't think my answers are any good.

The other police is a he maybe, I never saw hair like that for real, it's nearly see-through. He says, "We're at Navaho and Alcott, got a disturbed juvenile, possible domestic." I think he's talking to his phone. It's like playing Parrot, I know the words but I don't know what they mean. He comes closer to Officer Oh. "Any joy?"

"Slow going."

1 **easy-peasy** children's language for "very easy" – 26 **see-through** so thin that you can see through it – 26 **Navaho and Alcott** *AE* the crossroads of the two streets with these names – 27 **juvenile** a young person – 27 **domestic** *(n) here*: a disturbed family situation – 30 **Any joy?** *inf* "Are you having any luck / success?"

"Same with the witness. Suspect's white male, maybe five ten, forties, fifties, fled the scene in a maroon or dark brown pickup, possibly an F one-fifty or a Ram, starts K nine three, could be a *B* or a *P*, no state ..."

"The man you were with, was that your dad?" Officer Oh is talking to me again.

"I don't have one."

"Your Mom's boyfriend?"

"I don't have one." I said that before, am I allowed say twice?

"Do you know his name?"

I make me remember. "Ajeet."

"No, the other guy, the one who went off in the truck." "Old Nick." I whisper it because he wouldn't like me saying. "What's that?"

"Old Nick."

"That's negative," the man police says at his phone. "Suspect GOA, first name Nick, Nicholas, no second name."

"And what's your ma called?" asks Officer Oh.

"Ma."

"Has she got another name?"

I hold up two fingers.

"Two of them? Great. Can you remember what they are?"

They were in the note that he disappeared. I suddenly remember a bit. "He stole us."

Officer Oh sits down beside me on the ground. It's not like Floor, it's all hard and shivery. "Jack, would you like a blanket?"

I don't know. Blanket's not here.

"You've got some nasty cuts there. Did this Nick guy hurt you?" The man police is back, he holds out a blue thing to me, I don't touch. "Go ahead," he says at his phone.

Officer Oh folds the blue thing around me, it's not fleecy gray like Blanket, it's rougher. "How did you get those cuts?"

1 **five ten** 5 foot 10 (inches) *(ca. 1,80m)* – 17 **GOA** police code for "Gone on arrival" (Old Nick has run away) – 26 **shivery** Jack means: "you shiver because it is very cold"

"The dog is a vampire." I look for Raja and his humans but they're disappeared. "This finger it bit, and my knee was the ground."

"Beg your pardon?"

"The street, it hit me."

"Go ahead." The man police says that, he's talking at his phone again. Then he looks at Officer Oh and says, "Should I get on to Child Protection?"

"Give me another couple minutes," she says. "Jack, I bet you're good at telling stories."

How does she know? The man police looks at his watch that he's got stuck on his wrist. I remember Ma's wrist that doesn't work right. Is Old Nick there now, is he twisting her wrist or her neck, is he ripping her in pieces?

"Do you think you could tell me what happened tonight?" Officer Oh grins at me. "And maybe you could talk real slow and clear, because my ears don't work too well." Maybe she's deaf, but she doesn't talk with her fingers like deafs on TV.

"Copy," says the man police.

"You ready?" says Officer Oh.

It's me her eyes are on. I shut mine and pretend it's Ma I'm talking to, that makes me brave. "We did a trick," I say very slow, "me and Ma, we were pretending I was sick and then I was dead but really I'll unwrap myself and jump out of the truck, only I was meant to jump at the first slowing down but I didn't manage."

"OK, what happened then?" That's Officer Oh's voice right beside my head.

I still don't look or I'll forget the story. "I had a note in my underwear but he disappeared it. I've still got Tooth." I put my fingers in my sock for him. I open my eyes.

"Can I see that?"

She tries to take Tooth but I don't let her. "It's of Ma." "That's your ma that you were talking about?"

8 **Child Protection** an organization which specializes in helping children in danger

I think her brain's not working like her ears aren't, how could Ma be a tooth? I shake my head. "Just a bit of her dead spit that fell out."

Officer Oh looks at Tooth up close and her face gets all hard. The man police shakes his head and says something I can't hear.

"Jack," she says, "you told me you were supposed to jump out of the truck the first time it slowed down?"

"Yeah but I was still in Rug, then I unpeeled the banana but I wasn't scave enough." I'm looking at Officer Oh and I'm talking at the same time. "But after the third time stopping, the truck went *wooooo*—"

"It went what?"

"Like—" I show her. "All a different way."

"It turned."

"Yeah, and I got banged and he, Old Nick, he climbed out all mad and that's when I jumped."

"Bingo." Officer Oh claps her hands.

"Huh?" says the man police.

"Three stop signs and a turn. Left or right?" She waits. "Never mind, great job, Jack." She's staring down the street and then she's got a thing in her hand like a phone, where did that come from? She's watching the little screen, she says, "Get them to cross-ref the partial plates with ... try Carlingford Avenue, maybe Washington Drive ..."

I don't see Raja and Ajeet and Naisha anymore at all. "Did the dog go to jail?"

"No, no," says Officer Oh, "it was an honest mistake."

"Go ahead," the man police tells his phone. He shakes his head at Officer Oh.

She stands up. "Hey, maybe Jack can find the house for us. Would you like a ride in a patrol car?"

I can't get up, she puts out her hand but I pretend I don't see. I put one foot under then another and I'm up a bit dizzy. At the

24 **to cross-ref** *abb* to get a cross-reference *here*: to check

car I climb in where the door's open. Officer Oh sits in the back too and clicks the seat belt on me, I go small so her hand doesn't touch except the blue blanket.

The car's moving now, not so rattly like the truck, it's soft and humming. A bit like that couch in the TV planet with the puffy-hair lady asking questions, only it's Officer Oh. "This room," she says, "is it in a bungalow, or are there stairs?"

"It's not a house." I'm watching the shiny bit in the middle, it's like Mirror but tiny. I see the man police's face in it, he's the driver. His eyes are looking at me backwards in the little mirror so I look out the window instead. Everything's slipping past making me giddy. There's all light that comes out of the car onto the road, it paints over everything. Here comes another car, a white one super fast, it's going to crash into—

"It's OK," says Officer Oh.

When I take my hands off my face the other car's gone, did this one disappear it?

"Anything ringing a bell?"

I don't hear any bells. It's all trees and houses and cars dark. *Ma, Ma, Ma*. I don't hear her in my head, she's not talking. His hands are so tight around her, tighter tighter tighter, she can't talk, she can't breathe, she can't anything. Alive things bend but she's bent and bent and—

"Does this look like it might be your street?" asks Officer Oh.

"I haven't got a street."

"I mean the street this Nick guy took you from tonight." "I never saw it."

"What's that?"

I'm tired of saying.

Officer Oh clicks with her tongue.

"No sign of any pickups except that black one back there," says the man police.

"Might as well pull over."

The car stops, I'm sorry.

12 **giddy** unstable, dizzy – 18 **to ring a bell** *inf* to remind one of sth *here*: to look familiar

"You figure some kind of cult?" he says. "The long hair, no surnames, the state of that tooth ..."

Officer Oh twists her mouth. "Jack, is there daylight in this room of yours?"

"It's night," I tell her, didn't she notice?

"I mean in the daytime. Where does the light come in?"

"Skylight."

"There's a skylight, excellent."

"Go ahead," the man police says at his phone.

Officer Oh is looking at her shiny screen again. "Sat's showing a couple houses with attic skylights on Carlingford ..."

"Room's not in a house," I say again.

"I'm having trouble understanding, Jack. What's it in, then?"

"Nothing. Room's inside."

Ma's there and Old Nick too, he wants somebody to be dead and it's not me.

"So what's outside it?"

"Outside."

"Tell me more about what's outside."

"Got to hand it to you," the man police says, "you don't give up."

Am I the *you?*

"Go on, Jack," says Officer Oh, "tell me about what's just outside this room."

"Outside," I shout. I have to explain fast for Ma, *wait Ma wait for me*. "It's got stuff for real like ice cream and trees and stores and airplanes and farms and the hammock."

Officer Oh is nodding.

I have to try harder, I don't know what. "But it's locked and we don't know the code."

"You wanted to unlock the door and get outside?"

"Like Alice."

"Is Alice another friend of yours?"

I nod. "She's in the book."

10 **Sat** *abb* satellite

"*Alice in Wonderland.* For crying out loud," says the man police.

I know that bit. But how did he read our book, he wasn't ever in Room. I say to him, "Do you know the bit where her crying makes a pond?"

"What's that?" He looks at me backwards in the little mirror.

"Her crying makes a pond, remember?"

"Your ma was crying?" asks Officer Oh.

Outsiders don't understand anything, I wonder do they watch too much TV. "No, Alice. She's always wanting to get into the garden, like us."

"You wanted to get into the garden too?"

"It's a backyard, but we don't know the secret code."

"This room's right by the backyard?" she asks.

I shake my head.

Officer Oh rubs her face. "Work with me here, Jack. Is this room near a backyard?"

"Not near."

"OK."

Ma, Ma, Ma. "It's all around."

"This room's *in* the backyard?"

"Yeah."

I made Officer Oh happy but I don't know how. "Here we go, here we go," she's looking at her screen and pressing buttons, "freestanding rear structures on Carlingford and Washington ..."

"Skylight," says the man police.

"Right, with a skylight ..."

"Is that TV?" I ask.

"Hmm? No, it's a photo of all these streets. The camera's way up in space."

"Outer Space?"

"Yeah."

"Cool."

1 **for crying out loud** *inf* people use this expression when they are annoyed or surprised – 5 **pond** a small lake – 25 **rear** *adj* back

Officer Oh's voice gets all excited. "Three four nine Washington, shed in the rear, lit skylight … Got to be."

"That's three four nine Washington," the man police is saying at his phone. "Go ahead." He looks back in the mirror. "Owner's name doesn't match, but Caucasian male, DOB twelve-ten-sixty-one …"

"Vehicle?"

"Go ahead," he says again. He waits. "Two thousand one Silverado, brown, K nine three P seven four two."

"Bingo," says Officer Oh.

"We're en route," he's saying, "request backup to three four nine Washington."

The car's turning right around the other way. Then we're moving faster, it swirls me.

We're stopped. Officer Oh's looking out the window at a house. "No lights on," she says.

"He's in Room," I say, "he's making her be dead," but the crying is melting my words so I can't hear them.

Behind us there's another car just like this one. More police persons getting out. "Sit tight, Jack." Officer Oh's opening the door. "We're going to go find your ma."

I jump, but her hand is making me stay in the car. "Me too," I'm trying to say but all that comes out is tears.

She's got a big flashlight she switches on. "This officer will stay right here with you—"

A face I never saw before pushes in.

"No!"

"Give him some space," Officer Oh tells the new police.

"The blowtorch," I remember, but it's too late, she's gone already.

There's a creak and the back of the car pops up, the trunk, that's what it's called.

5 **Caucasian** [ˌkɑːˈkeɪʒən] *adj* white (person) – 5 **DOB** *abb* date of birth – 11 **to request backup** *here*: the policeman is asking for further support – 14 **to swirl** to move round and round quickly – 31 **creak** a harsh sound – 31 **to pop up** *inf* to open

I put my hands over my head so nothing can get in, not faces not lights not noises not smells. *Ma Ma don't be dead don't be dead don't be dead …*

I count to one hundred like Officer Oh said but I'm not any calmer. I do to five hundred, the numbers aren't working. My back is jumping and shaking, it must be from being cold, where's the blanket fallen?

A terrible sound. The police in the front seat is blowing his nose. He does a tiny smile and pokes the tissue in his nose, I look away.

I stare out the window at the house with no lights. A bit of it is open now that wasn't before I don't think, the garage, a huge dark square. I'm looking for hundreds of hours, my eyes get prickly. Someone comes out of the dark but it's another police I never saw before. Then a person that's Officer Oh and beside her—

I'm thumping banging on the car door but I don't know how, I have to smash the glass but I can't, *Ma Ma Ma Ma Ma Ma Ma Ma—*

Ma makes the door be open and I fall halfway out. She's got me, she's scooped me all up. It's her for real, she's one hundred percent alive.

"We did it," she says, when we're both in the back of the car together. "Well, *you* did it, really."

I'm shaking my head. "I kept messing up the plan."

"You saved me," says Ma, she kisses my eye and holds me tight.

"Was he there?"

"No, I was all by myself just waiting, it was the longest hour of my life. The next thing I knew was, the door exploded open, I thought I was having a heart attack."

"The blowtorch!"

"No, they used a shotgun."

"I want to see the explosion."

8 **to blow one's nose** *die Nase putzen* – 9 **to poke** to push – 14 **prickly** *kratzig*

"It was only for a second. You can see another some time, I promise." Ma's grinning. "We can do anything now."

"Why?"

"Because we're free."

I'm dizzy, my eyes shut without me. I'm so sleepy I think my head's going to fall off.

Ma's talking in my ear, she says we need to go talk to some more police. I snuggle against her, I say, "Want to go to Bed."

"They'll find us somewhere to sleep in a little while."

"No. *Bed*."

"You mean in Room?" Ma's pulled back, she's staring in my eyes.

"Yeah. I've seen the world and I'm tired now."

"Oh, Jack," she says, "we're never going back."

The car starts moving and I'm crying so much I can't stop.

8 **to snuggle** to settle into a warm and comfortable position

After

Officer Oh is riding in front, she looks different backwards. She turns around and smiles at me, she says, "Here's the precinct."

"Can you climb out?" asks Ma. "I'll carry you." She opens the car and cold air jumps in. I go small. She pulls at me, makes me stand up and I bang my ear on the car. She's walking with me up on her hip, I cling onto her shoulders. It's dark but then there's lights quick quick like fireworks.

"Vultures," says Officer Oh.

Where?

"No pictures," shouts the man police.

What pictures? I don't see any vultures, I only see person faces with machines flashing and black fat sticks. They're shouting but I can't understand. Officer Oh tries to put the blanket over my head, I push it off. Ma's running, I'm shaking all about, we're inside a building and it's a thousand percent bright so I put my hand over my eyes.

The floor's all shiny hard not like Floor, the walls are blue and more of them, it's too loud. There's persons everywhere not friends of mine. A thing like a spaceship all lit up with things inside all in their little squares like bags of chips and chocolate bars, I go look and try and touch but they're locked up in the glass. Ma pulls my hand.

"This way," says Officer Oh. "No, right in here—"

We're in a room that's quieter. A huge wide man says, "I do apologize about the media presence, we've upgraded to a trunk system but they've got these new tracking scanners ..." He's sticking out his hand. Ma puts me down and does his hand up and down like persons in TV.

"And you, sir, I understand you've been a remarkably courageous young man."

2 **backwards** *here*: from behind – 3 **precinct** *here*: the area around the police headquarters – 9 **vulture** a bird that feeds on dead animals *(Geier)* – 26 **to upgrade** to improve

That's me he's looking at. But he doesn't know me and why he says I'm a man? Ma sits down in a chair that's not our chairs and lets me in her lap. I try to rock but it's not Rocker. Everything's wrong.

"Now," says the wide man, "I appreciate it's late, and your son's got some abrasions that need looking at, and they're on standby for you at the Cumberland Clinic, it's a very nice facility."

"What kind of facility?"

"Ah, psychiatric."

"We're not—"

He butts in. "They'll be able to give you all the appropriate care, it's very private. But as a matter of priority I do need to go over your statement tonight in more detail as you're able."

Ma's nodding.

"Now, certain of my lines of questioning may be distressing, would you prefer Officer Oh remain for this interview?"

"Whatever, no," says Ma, she yawns.

"Your son's been through a lot tonight, perhaps he should wait outside while we cover, ah …"

But we're in Outside already.

"That's OK," says Ma, wrapping the blue blanket around me.

"Don't shut it," she says very fast to Officer Oh going out.

"Sure," says Officer Oh, she makes the door stay halfway open. Ma's talking to the huge man, he's calling her by one of her other names. I'm looking on the walls, they've turned creamish like no color. There's frames with lots of words in, one with an eagle, he says *The Sky's No Limit*. Somebody goes by the door, I jump. I wish it was shut. I want some so bad.

Ma pulls her T-shirt down to her pants again. "Not right this minute," she whispers, "I'm talking to the captain."

6 **abrasion** [ə'breɪʒn] a wound where the skin has been worn away (*Hautabschürfung*) – 6 **on standby** *here*: waiting – 7 **facility** [fə'sɪləṭi] *Einrichtung* – 12 **appropriate** necessary, suitable – 18 **to yawn** you yawn when you are tired or bored

"And this took place—any recollection of the date?" he asks. She shakes her head. "Late January. I'd only been back at school a couple weeks ..."

I'm still thirsty, I lift her T-shirt again and this time she puffs her breath and lets me, she curls me against her chest.

"Would you, ah, prefer ... ?" asks the Captain.

"No, let's just carry on," says Ma. It's the right, there's not much but I don't want to climb off and switch sides because she might say *that's enough* and it's not enough.

Ma's talking for ages about Room and Old Nick and all that, I'm too tired for listening. A she person comes in and tells the Captain something.

Ma says, "Is there a problem?"

"No no," says the Captain.

"Then why is she staring at us?" Her arm goes around me tight. "I'm nursing my son, is that OK with you, lady?"

Maybe in Outside they don't know about having some, it's a secret.

Ma and the Captain talk a lot more. I'm nearly asleep but it's too bright and I can't get comfy.

"What is it?" she asks.

"We really have to go back to Room," I tell her. "I need Toilet." "That's OK, they've got them here in the precinct."

The Captain shows us the way past the amazing machine and I touch the glass nearly at the chocolate bars. I wish I knowed the code to let them out.

There's one two three four toilets, each in a little room inside a bigger room with four sinks and all mirrors. It's true, toilets in Outside have lids on their tanks, I can't look in. When Ma pees and stands up there's awful roaring, I cry. "It's OK," she says, wiping my face with the flat bits of her hands, "it's just an automatic flush. Look, the toilet sees with this little eye when we're all done and it flushes by itself, isn't that clever?"

4 **to puff one's breath** to breathe loudly – 16 **to nurse** to breast-feed (*stillen*) – 20 **comfy** *sl* (short for:) comfortable – 23 **precinct** *here*: the police headquarters – 29 **lid** *Deckel* – 29 **tank** *here*: the part of a toilet which contains the water used for flushing

I don't like a clever toilet looking at our butts.

Ma gets me to step out of my underwear. "I pooed a bit by accident when Old Nick carried me," I tell her.

"Don't worry about it," she says and she does something weird, she throws my underwear in a trash.

"But—"

"You don't need them anymore, we'll get you new ones."

"For Sundaytreat?"

"No, any day we like."

That's weird. I'd rather on a Sunday.

The faucet's like the real ones in Room but wrong shaped. Ma turns it on, she wets paper and wipes my legs and my butt. She puts her hands under a machine, then hot air puffs out, like our vents but hotter and noisy again. "It's a hand dryer, look, do you want to try?" She's smiling at me but I'm too tired for smiling. "OK, just wipe your hands on your T-shirt." Then she wraps the blue blanket around me and we go out again. I want to look in the machine where all the cans and bags and chocolate bars are in jail. But Ma pulls me along to the room where the Captain is for more talking.

After hundreds of hours Ma's standing me up, I'm all wobbly. Sleep not in Room makes me feel sick.

We're going to a kind of hospital, but wasn't that the old Plan A, *Sick, Truck, Hospital?* Ma's got a blue blanket around her now, I think it's the one that was on me but that one's still on me so hers must be a different. The patrol car looks like the same car but I don't know, things in Outside are tricksy. I trip on the street and nearly fall but Ma grabs me.

We're driving along. When I see a car coming I squeeze my eyes every time.

"They're on the other side, you know," says Ma.

"What other side?"

21 **wobbly** unsteady, shaky – 27 **tricksy** Jack means "tricky, full of difficulties" – 27 **to trip** to lose one's balance and fall over (or almost fall over) – 29 **to squeeze** [skwi:z] to press together *here*: to shut tightly

"See that line down the middle? They always have to stay on that side of it, and we stay on this side, so we don't crash."

Suddenly we're stopped. The car opens and a person with no face looks in. I'm screaming.

"Jack, Jack," says Ma.

"It's a zombie."

I keep my face on her tummy.

"I'm Dr. Clay, welcome to the Cumberland," says the no face with the deepest voice ever booming. "The mask is just to keep you safe. Want to see under?" It pulls the white bit up and a man person smiling, an extra-brown face with the tiniest triangle of black chin. He lets the mask back on, snap. His talk comes through the white. "Here's one for each of you."

Ma takes the masks. "Do we have to?"

"Think of everything floating around that your son's probably never come in contact with before."

"OK." She puts one mask on her and one on me with loops around my ears. I don't like the way it presses. "I don't see anything floating around," I whisper to Ma.

"Germs," she says.

I thought they were only in Room, I didn't know the world was all full of them too.

We're walking in a big lighted building, I think it's the Precinct again but then it's not. There's a somebody called the Admission Coordinator tapping on a—I know, it's a computer, just like in TV. They all look like the persons on the medical planet, I have to keep remembering they're real.

I see the most coolest thing, it's a huge glass with corners but instead of cans and chocolate there's fish alive, swimming and hiding with rocks. I pull Ma's hand but she won't come, she's still talking to the Admission Coordinator that has a name on her label too, it's Pilar.

9 **to boom** to make a deep hollow sound – 17 **loop** *Schlaufe* – 24 **Admission coordinator** a person who does the paperwork when a new patient comes in – 32 **label** *here*: name tag on a jacket

“Listen, Jack,” Dr. Clay says, he bends down his legs so he’s like a giant frog, why is he doing that? His head is nearly beside mine, his hair is just fuzz like a quarter of an inch long. He doesn’t have his mask anymore, it’s only me and Ma. “We need to take a look at your mom in that room across the hall, OK?”

It’s me he’s saying. But didn’t he look at her already?

Ma’s shaking her head. “Jack stays with me.”

“Dr. Kendrick—she’s our general medical resident on duty—she’s going to have to administer the evidence collection kit right away, I’m afraid. Blood, urine, hair, fingernail scrapings, oral swabs, vaginal, anal—”

Ma stares at him. She lets out her breath. “I’ll be just in there,” she tells me, pointing at a door, “and I’ll be able to hear you if you call, OK?”

“Not OK.”

“Please. You’ve been such a brave JackerJack, just a bit longer, OK?”

I grab onto her.

“Hmm, maybe he could come in and we could put up a screen?” says Dr. Kendrick. Her hair is all creamy colored and twisted up on her head.

“A TV?” I whisper to Ma. “There’s one over there.” It’s way bigger than the one in Room, there’s dancing and the colors are much dazzlier.

“Actually, yeah,” says Ma, “could he maybe sit there at Reception? That would distract him better.”

The Pilar woman is behind the table talking on the phone, she smiles at me but I pretend I don’t see. There’s lots of chairs, Ma chooses one for me. I watch her going with the doctors. I have to grip onto the chair not to run after her.

3 **fuzz** *inf* a mass of sth soft and thin (*here*: his hair) – 8 **medical resident on duty** one of the regular doctors of the clinic working in this particular shift – 9 **evidence collection kit** *here:* several examinations necessary for a court case – 11 **swab** a small piece used for a test – 20 **screen** a movable wall to protect people from view – 24 **dazzlier** Jack means “extremely bright”

The planet's changed to a game of football with persons with huge shoulders and helmets. I wonder if it's really happening for real or just pictures. I look at the fish glass but it's too far, I can't see the fish but they must be still there, they can't walk. The door where Ma went is a bit apart, I think I hear her voice. Why are they taking her blood and pee and fingernails? She's still there even though I don't see her, like she was in Room all the time I was doing our Great Escape. Old Nick zoomed off in his truck, now he's not in Room and he's not in Outside, I don't see him in TV. My head's worn out from wondering.

I hate the mask pressing, I put it up on my head, it's got a stiff bit with a wire inside I think. It keeps my hair out of my eyes. Now there's tanks in a city that's all smashed into bits, an old person crying. Ma's a long long time in the other room, are they hurting her? The Pilar woman is still talking on the phone. Another planet with men in a ginormous room talking, all in jackets, I think they're kind of fighting. They talk for hours and hours.

Then it changes again and there's Ma and she's carrying somebody and *it's me.*

I jump up and go right to the screen. There's a me like in Mirror only I'm tiny. Words sliding underneath *LOCAL NEWS AS IT HAPPENS.* A she person is talking but I can't see: "... bachelor loner converted the garden shed into an impregnable twenty-first-century dungeon. The despot's victims have an eerie pallor and appear to be in a borderline catatonic state after the long nightmare of their incarceration." There's when Officer Oh tried to put the blanket on my head and I don't let her. The invisible voice says, "The malnourished boy, unable

1 **persons with huge shoulders and helmets** American football players wear protection on their shoulders and heads – 10 **to be worn out** to be tired – 12 **wire** a thin metal in the form of a thread (*Draht*) – 16 **ginormous** Jack's language for "enormous" – 22 **to slide** *here*: to move – 23 **bachelor** a man who is unmarried – 24 **to convert** to change – 24 **impregnable** which cannot be entered – 25 **dungeon** a dark underground prison – 25 **pallor** [ˈpælɚ] unhealthy paleness of the skin – 26 **a borderline catatonic state** almost unable to control body movements – 27 **incarceration** imprisonment – 29 **malnourished** [ˌmælˈnɜrɪʃt] a state of bad health because of the wrong food

to walk, is seen here lashing out convulsively at one of his rescuers."

"Ma," I shout.

She doesn't come. I hear her calling, "Just a couple more minutes."

"It's us. It's us in TV!"

But it's gone blank. Pilar is standing up pointing at it with a remote and staring at me. Dr. Clay comes out, he says mad things to Pilar.

"On again," I say. "It's us, I want to see us."

"I'm terribly, terribly sorry—," says Pilar.

"Jack, would you like to join your mom now?" Dr. Clay holds out his hand, he's got funny white plastic on it. I don't touch. "Mask on, remember?" I put it over my nose. I walk behind not too near.

Ma's sitting on a little high bed in a dress made out of paper and it's split at the back. Persons wear funny things in Outside. "They had to take away my real clothes." It's her voice though I can't see where it comes out of the mask.

I climb up to her lap all crinkly. "I saw us in TV."

"So I heard. How did we look?"

"Small."

I'm pulling at her dress but there's no way in. "Not right this minute." She kisses me instead on the side of the eye but it's not a kiss I want. "You were saying …"

I wasn't saying anything.

"About your wrist, yes," says Dr. Kendrick, "it'll probably need to be broken again at some point."

"No!"

"Shh, it's OK," Ma tells me.

"She'll be asleep when it happens," says Dr. Kendrick, looking at me. "The surgeon will put a metal pin in to help the joint work better."

"Like a cyborg?"

1 **convulsive** as if in a fit – 20 **crinkly** *zerknittert* – 32 **surgeon** a doctor who performs operations – 32 **joint** the connection between two bones (*Gelenk*)

"What's that?"

"Yeah, a bit like a cyborg," says Ma, grinning at me.

"But in the short term I'd say dentistry is the top priority," says Dr. Kendrick, "so I'm going to put you on a course of antibiotics right away, as well as extra-strength analgesics ..."

I do a huge yawn.

"I know," says Ma, "it's hours past bedtime."

Dr. Kendrick says, "If I could just give Jack a quick checkup?" "I said no already."

What does she want to give me? "Is it a toy?" I whisper to Ma. "It's unnecessary," she says to Dr. Kendrick. "Take my word for it."

"We're just following the protocol for cases like this," says Dr. Clay.

"Oh, you see lots of cases like this here, do you?" Ma's mad, I can hear it.

He shakes his head. "Other trauma situations, yes, but I'll be honest with you, nothing like yours. Which is why we need to get it right and give you both the best possible treatment from the start."

"Jack doesn't need *treatment,* he needs some sleep." Ma's talking through her teeth. "He's never been out of my sight and nothing happened to him, nothing like what you're insinuating."

The doctors look at each other. Dr. Kendrick says, "I didn't mean—"

"All these years, I kept him safe."

"Sounds like you did," says Dr. Clay.

"Yes, I did." There's tears all down Ma's face, now, there's one all dark on the edge of her mask. Why are they making her cry? "And tonight, what he's had to—he's asleep on his feet—"

I'm not asleep.

"I understand completely," says Dr. Clay. "Height and weight and she'll deal with his cuts, how about that?"

5 **analgesics** painkillers – 24 **to insinuate** to imply, to suggest

After a second Ma nods.

I don't want Dr. Kendrick to touch me, but I don't mind standing on the machine that shows my heavy, when I lean on the wall by accident Ma straightens me up. Then I stand against the numbers, just like we did beside Door but there's more of them and the lines are straighter. "You're doing great," says Dr. Clay.

Dr. Kendrick writes things down a lot. She points machines in my eyes and my ears and my mouth, she says, "Everything seems to be sparkling."

"We brush all the times we eat."

"Beg your pardon?"

"Slow down and speak up," Ma tells me.

"We brush after we eat."

Dr. Kendrick says, "I wish all my patients took such care of themselves."

Ma helps me pull my T-shirt over my head. It makes the mask fall off and I put it back on. Dr. Kendrick gets me to move all my pieces. She says my hips are excellent but I could do with a bone density scan at some point, that's a kind of X-ray. There's scratchy marks on my inside hands and my legs that's from when I jumped out of the truck. The right knee has all dried blood. I jump when Dr. Kendrick touches it.

"I'm sorry," she says.

I'm against Ma's tummy, the paper's in creases. "Germs are going to jump in the hole and I'll be dead."

"Don't worry," says Dr. Kendrick, "I've got a special wipe that takes them all away."

It stings. She does my bitten finger too, on the left hand where the dog drank my blood. Then she puts something on my knee, it's like a sticky tape but with faces on it, they're Dora and Boots waving at me. "Oh, oh—"

3 **heavy** Jack means "weight" – 10 **sparkling** *inf* shining bright, i.e. all right – 20 **bone density** *Knochendichte* – 20 **scan** a close examination – 20 **X-ray** *Röntgenaufnahme* – 25 **in creases** *here*: crumbly – 27 **wipe** medical cloth or cotton wool which is sterile – 29 **to sting** to hurt

"Does that hurt?"

"You've made his day," Ma says to Dr. Kendrick.

"You're a Dora fan?" says Dr. Clay. "My niece and nephew too." His teeth are smiling like snow.

Dr. Kendrick puts another Dora and Boots on my finger, it's tight.

Tooth is still safe down the side of my right sock. When I have my T-shirt and blanket back on, the doctors are talking all quiet, then Dr. Clay asks, "Do you know what a needle is, Jack?"

Ma groans. "Oh, come on."

"This way the lab can do a full blood count first thing in the morning. Markers of infection, nutritional deficiencies… . It's all admissible evidence, and more importantly, it'll help us figure out what Jack needs right away."

Ma looks at me. "Can you be a superhero for one more minute and let Dr. Kendrick prick your arm?"

"No." I hide both under the blanket.

"Please."

But no, I used all my brave up.

"I just need this much," says Dr. Kendrick, holding up a tube. That's way more than the dog or the mosquito, I won't have hardly any left.

"And then you'll get … What would he like?" she asks Ma.

"I'd like to go to Bed."

"She means a treat," Ma tells me. "Like cake or something."

"Hmm, I don't think we've got any cake right now, the kitchens are shut," says Dr. Clay. "What about a sucker?"

Pilar brings in a jar that's full of lollipops, that's what suckers are.

Ma says, "Go on, choose one."

But there's too many, they're yellow and green and red and blue and orange. They're all flat like circles not balls like the one from Old Nick that Ma threw in Trash and I ate anyway. Ma chooses for me, it's a red but I shake my head because the one

11 **lab** *abb* laboratory – 12 **nutritional deficiencies** lack of healthy food – 13 **admissible evidence** *zulässiges Beweismaterial*

from him was red and I think I'm going to cry again. Ma chooses a green. Pilar gets the plastic off. Dr. Clay stabs the needle inside my elbow and I scream and try to get away but Ma's holding me, she puts the lollipop in my mouth and I suck but it doesn't stop the hurting at all. "Nearly done," she says.

"I don't like it."

"Look, the needle's out."

"Good work," says Dr. Clay.

"No, the lollipop."

"You've got your lollipop," says Ma.

"I don't like it, I don't like the green."

"No problem, spit it out."

Pilar takes it. "Try an orange instead, I like the orange ones best," she says.

I didn't know I was allowed two. Pilar opens an orange for me and it's good.

* * *

First it's warm, then it gets cold. The warm was nice but the cold is a wet cold. Ma and me are in Bed but it's shrunk and it's getting chilly, the sheet under us and the sheet on us too and the Duvet's lost her white, she's all blue—

This isn't Room.

Silly Penis is standing up. "We're in Outside," I whisper to him.

"Ma—"

She jumps like an electric shock.

"I peed."

"That's OK."

"No, but it's all wetted. My T-shirt on the tummy bit as well."

"Forget about it."

I try forgetting. I'm looking past her head. The floor is like Rug but fuzzy with no pattern and no edges, sort of gray, it goes

2 **to stab** *here*: to push – 21 **duvet** [duːˈveɪ] a warm cover filled with feathers – 32 **fuzzy** having a hairy surface

all the way to the walls, I didn't know walls are green. There's a picture of a monster, but when I look it's actually a huge wave of the sea. A shape like Skylight only in the wall, I know what it is, it's a sideways window, with hundreds of wooden stripes across it but there's light coming between. "I'm still remembering," I tell Ma.

"Of course you are." She finds my cheek to kiss it.

"I can't forget it because I'm all still wet."

"Oh, that," she says in a different voice. "I didn't mean you had to forget you wet the bed, just don't worry about it." She's climbing out, she's still in her paper dress, it's crunched up. "The nurses will change the sheets."

I don't see the nurses.

"But my other T-shirts—" They're in Dresser, in the lower drawer. They were yesterday so I guess they are now too. But is Room still there when we're not in it?

"We'll figure something out," says Ma. She's at the window, she's made the wooden stripes go more apart and there's lots of light.

"How you did that?" I run over, the table hits my leg *bam*.

She rubs it better. "With the string, see? It's the cord of the blind."

"Why it's—?"

"It's the cord that opens and closes the blind," she says. "This is a window blind, it's called a blind—I guess because it stops you seeing."

"Why it stops me seeing?"

"I mean you as in anyone."

Why I am as in anyone?

"It stops people looking in or out," says Ma.

But I'm looking out, it's like TV. There's grass and trees and a bit of a white building and three cars, a blue and a brown and a silver with stripey bits. "On the grass—"

"What?"

22 **blind** *Jalousie* (Jack confuses this with the other meaning of the word, i.e. not being able to see) – 33 **stripey** *gestreift*

"Is that a vulture?"

"It's just a crow, I think."

"Another one—"

"That's a, a what-do-you-call-it, a pigeon. Early Alzheimer's! OK, let's get cleaned up."

"We haven't had breakfast," I tell her.

"We can do that after."

I shake my head. "Breakfast comes before bath."

"It doesn't have to, Jack."

"But—"

"We don't have to do the same as we used to," says Ma, "we can do what we like."

"I like breakfast before bath."

But she's gone around a corner and I can't see her, I run after. I find her in another little room inside this one, the floor's turned into shiny cold white squares and the walls are gone white too. There's a toilet that's not Toilet and a sink that's twice the big of Sink and a tall invisible box that must be a shower like TV persons splash in. "Where's the bath hiding?"

"There's no bath." Ma bangs the front of the box sideways so it's open. She takes off her paper dress and crumples it up in a basket that I think is a trash, but it hasn't got a lid that goes *ding*. "Let's get rid of that filthy thing too." My T-shirt pulls my face coming off. She scrunches it up and throws it in the trash.

"But—"

"It's a rag."

"It's not, it's my T-shirt."

"You'll get another, lots of them." I can hardly hear her because she's switched on the shower, all crashy. "Come on in."

"I don't know how."

"It's lovely, I promise." Ma waits. "OK, then, I won't be long." She steps in and starts closing the invisible door.

"No."

2 **crow** [kroʊ] a shiny black bird which can make loud noises – 4 **pigeon** [ˈpɪdʒən] a common, gray bird – 18 **invisible** Jack's way of saying "transparent" – 22 **trash** (trash can) bin for garbage – 26 **rag** an old piece of cloth – 29 **crashy** Jack's word for "noisy"

"I've got to, or the water will spill out."

"No."

"You can watch me through the glass, I'm right here." She slides it *bang,* I can't see her anymore except blurry, not like the real Ma but some ghost that makes weird sounds.

I hit it, I can't figure out the way, then I do and I slam it open. "Jack—"

"I don't like when you're in and I'm out."

"Then get on in here."

I'm crying.

Ma wipes my face with her hand, that spreads the tears. "Sorry," she says, "sorry. I guess I'm moving too fast." She gives me a hug that wets me all down me. "There's nothing to cry about anymore."

When I was a baby I only cried for a good reason. But Ma going in the shower and shutting me on the wrong side, that's a good reason.

This time I come in, I stand flat against the glass but I still get splashed. Ma puts her face into the noisy waterfall, she makes a long groan.

"Are you hurting?" I shout.

"No, I'm just trying to enjoy my first shower in seven years."

There's a tiny packet that says *Shampoo,* Ma opens it with her teeth, she's using it all up so there's nearly none left. She waters her hair for ages and puts on more stuff from another little packet that says *Conditioner* for making silky. She wants to do mine but I don't want to be silky, I won't put my face in the splash. She washes me with her hands because there's no cloth. There's bits of my legs gone purple from where I jumped out of the brown truck ages ago. My cuts hurt everywhere, especially on my knee under my Dora and Boots Band-Aid that's going curly, Ma says that means the cut's getting better. I don't know why hurting means getting better.

4 **blurry** Jack means "not clear" – 6 **to slam it open** Jack's words for "to push/pull it open violently" – 26 **silky** shiny like silk – 32 **curly** opp of straight

There's a super thick white towel we can use each, not one to share. I'd rather share but Ma says that's silly. She wraps another third towel around her head so it's all huge and pointy like an ice-cream cone, we laugh.

I'm thirsty. "Can I have some now?"

"Oh, in a little while." She holds out a big thing to me, with sleeves and a belt like a costume. "Wear this robe for now."

"But it's a giant's."

"It'll do." She folds up the sleeves till they're shorter and all puffy. She smells different, I think it's the conditioner. She ties the robe around my middle. I lift up the long bits to walk. "Ta-da," she says, "King Jack."

She gets another robe just the same out of the wardrobe that's not Wardrobe, it goes down just to her ankles.

" 'I will be king, diddle diddle, you can be queen,' " I sing.

Ma's all pink and grinning, her hair is black from being wet. Mine is back in ponytail but tangledy because there's no Comb, we left him in Room. "You should have brung Comb," I tell her.

"Brought," she says. "Remember, I was kind of in a hurry to see you."

"Yeah, but we need it."

"That old plastic comb with half its teeth snapped off? We need it like a hole in the head," she says.

I find my socks beside the bed, I'm putting them on but Ma says stop because they're all filthy from the street when I ran and ran and with holes in. She throws them in the trash too, she's wasting everything.

"But Tooth, we forgot him." I run to get the socks out of the trash and I find Tooth in the second one.

Ma rolls her eyes.

"He's my friend," I tell her, putting Tooth in the pocket in my robe. I'm licking my teeth because they feel funny. "Oh no, I

17 **tangledy** Jack means "tangled, disordered" – 22 **to snap off** *here*: broken – 23 **like a hole in the head** *inf* here: not at all – 27 **to waste** *verschwenden* (Jack means rather: "to get rid of")

didn't brush after the lollipop." I press them hard with my fingers so they won't fall out, but not the bitten finger.

Ma shakes her head. "It wasn't a real one."

"It tasted real."

"No, I mean it was sugarless, they make them with a kind of not-real sugar that's not bad for your teeth."

That's confusing. I point at the other bed. "Who sleeps there?"

"It's for you."

"But I sleep with you."

"Well, the nurses didn't know that." Ma's staring out the window. Her shadow's all long across the soft gray floor, I never saw such a long one. "Is that a cat in the parking lot?"

"Let's see." I run to look but my eyes don't find it.

"Will we go explore?"

"Where?"

"Outside."

"We're in Outside already."

"Yeah, but let's go out in the fresh air and look for the cat," says Ma.

"Cool."

She finds us two pairs of slippers but they don't fit me so I'm falling over, she says I can be barefoot for now. When I look out the window again, a thing zooms up near the other cars, it's a van that says *The Cumberland Clinic.*

"What if he comes?" I whisper.

"Who?"

"Old Nick, if he comes in his truck." I was nearly forgetting him, how could I be forgetting him?

"Oh, he couldn't, he doesn't know where we are," says Ma.

"Are we a secret again?"

"Kind of, but the good kind."

Beside the bed there's a—I know what it is, it's a phone. I lift the top bit, I say, "Hello," but nobody's talking, only a sort of hum. "Oh, Ma, I didn't have some yet."

"Later."

23 **to zoom up** *inf* to go quickly with a loud noise

Everything's backwards today.

Ma does the door handle and makes a face, it must be her bad wrist. She does it with the other hand. We go out in a long room with yellow walls and windows all along and doors the other side. Every wall's a different color, that must be the rule. Our door is the door that says *Seven* all gold. Ma says we can't go in the other doors because they belong to other persons.

"What other persons?"

"We haven't met them yet."

Then how does she know? "Can we look out the sideways windows?"

"Oh, yeah, they're for anyone."

"Is anyone us?"

"Us and anyone else," says Ma.

Anyone else isn't there so it's just us. There's no blind on these windows to stop seeing. It's a different planet, it shows more other cars like green and white and a red one and a stony place and there's things walking that are persons. "They're tiny, like fairies."

"Nah, that's just because they're far away," Ma says.

"Are they real for real?"

"As real as you and me."

I try and believe it but it's hard work.

There's one woman that's not really one, I can tell because she's gray, she's a statue and all naked.

"Come on," says Ma, "I'm starving."

"I'm just—"

She pulls me by the hand. Then we can't go anymore because there's stairs down, lots of them. "Hold on to the banister."

"The what?"

"This thing here, the rail."

I do.

"Climb down one step at a time."

I'm going to fall. I sit down.

19 **fairy** a tiny, fictional, human-like creature with magical powers – 29 **banister** *Treppengeländer* – 31 **rail** metal bar (*here:* banister)

"OK, that works too."

I go on my butt, one step then another then another and the giant robe comes loose. A big person rushes up the steps quick quick like she's flying, but she's not, she's a real human all in white. I put my face on Ma's robe to be not seen. "Oh," says the she, "you should have buzzed—"

Like bees?

"The buzzer right by your bed?"

"We managed," Ma tells her.

"I'm Noreen, let me get you a couple of fresh masks."

"Oh sorry, I forgot," says Ma.

"Sure, why don't I bring them up to your room?"

"That's OK, we're coming down."

"Grand. Jack, will I page an aide to carry you down the stairs?" I don't understand, I put my face away again.

"It's OK," says Ma, "he's doing it his way."

I go on my butt down the next eleven. At the bottom Ma ties up my robe again so we're still the king and the queen like "Lavender's Blue." Noreen gives me another mask I have to wear, she says she's a nurse and she comes from another place called Ireland and she likes my ponytail. We go in a huge bit that has all tables, I never saw so many with plates and glasses and knives and one of them stabs me in the tummy, one table I mean. The glasses are invisible like ours but the plates are blue, that's disgusting.

It's like a TV planet that's all about us, persons saying "Good morning" and "Welcome to the Cumberland" and "Congratulations," I don't know for what. Some are in robes the exact as ours and some in pajamas and some in different uniforms. Most are huge but don't have long of hair like us, they move fast and they're suddenly on all the sides, even behind. They walk up close and have so many teeth, they smell wrong. A he with a beard all over says, "Well, buddy, you're some kind of hero."

6 **to buzz** to push a button, to call sb. Bees buzz. (*summen*) – 14 **to page** to call sb for help

That's me he means. I don't look.

"How're you liking the world so far?"

I don't say anything.

"Pretty nice?"

I nod. I hold on tight to Ma's hand but my fingers are slipping, they've wet themselves. She's swallowing some pills Noreen gives her.

I know one head high up with a fuzzy small hair, that's Dr. Clay with no mask on. He shakes Ma's hand with his white plastic one and he asks if we slept well.

"I was too wired," says Ma.

Other uniformy persons walk up, Dr. Clay says names but I don't understand them. One has curves of hair that's all gray and she's called the Director of the Clinic that means the boss but she laughs and says not really, I don't know what's the joke.

Ma's pointing me a chair to sit beside her. There's the most amazing thing at the plate, it's silver and blue and red, I think it's an egg but not a real one, a chocolate.

"Oh, yeah, Happy Easter," says Ma, "it totally slipped my mind." I hold the pretend egg in my hand. I never knowed the Bunny came in buildings.

Ma's put her mask down on her neck, she's drinking juice that's a funny color. She puts my mask up on my head so I can try the juice but there's invisible bits in it like germs going down my throat so I cough it back in the glass real quiet. There's anyones too near eating strange squares with little squares all over and curly bacons. How can they let the food go on the blue plates and get all color on? It does smell yummy but too much and my hands are slippy again, I put the Easter back in the exactly middle of the plate. I rub my hands on the robe but not my bitten finger. The knives and forks are wrong too, there's no white on the handle, just the metal, that must hurt.

11 **wired** *here*: thinking of too many things – 19 **to slip one's mind** *inf* to forget – 26 **square** shape with four equal sides

The persons are with huge eyes, they have all faces different shapes with some mustaches and dangling jewels and painted bits. “No kids,” I whisper to Ma.

“What’s that?”

“Where are the kids?”

“I don’t think there are any.”

“You said there was millions in Outside.”

“The clinic’s only a little piece of the world,” says Ma. “Drink your juice. Hey, look, there’s a boy over there.”

I peek where she points, but he’s long like a man with nails in his nose and his chin and his over-eyes. Maybe he’s a robot?

Ma drinks a brown steaming stuff, then she makes a face and puts it down. “What would you like?” she asks.

The Noreen nurse is right beside me, I jump. “There’s a buffet,” she says, “you could have, let’s see, waffles, omelet, pancakes …”

I whisper, “No.”

“You say, *No, thanks,*” says Ma, “that’s good manners.”

Persons not friends of mine watching at me with invisible rays zap, I put my face against Ma.

“What d’you fancy, Jack?” asks Noreen. “Sausage, toast?” “They’re looking,” I tell Ma.

“Everybody’s just being friendly.”

I wish they’d stop.

Dr. Clay’s here again too, he leans near us. “This must be kind of overwhelming for Jack, for you both. Maybe a little ambitious for day one?”

What’s Day One?

Ma puffs her breath. “We wanted to see the garden.”

No, that was Alice.

“There’s no rush,” he says.

18 **good manners** *here:* polite – 20 **ray** a beam of light – 20 **to zap** *inf* to attack or destroy – 26 **overwhelming** too much – 26 **ambitious** having a desire to be successful (*ehrgeizig*)

"Have a few bites of something," she tells me. "You'll feel better if you drink your juice at least."

I shake my head.

"Why don't I make up a couple of plates and bring them up to your room?" says Noreen.

Ma snaps her mask back over her nose. "Come on, then." She's mad, I think.

I hold on to the chair. "What about the Easter?"

"What?"

I point.

Dr. Clay swipes the egg and I nearly shout. "There you go," he says, he drops it into the pocket of my robe.

The stairs are more harder going up so Ma carries me. Noreen says, "Let me, can I?"

"We're fine," says Ma, nearly shouting.

Ma shuts our door Number Seven all tight after Noreen's gone. We can take the masks off when it's just us, because we have the same germs. Ma tries to open the window, she bangs it, but it won't.

"Can I have some now?"

"Don't you want your breakfast?"

"After."

So we lie down and I have some, the left, it's yummy.

Ma says the plates aren't a problem, the blue doesn't go on the food, she gets me to rub it with my finger to see. Also the forks and knives, the metal feels weird with no white handles but it doesn't actually hurt. There's a syrup that's to put on the pancakes but I don't want mine wet. I have a bit of all the foods and everything are good except the sauce on the scrambled eggs. The chocolate one, the Easter, it's meltedy inside. It's double more chocolatier than the chocolates we got sometimes for Sundaytreat, it's the best thing I ever ate.

11 **to swipe** to take away – 24 **blue** *here*: the blue colour – 29 **scrambled eggs** *Rühreier* – 30 **meltedy** Jack means "soft"

"Oh! We forgot to say thanks to Baby Jesus," I tell Ma. "We'll say it now, he doesn't mind if we're late."

Then I do a huge burp.

Then we go back to sleep.

* * *

When the door knocks, Ma lets Dr. Clay in, she puts her mask back on and mine. He's not very scary now. "How're you doing, Jack?" "OK."

"Gimme five?"

His plastic hand is up and he's waggling his fingers, I pretend I don't see. I'm not going to give him my fingers, I need them for me.

He and Ma talk about stuff like why she can't get to sleep, *tachycardia* and *re-experiencing*. "Try these, just one before bed," he says, writing something on his pad. "And anti-inflammatories might work better for your toothache ..."

"Can I please hold on to my medications instead of the nurses doling them out like I'm a sick person?"

"Ah, that shouldn't be a problem, as long as you don't leave them lying around your room."

"Jack knows not to mess with pills."

"Actually I was thinking of a few of our patients who've got histories of substance abuse. Now, for you, I've got a magic patch." "Jack, Dr. Clay's talking to you," says Ma.

The patch is to put on my arm that makes a bit of it feel not there. Also he's brought cool shades to wear when it's too bright in the windows, mine are red and Ma's are black. "Like rap stars," I tell her. They go darker if we'll be in the outside of Outside and lighter if we'll be in the inside of Outside. Dr. Clay

3 **burp** [bɜrp] *inf* belch *(Rülpser)* – 9 **to waggle** *inf* to move from side to side – 13 **tachycardia and re-experiencing** a state of going through the past again and again – 14 **anti-inflammatory** *entzündungshemmend* – 17 **to dole out** *inf* to distribute – 22 **substance abuse** wrong use of drugs – 23 **patch** a small piece of material to cover a wound

says my eyes are super sharp but they're not used to looking far away yet, I need to stretch them out the window. I never knowed there were muscles inside my eyes, I put my fingers to press but I can't feel them.

"How's that patch," says Dr. Clay, "are you numb yet?" He peels it off and touches me under, I see his finger on me but I can't feel it. Then the bad thing, he's got needles and he says he's sorry but I need six shots to stop me to get horrible sicknesses, that's what the patch is for, for making the needles not hurt. Six is not possible, I run in the toilet bit of the room.

"They could kill you," says Ma, pulling me back to Dr. Clay.

"No!"

"The germs, I mean, not the shots."

It's still no.

Dr. Clay says I'm really brave but I'm not, I used my brave all up doing Plan B. I scream and scream. Ma holds me on her lap while he sticks his needles in over and over and they do hurt because he took the patch off, I cry for it and in the end Ma puts it back on me.

"All done for now, I promise." Dr. Clay puts the needles in a box on the wall called *Sharps*. He has a lollipop for me in his pocket, an orange, but I'm too full. He says I can keep it for another time.

"… like a newborn in many ways, despite his remarkably accelerated literacy and numeracy," he's saying to Ma. I'm listening hard because it's me that's the he. "As well as immune issues, there are likely to be challenges in the areas of, let's see, social adjustment, obviously, sensory modulation—filtering and sorting all the stimuli barraging him—plus difficulties with spatial perception …"

Ma asks, "Is that why he keeps banging into things?"

25 **accelerated** *here*: very advanced – 25 **literacy and numeracy** *Fähigkeit zu lesen und zu rechnen* – 27 **social adjustment** to find one' s way in new surroundings – 28 **sensory modulation** flexibility of the senses – 29 **to barrage** [bəˈrɑːdʒ] hitting him with too many questions and impressions at the same time – 30 **spacial perception** *räumliche Wahrnehmung*

"Exactly. He's been so familiar with his confined environment that he hasn't needed to learn to gauge distance."

Ma's got her head in her hands. "I thought he was OK. More or less."

Am I not OK?

"Another way to look at this—"

But he stops because there's a knock, when he opens it's Noreen with another tray.

I do a burp, my tummy's still crammed from breakfast.

"Ideally a mental health OT with qualifications in play and art therapy," Dr. Clay is saying, "but at our meeting this morning it was agreed that the immediate priority is to help him feel safe. Both of you, rather. It's a matter of slowly, slowly enlarging the circle of trust." His hands are in the air moving wider. "As I was lucky enough to be the admitting psychiatrist on duty last night—"

"Lucky?" she says.

"Poor word choice." He does a sort of grin. "I'm going to be working with you both for the moment—"

What working? I didn't know kids had to work.

"—with input of course from my colleagues in child and adolescent psychiatry, our neurologist, our psychotherapists, we're going to bring in a nutritionist, a physio—"

Another knock. It's Noreen again with a police, a he but not the yellow-hair one from last night.

That's three persons in the room now and two of us, that equals five, it's nearly full of arms and legs and chests. They're all saying till I hurt. "Stop all saying at the same time." I say it only on mute. I squish my fingers in my ears.

"You want a surprise?"

It was me Ma was saying, I didn't know. Noreen's gone and the police too. I shake my head.

Dr. Clay says, "I'm not sure this is the most advisable—"

2 **to gauge** [geɪdʒ] to judge (*abschätzen*) – 10 **OT Occupational Therapy** *(Ergotherapie)* – 13 **to enlarge** to make bigger – 22 **adolescent** *adj* young adult

"Jack, it's the best news," Ma butts in. She holds up pictures. I see who it is without even going close, it's Old Nick. The same face as when I peeked at him in Bed in the night that time, but he has a sign around his neck and he's against numbers like we marked my tall on birthdays, he's nearly at the six but not quite. There's a picture where he's looking sideways and another where he's looking at me.

"In the middle of the night the police caught him and put him in jail, and that's where he'll stay," says Ma.

I wonder is the brown truck in jail too.

"Does looking at them trigger any of the symptoms we were talking about?" Dr. Clay is asking her.

She rolls her eyes. "After seven years of the real deal, you think I'm going to crumble at a photo?"

"What about you, Jack, how does it feel?"

I don't know the answer.

"I'm going to ask a question," says Dr. Clay, "but you don't have to answer it unless you want to. OK?"

I look at him then back at the pictures. Old Nick's stuck in the numbers and he can't get out.

"Did this man ever do anything you didn't like?"

I nod.

"Can you tell me what he did?"

"He cutted off the power so the vegetables went slimy."

"Right. Did he ever hurt you?"

Ma says, "Don't—"

Dr. Clay puts his hand up. "Nobody's doubting your word," he tells her. "But think of all the nights you were asleep. I wouldn't be doing my job if I didn't ask Jack himself, now, would I?"

Ma lets her breath out very long. "It's OK," she says to me, "you can answer. Did Old Nick ever hurt you?"

"Yeah," I say, "two times."

They're both staring.

11 **to trigger** to bring out again, cause – 14 **to crumble** *here*: to break down – 24 **slimy** food goes slimy when it is old or rotten

"When I was doing the Great Escape he dropped me in the truck and also on the street, the second was the hurtest."

"OK," says Dr. Clay. He's smiling, I don't know why. "I'll get onto the lab right away to see if they need another sample from you both for DNA," he tells Ma.

"DNA?" She's got her crazy voice again. "You think I had *other visitors?*"

"I think this is how the courts work, every box has got to be ticked."

Ma's sucking her whole mouth in so her lips are invisible. " Monsters are let off on technicalities every day." He sounds all fierce. "OK?"

"OK."

When he's gone I rip my mask off and I ask, "Is he mad at us?" Ma shakes her head. "He's mad at Old Nick."

I didn't think Dr. Clay even knows him, I thought we were the only ones.

I go look at the tray Noreen brought. I'm not hungry but when I ask Ma she says it's after one o'clock, that's too late for lunch even, lunch should be twelve something but there's no room in my tummy yet.

"Relax," Ma tells me. "Everything's different here."

"But what's the rule?"

"There is no rule. We can have lunch at ten or one or three or the middle of the night."

"I don't want lunch in the middle of the night."

Ma puffs her breath. "Let's make a new rule that we'll have lunch ... anytime between twelve and two. And if we're not hungry we'll just skip it."

"How do we skip it?"

"Eat nothing. Zero."

"OK." I don't mind eating zero. "But what will Noreen do with all the food?"

2 **the hurtest** Jack means "the second one hurt most" – 8 **every box has got to be ticked** every question has to be answered – 11 **monsters** *here*: criminals – 12 **fierce** angry – 29 **to skip** to leave out

"Throw it away."

"That's waste."

"Yeah, but it has to go in the trash because it's—it's like it's dirty."

I look at the food all multicolored on the blue plates. "It doesn't look dirty."

"It's not actually, but nobody else here would want it after it's been on our plates," says Ma. "Don't worry about it."

She keeps saying that but I don't know to not worry.

I yawn so huge it nearly knocks me over. My arm still hurts from where it wasn't numb. I ask if we can go back to sleep again and Ma says sure, but she's going to read the paper. I don't know why she wants to read the paper instead of being asleep with me.

* * *

When I wake up the light's in the wrong place.

"It's all right," says Ma, she puts her face touching mine, "everything's all right."

I put on my cool shades to watch God's yellow face in our window, the light slides right across the fuzzy gray carpet.

Noreen comes in with bags.

"You could knock." Ma's nearly shouting, she puts my mask on and hers.

"Sorry," says Noreen. "I did, actually, but I'll be sure and do it louder next time."

"No, sorry, I didn't—I was talking to Jack. Maybe I heard it but I didn't know it was the door."

"No bother," says Noreen.

"There's sounds from—the other rooms, I hear things and I don't know if it's, where it is or what."

"It must all seem a bit strange."

Ma kind of laughs.

27 **No bother** *inf* no problem

"And as for this young lad—" Noreen's eyes are all shiny. "Would you like to see your new clothes?"

They're not our clothes, they're different ones in bags and if they don't fit or we don't like them Noreen will take them right back to the store to get other ones. I try on everything, I like the pajamas best, they're furry with astronauts on them. It's like a costume of a TV boy. There's shoes that do on with scratchy stuff that sticks called Velcro. I like putting them open and shut like *rrrrrpppp rrrrrpppp*. It's hard to walk though, they feel heavy like they'll trip me up. I prefer to wear them when I'm on the bed, I wave my feet in the air and the shoes fight each other and make friends again.

Ma's in a jeans that's too tight. "That's how they're wearing them these days," says Noreen, "and God knows you've got the figure for it."

"Who's they?"

"Youngsters."

Ma grins, I don't know why. She puts on a shirt that's too tight too.

"Those aren't your real clothes," I whisper to her.

"They are now."

The door goes knock, it's another nurse, the same uniform but the different face. She says we should put our masks back on because we have a visitor. I never had a visitor before, I don't know how.

A person comes in and runs at Ma, I jump up with fists but Ma's laughing and crying at the same time, it must be happysad.

"Oh, Mom." That's Ma saying. "Oh, Mom."

"My little—"

"I'm back."

"Yes, you are," says the she person. "When they called I was sure it was another hoax—"

"Did you miss me?" Ma starts to laugh, a weird way.

6 **furry** very soft (*flauschig*) – 7 **scratchy** rough – 10 **to trip up** to lose one's balance – 33 **hoax** trick, lie

The woman is crying too, there's all black drips under her eyes, I wonder why her tears come out black. Her mouth is all blood color like women on TV. She has yellowy hair short but not all short and big gold knobs stuck in her ears below the hole. She's still got Ma all tied up in her arms, she's three times as round as her. I never saw Ma hug a someone else.

"Let me see you without this silly thing for a second."

Ma pulls her mask down, smiling and smiling.

The woman's staring at me now. "I can't believe it, I can't believe any of this."

"Jack," says Ma, "this is your grandma."

So I really have one.

"What a treasure." The woman opens her arms like she's going to wave them but she doesn't. She walks over at me. I get behind the chair.

"He's very affectionate," says Ma, "he's just not used to anyone but me."

"Of course, of course." The Grandma comes a bit closer. "Oh, Jack, you've been the bravest little guy in the world, you've brought my baby back."

What baby?

"Lift up your mask for a second," Ma tells me.

I do then snap it back.

"He's got your jaw," the Grandma says.

"You think so?"

"Of course you were always wild about kids, you'd babysit for free …"

They talk and talk. I look under my Band-Aid to see if my finger's going to fall off still. The red dots are scaly now.

Air coming in. There's a face in the door, a face with beard all over it on the cheeks and the chin and under the nose but none on the head.

1 **drip** *here*: drop – 4 **knob** a round thing – 16 **affectionate** showing love – 23 **to snap** to move sth suddenly so as to cause a sharp sound – 24 **jaw** *Kinn* – 29 **scaly** *schuppig*

“I told the nurse we didn’t want to be disturbed,” says Ma. “Actually, this is Leo,” says Grandma.

“Hey,” he says, he wiggles his fingers.

“Who’s Leo?” asks Ma, not smiling.

“He was meant to stay in the corridor.”

“No problemo,” says Leo, then he’s not there anymore. “Where’s Dad?” asks Ma.

“In Canberra right now, but he’s on his way,” says Grandma. “There’s been a lot of changes, sweetheart.”

“Canberra?”

“Oh, honey, it’s probably too much for you to take in …”

It turns out the hairy Leo person isn’t my real Grandpa, the real one went back to live in Australia after he thought Ma was dead and had a funeral for her, Grandma was mad at him because she never stopped hoping. She always told herself their precious girl must have had her reasons for disappearing and one fine day she’d get in touch again.

Ma is staring at her. “One fine day?”

“Well, isn’t it?” Grandma waves at the window.

“What kind of *reasons* would I—?”

“Oh, we racked our brains. A social worker told us kids your age sometimes just take off out of the blue. Drugs, possibly, I scoured your room—”

“I had a three-point-seven grade average.”

“Yes you did, you were our pride and joy.”

“I was snatched off the street.”

“Well I know that *now*. We stuck up posters all over the city, Paul made a website. The police talked to everyone you knew from college and high school too, to find out who else you might have been hanging around with that we didn’t know. I kept thinking I saw you, it was torture,” says Grandma. “I used

8 **Canberra** a big city in Australia – 11 **to take in** to understand – 14 **funeral** ['fju:nərəl] a ceremony of burying a dead person – 16 **precious** ['preʃəs] valuable – 21 **to rack one’s brain** to think hard – 22 **out of the blue** without a reason – 23 **to scour** [skaʊɚ] to search every part of (a room) thoroughly – 24 **three-point-seven grade average** *ein sehr guter Schulabschluß* – 31 **torture** *Folter*

to pull up beside girls and slam on my horn, but they'd turn out to be strangers. For your birthday I always baked your favorite just in case you walked in, remember my banana chocolate cake?"

Ma nods. She's got tears all down her face.

"I couldn't sleep without pills. The not knowing was eating me up, it really wasn't fair to your brother. Did you know—well, how could you?—Paul's got a little girl, she's almost three and potty-trained already. His partner's lovely, a radiologist."

They talk a lot more, my ears get tired listening. Then Noreen comes in with pills for us and a glass of juice that's not orange, it's apple and the best I ever drunk.

Grandma's going to her house now. I wonder if she sleeps in the hammock. "Will I—Leo could pop in for a quick hello," she says when she's at the door.

Ma says nothing. Then, "Maybe next time."

"Whatever you like. The doctors say to take it slow."

"Take what slow?"

"Everything." Grandma turns to me. "So. Jack. Do you know the word *bye-bye?*"

"Actually I know all the words," I tell her.

That makes her laugh and laugh.

She kisses her own hand and blows it at me. "Catch?"

I think she wants me to play like I'm catching the kiss, so I do it and she's glad, she has more tears.

"Why did she laugh about me knowing all the words when I wasn't making a joke?" I ask Ma after.

"Oh, it doesn't matter, it's always good to make people laugh."

At 06:12 Noreen brings another whole different tray that's dinner, we can have dinner at five something or six something or even seven something, Ma says. There's green crunchy stuff called arugula that tastes too sharp, I like the potatoes with crispy edges and meats with stripes all on them. The bread has

1 **to slam the horn** *(ganz fest) hupen* – 9 **to potty-train** to teach a baby to use a potty or toilet – 30 **whole** Jack means "completely" – 33 **arugula** *AE* a kind of lettuce (*Rucola*)

bits that scratch my throat, I try to pick them out but then there's holes, Ma says to just leave it. There's strawberries she says taste like Heaven, how does she know what Heaven tastes like? We can't eat it all. Ma says most people stuff themselves too much anyway, we should just eat what we like and leave the rest.

My favorite bit of Outside is the window. It's different every time. A bird goes right by *zoom,* I don't know what it was. The shadows are all long again now, mine waves right across our room on the green wall. I watch God's face falling slow slow, even orangier and the clouds are all colors, then after there's streaks and dark coming up so bit-at-a-time I don't see it till it's done.

* * *

Ma and me keep knocking into each other in the night. The third time I wake up I'm wanting Jeep and Remote but they're not here.

No one's in Room now, just things, everything lying extra still with dust falling, because Ma and me are at the Clinic and Old Nick is in the jail. He has to stay forever locked in.

I remember I'm in the pajamas with the astronauts. I touch my leg through the cloth, it doesn't feel like mine. All our stuff that was ours is locked in Room except my T-shirt that Ma threw in the trash here and it's gone now, I looked at bedtime, a cleaner must have took it away. I thought that meant a person cleaner than everybody else, but Ma says it's one who does the cleaning. I think they're invisible like elves. I wish the cleaner would bring back my old T-shirt but Ma would only get cranky again.

We have to be in the world, we're not ever going back to Room, Ma says that's how it is and I should be glad. I don't know why we can't go back just to sleep even. I wonder do we have to

12 **streak** a thin line – 20 **jail** prison – 27 **elf** (*pl*: elves) a small fairy with pointed ears that plays tricks on people – 28 **cranky** *inf* bad-tempered

stay always in the Clinic bit or can we go in others of Outside like the house with the hammock, except the real Grandpa's in Australia that's too far away. "Ma?"

She groans. "Jack, I was finally dropping off …"

"How long are we here?"

"It's only been twenty-four hours. It just feels longer."

"No, but—how long do we still be here after now? How many days and nights?"

"I don't actually know."

But Ma always knows things. "Tell me."

"Shh."

"But how long?"

"Just a while," she says. "Now shush, there's other people next door, remember, and you're disturbing them."

I don't see the persons but they're there anyway, they're the ones from the dining room. In Room I was never disturbing anybody only sometimes Ma if Tooth was really bad. She says the persons are here at the Cumberland because they're a bit sick in the head, but not very. They can't sleep maybe from worrying, or they can't eat, or they wash their hands too much, I didn't know washing could be too much. Some of them have hit their heads and don't know themselves anymore, and some are sad all the time or scratch their arms with knives even, I don't know why. The doctors and nurses and Pilar and the invisible cleaners aren't sick, they're here to help. Ma and me aren't sick either, we're just here for a rest, also we don't want to be bugged by the paparazzi which is the vultures with their cameras and microphones, because we're famous now, like rap stars but we didn't do it on purpose. Ma says basically we just need a bit of help while we sort things out. I don't know which things.

I reach under the pillow now to feel has Tooth turned into money but no. I think the Fairy doesn't know where the Clinic is.

27 **to bug** *inf* to annoy – 29 **on purpose** intentionally – 30 **to sort things out** to solve problems, get things organized

"Ma?"

"What?"

"Are we locked in?"

"No." She nearly barks it. "Of course not. Why, are you not liking it here?"

"I mean but do we *have* to stay?"

"No, no, we're free as a bird."

* * *

I thought all the weird things happened yesterday but there's lots more today.

My poo is hard to push out because my tummy's not used to so much food.

We don't have to wash our sheets in the shower because the invisible cleaners do that too.

Ma writes in a notebook Dr. Clay gave her for homework. I thought just kids going to school do that, it means work for doing at home but Ma says the Clinic's not anybody's actual home, everyone goes home in the end.

I hate my mask, I can't breathe through it but Ma says I can really.

We have our breakfast in the dining room that's for eating just, persons in the world like to go in different rooms for each thing. I remember manners, that's when persons are scared to make other persons mad. I say, "Please may you have me more pancakes?"

The she with the apron says, "He's a doll."

I'm not a doll, but Ma whispers it means the woman likes me so I should let her call me one.

I try the syrup, it's super extra sweet, I drink a whole little tub before Ma stops me. She says it's only for putting on pancakes but I think that's yucky.

4 **to bark** to shout in a rough way (Dogs bark.) – 17 **actual** real – 26 **apron** worn in the kitchen to keep one's clothes clean (*Schürze*) – 31 **yucky** *inf* terrible

People keep coming at her with jugs of coffee, she says no. I eat so many bacon I lose count, when I say, "Thank you, Baby Jesus," people stare because I think they don't know him in Outside.

Ma says when a person acts funny like that long boy with the metal bits in his face called Hugo doing the humming or Mrs. Garber scratching her neck all the time, we don't laugh except inside behind our faces if we have to.

I never know when sounds are going to happen and make me jump. Lots of times I can't see what makes them, some are tiny like little bugs whining but some hurt my head. Even though everything's always so loud, Ma keeps telling me not to shout so I don't disturb persons. But often when I talk they don't hear me.

Ma says, "Where are your shoes?"

We go back and find them in the dining room under the table, one has a piece of bacon on it that I eat.

"Germs," says Ma.

I carry my shoes by the Velcro straps. She tells me to put them on. "They make my feet sore."

"Aren't they the right size?"

"They're too heavy."

"I know you're not used to them, but you just can't go around in your socks, you might step on something sharp."

"I won't, I promise."

She waits till I put them on. We're in a corridor but not the one on top of the stairs, the Clinic has all different bits. I don't think we went here before, are we lost?

Ma's looking out a new window. "Today we could go outside and see the trees and the flowers, maybe."

"No."

"Jack—"

"I mean no, thanks."

2 **to lose count** to not know the exact number – 11 **bug** *AE* insect – 11 **to whine** [waɪn] to make a high (but not loud) sound – 19 **strap** *here*: a narrow band of material to fasten the shoe – 20 **sore** painful from a wound

"Fresh air!"

I like the air in Room Number Seven, Noreen brings us back there. Out our window we can see cars parking and unparking and pigeons and sometimes that cat.

Later we go play with Dr. Clay in another new room that has a rug with long hair, not like Rug who's all flat with her zigzag pattern. I wonder if Rug misses us, is she still in the back of the pickup truck in jail?

Ma shows Dr. Clay her homework, they talk more about not very interesting stuff like *depersonalization* and *jamais vu*. Then I help Dr. Clay unpack his toy trunk, it's the coolest. He talks into a cellphone that's not a real one, "Great to hear from you, Jack. I'm at the clinic right now. Where are you?"

There's a plastic banana, I say, "Me too," into it.

"What a coincidence. Are you enjoying it here?"

"I'm enjoying the bacon."

He laughs, I didn't know I made a joke again. "I enjoy bacon too. Too much."

How can enjoying be too much?

In the bottom of the trunk I find tiny puppets like a spotty dog and a pirate and a moon and a boy with his tongue stuck out, my favorite is the dog.

"Jack, he's asking you a question."

I blink at Ma.

"So what do you not like so much here?" says Dr. Clay. "Persons looking."

"Mmm?"

He says that a lot instead of words.

"Also sudden things."

"Certain things? Which ones?"

"Sudden things," I tell him. "That come quick quick." "Ah, yes. 'World is suddener than we fancy it.' "

"Huh?"

10 **depersonalization** *Entpersonalisierung* – 10 **jamais vu** *Fr* never seen before – 11 **trunk** a large box – 15 **coincidence** sth happening by chance (*Zufall*) – 24 **to blink** to open and shut your eyes quickly – 32 **to fancy** *inf* to like

"Sorry, just a line from a poem." Dr. Clay grins at Ma. "Jack, can you describe where you were before the clinic?"

He never went to Room, so I tell him all about all the bits of it, what we did every day and stuff, Ma says anything I forget to say. He's got goo I saw in TV in all colors, he makes it into balls and worms while we're talking. I stick my finger into a yellow bit, then there's some in my nail and I don't like it to be yellow.

"You never got Play-Doh for one of your Sunday treats?" he asks.

"It dries out." That's Ma butting in. "Ever think of that? Even if you put it back in the tub, like, religiously, after a while it starts going leathery."

"I guess it would," says Dr. Clay.

"That's the same reason I asked for crayons and pencils, not markers, and cloth diapers, and—whatever would last, so I wouldn't have to ask again a week later."

He keeps nodding.

"We made flour dough, but it was always white." Ma's sounding mad. "You think I wouldn't have given Jack a different color of Play-Doh every day if I could have?"

Dr. Clay says Ma's other name. "Nobody's expressing any judgment about your choices and strategies."

"Noreen says it works better if you add as much salt as flour, did you know that? I didn't know that, how would I? I never thought to ask for food coloring, even. If I'd only had the first freakin' clue—"

She keeps telling Dr. Clay she's fine but she doesn't sound fine. She and him talk about *cognitive distortions,* they do a breathing exercise, I play with the puppets. Then our time's up because he has to go play with Hugo.

"Was he in a shed too?" I ask.

Dr. Clay shakes his head.

11 **religiously** i.e. you never fail to do it, like a religious ritual; carefully – 14 **crayon** a stick of coloured wax used to draw with (*Wachsmalstift*) – 15 **diaper** ['daɪpɚ] *AE* babies wear diapers (*Windel*) – 18 **flour dough** *Mehlteig* – 26 **freakin' clue** *sl* an idea ("freakin'" is often used instead of the much stronger "fucking", i.e. it is an 'intensifier' – Ma is very angry) – 28 **cognitive distortion** *Wahrnehmungsstörung*

"What happened to him?"

"Everyone's got a different story."

When we go back to our room Ma and I get into the bed and I have lots. She still smells wrong from the conditioner, too silky.

* * *

Even after the nap I'm still tired. My nose keeps dripping and my eyes too, like they're melting inside. Ma says I've picked up my first cold, that's all.

"But I wore my mask."

"Still, germs just sneak in. I'll probably catch it from you by tomorrow."

I'm crying. "We're not done playing."

She's holding me.

"I don't want to go to Heaven yet."

"Sweetie—" Ma never called me that before. "It's OK, if we get sick the doctors will make us better."

"I want it."

"You want what?"

"I want Dr. Clay making me better now."

"Well, actually, he can't cure a cold." Ma chews her mouth. "But it'll be all gone in a few days, I promise. Hey, would you like to learn to blow your nose?"

It takes me just four tries, when I get all the snot out in the tissue, she claps.

Noreen brings up lunch that's soups and kebabs and a rice that's not real called quinoa. For after there's a salad of fruits and I guess all them, apple and orange and the ones I don't know are pineapple and mango and blueberry and kiwi and watermelon, that's two right and five wrong, that's minus three. There's no banana.

11 **we're not done** *inf, AE* we have not finished – 19 **to cure** to heal – 21 **to blow one's nose** *schneuzen* – 22 **snot** *inf* liquid produced in the nose – 25 **quinoa** grain-like crop, originally from South America – 27 **blueberry** a very small North American fruit

I want to see the fish again so we go down in the bit called Reception. They've got stripes. "Are they sick?"

"They look lively enough to me," says Ma. "Especially that big, bossy one in the seaweed."

"No, but in the head? Are they crazy fish?"

She laughs. "I don't think so."

"Are they just resting for a little while because they're famous?" "These ones were born here, actually, right in this tank." It's the Pilar woman.

I jump, I didn't see her coming out of her desk. "Why?" She stares at me still smiling. "Ah—"

"Why are they here?"

"For us all to look at, I guess. Aren't they pretty?"

"Come on, Jack," says Ma, "I'm sure she's got work to do."

In Outside the time's all mixed up. Ma keeps saying, "Slow down, Jack," and "Hang on," and "Finish up now," and "Hurry up, Jack," she says *Jack* a lot so I'll know it's me she's talking to not persons else. I can hardly ever guess what time it is, there's clocks but they have pointy hands, I don't know the secret and Watch isn't here with her numbers so I have to ask Ma and she gets tired of me asking. "You know what time it is, it's time to go outside."

I don't want to but she keeps saying, "Let's try, just try. Right now, why not?"

I have to put my shoes back on first. Also we have to have jackets and hats and sticky stuff on faces under our masks and on our hands, the sun might burn our skin off because we're from Room. Dr. Clay and Noreen are coming with us, they don't have any cool shades or anything.

The way to out isn't a door, it's like an airlock on a spaceship. Ma can't remember the word, Dr. Clay says, "Revolving door."

4 **seaweed** green plant species that grows in the sea – 19 **pointy** sharp – 19 **hands** the two parts of an analogue clock that show the time (*Zeiger*) – 31 **revolving** turning in a circle

"Oh yeah," I say, "I know it in TV." I like the going around bit but then we're outside and the light hurts my shades all dark, the wind smacks my face and I have to get back in.

"It's OK," Ma keeps saying.

"I don't like it." The revolving's stuck, it won't revolve, it's squeezing me out.

"Hold my hand."

"The wind's going to rip us."

"It's only a breeze," says Ma.

The light's not like in a window, it's coming all ways around the sides of my cool shades, it wasn't like this on our Great Escape. Too much horrible shine and air freshing. "My skin's burning off."

"You're grand," says Noreen. "Big, slow breaths, that's a boy."

Why is that a boy? There aren't any breaths out here. There's spots on my shades, my chest's going *bang bang bang* and the wind's so loud I can't hear anything.

Noreen's doing something strange, she's pulling off my mask and putting a different paper on my face. I push it away with my sticky hands.

Dr. Clay says, "I'm not sure this is such a—"

"Breathe in the bag," Noreen tells me.

I do, it's warm, all I do is suck it in and suck it in.

Ma's holding my shoulders, she says, "Let's go back in."

Back in Room Number Seven I have some on the bed, still with my shoes on and the stickiness.

Later Grandma comes, I know her face this time. She's brung books from her hammock house, three for Ma with no pictures that she gets all excited and five for me with pictures, Grandma didn't even know five was my best best number. She says these ones were Ma's and my Uncle Paul's when they were kids, I don't think she's lying but it's hard for it to be true that Ma was ever a kid. "Would you like to sit in Grandma's lap and I'll read you one?"

3 **to smack** to hit – 6 **to squeeze** to press firmly – 8 **to rip** to tear violently – 9 **breeze** a light wind – 12 **shine** Jack means "bright light"

"No, thanks."

There's *The Very Hungry Caterpillar* and *The Giving Tree* and *Go, Dog, Go* and *The Lorax* and *The Tale of Peter Rabbit,* I look at all the pictures.

"I mean it, every detail," Grandma's saying to Ma really quiet, "I can take it."

"I doubt that."

"I'm ready."

Ma keeps shaking her head. "What's the point, Mom? It's over now, I'm out the other side."

"But, honey—"

"I'd actually rather not have you thinking about that stuff every time you look at me, OK?"

There's more tears rolling down Grandma. "Sweetie," she says, "all I think when I look at you is hallelujah."

When she's gone Ma reads me the rabbit one, he's a Peter but not the Saint. He wears old-fashioned clothes and gets chased by a gardener, I don't know why he bothers swiping vegetables. Swiping's bad but if I was a swiper I'd swipe good stuff like cars and chocolates. It's not a very excellent book but it's excellent to have so many new ones. In Room I had five but now it's plus five, that equals ten. Actually I don't have the old five books now so I guess I just have the new five. The ones in Room, maybe they don't belong to anyone anymore.

Grandma only stays a little while because we have another visitor, that's our lawyer Morris. I didn't know we had one, like the courtroom planet where people shout and the judge bangs the hammer. We meet him in a room in the not upstairs, there's a table and a smell like sweet. His hair is extra curly. While he and Ma talk I practice blowing my nose.

"This paper that's printed your fifth-grade photo, for instance," he's saying, "we'd have a strong case for breach of privacy there."

17 **to chase** to hunt, follow (with the purpose of catching sb) – 18 **to swipe** *inf* to steal – 26 **lawyer** a person who advises people about laws and represents them in court – 27 **courtroom** the main room in a court (*Gerichtssaal*) – 29 **curly** *opp of* straight – 32 **breach of privacy** *Verstoß gegen die Privatspäre*

The *you* means Ma, not me, I'm getting good at telling.

"You mean like suing? That's the last thing on my mind," she tells him. I show her my tissue with my blowing in it, she does a thumbs-up.

Morris nods a lot. "I'm just saying, you have to consider your future, yours and the boy's." That's me, the boy. "Yeah, the Cumberland's waiving its fees in the short term, and I've set up a fund for your fans, but I have to tell you, sooner or later there's going to be bills like you wouldn't believe. Rehab, fancy therapies, housing, educational costs for both of you ..."

Ma rubs her eyes.

"I don't want to rush you."

"You said—my fans?"

"Sure," says Morris. "Donations are pouring in, about a sack a day."

"A sack of what?"

"You name it. I grabbed some things at random—" He lifts up a big plastic bag from behind his chair and takes parcels out.

"You opened them," says Ma, looking in the envelopes. "Believe me, you need this stuff filtered. F-E-C-E-S, and that's just for starters."

"Why somebody sent us poo?" I ask Ma.

Morris is staring.

"He's a good speller," she tells him.

"Ah, you asked why, Jack? Because there's a lot of crazies out there."

I thought the crazies were in here in the Clinic getting helped.

"But most of what you're receiving is from well-wishers," he says. "Chocolates, toys, that kind of thing."

Chocolates!

2 **to sue** [suː] to take sb to court – 4 **thumbs-up** an expression of satisfaction or victory – 7 **to waive fees** [weɪv] *Gebühren erlassen* – 9 **bills like you wouldn't believe** very expensive costs – 9 **Rehab** *abb* rehabilitation – 9 **fancy** *inf* unusual, exotic – 14 **donation** money given for a good purpose/charity (*Spende*) – 14 **to pour** to flow steadily – 17 **at random** by chance – 20 **feces** [ˈfiːsɪz] *Kot*

"I thought I'd bring you the flowers first as they're giving my PA a migraine." He's lifting up lots of flowers in plastic invisible, that's what the smell.

"What toys are the toys?" I whisper.

"Look, here's one," says Ma, pulling it out of an envelope. It's a little wooden train. "Don't snatch."

"Sorry." I choo-choo it all along the table down the leg and over the floor up the wall that's blue in this room.

"Intense interest from a number of networks," Morris is saying, "you might consider doing a book, down the road ..."

Ma's mouth isn't friendly. "You think we should sell ourselves before somebody else does."

"I wouldn't put it like that. I'd imagine you've a lot to teach the world. The whole living-on-less thing, it couldn't be more zeitgeisty."

Ma bursts out laughing.

Morris puts his hands up flat. "But it's up to you, obviously. One day at a time."

She's reading some of the letters. " 'Little Jack, you wonderful boy, enjoy every moment because you deserve it because you have been quite literally to Hell and back!' "

"Who said that?" I ask.

She turns the page over. "We don't know her."

"Why she said I was wonderful?"

"She's just heard about you on the TV."

I'm looking in the envelopes that are fattest for more trains.

"Here, these look good," says Ma, holding up a little box of chocolates.

"There's more." I've finded a really big box.

"Nah, that's too many, they'd make us sick."

I'm sick already with my cold so I wouldn't mind.

"We'll give those to someone," says Ma.

"Who?"

"The nurses, maybe."

2 **PA** personal assistant – 6 **to snatch** to grab in an impolite way – 7 **choo-choo** the sound that a child makes to imitate a (steam) train – 21 **literally** really

"Toys and so forth, I can pass on to a kids hospital," says Morris.

"Great idea. Choose some you want to keep," Ma tells me. "How many?"

"As many as you like." She's reading another letter. " 'God bless you and your sweet saint of a son, I pray you discover all the beautiful things this world has to offer all your dreams come true and your path in life is paved with happiness and gold.' " She puts it on the table. "How am I going to find the time to answer all these?"

Morris shakes his head. "That bast—the accused, shall we say, he robbed you of the seven best years of your life already. Personally, I wouldn't waste a second more."

"How do you know they would have been the best years of my life?"

He shrugs. "I just mean—you were nineteen, right?"

There's super cool stuff, a car with wheels that go *zzzzzzhhhhhmmm,* a whistle shaped like a pig, I blow it.

"Wow! That's loud," says Morris.

"Too loud," says Ma.

I do it one more time.

"Jack—"

I put it down. I find a velvety crocodile as long as my leg, a rattle with a bell in it, a clown face when I press the nose it says *ha ha ha ha ha.*

"Not that either, it gives me the creeps," says Ma.

I whisper bye-bye to the clown and put it back in its envelope. There's a square with a sort of pen tied to it that I can draw on but it's hard plastic, not paper, and a box of monkeys with curly arms and tails to make into chains of monkeys. There's a fire truck, and a teddy bear with a cap on that doesn't come off even when I pull hard. On the label a picture of a baby face has a line

6 **saint** a holy person (*Heiliger*) – 8 **path** track or way – 8 **to pave** to cover – 11 **bast** Morris means "bastard" – 11 **accused** a person who is charged with a crime – 23 **velvety** soft, like velvet (*Samt*) – 26 **gives me the creeps** *inf* makes me feel uneasy – 30 **chain** a number of connected things

through it and *0–3,* maybe that means it kills babies in three seconds?

"Oh, come on, Jack," says Ma. "You don't need that many."

"How many do I need?"

"I don't know—"

"If you could sign here, there, and there," Morris tells her.

I'm chewing my finger in under my mask. Ma doesn't tell me not to do that anymore. "How many do I need?"

She looks up from the papers she's writing. "Choose, ah, choose five."

I count, the car and the monkeys and the writing square and the wooden train and the rattle and the crocodile, that's six not five, but Ma and Morris are talking and talking. I find a big empty envelope and I put all the six in.

"OK," says Ma, throwing all the rest of the parcels back into the huge bag.

"Wait," I say, "I can write on the bag, I can put *Presents from Jack for the Sick Kids*."

"Let Morris handle it."

"But—"

Ma puffs her breath. "We've got a lot to do, and we have to let people do some of it for us or my head's going to explode." Why her head's going to explode if I write on the bag? I take out the train again, I put it up my shirt, it's my baby and it pops out and I kiss it all over.

"January, maybe, October's the very earliest it could come to trial," Morris is saying.

There's a trial of tarts, Bill the Lizard has to write with his finger, when Alice knocks over the jury box she puts him back head down by accident, ha ha.

"No but, how long will he be in jail?" asks Ma.

She means him, Old Nick.

27 **trial** the act of hearing and judging a person in a court (*Prozess*) – 28 **tart** a kind of cake, Jack is refering to Alice in Wonderland

"Well, the DA tells me she's hoping for twenty-five to life, and for federal offenses there's no parole," says Morris. "We've got kidnapping for sexual purposes, false imprisonment, multiple counts of rape, criminal battery ..." He's counting on his fingers not in his head.

Ma's nodding. "What about the baby?"

"Jack?"

"The first one. Doesn't that count as some kind of murder?" I never heard this story.

Morris twists his mouth. "Not if it wasn't born alive."

"She."

I don't know who the *she* is.

"*She,* I beg your pardon," he says. "The best we could hope for is criminal negligence, maybe even recklessness ..."

They try to ban Alice from court for being more than a mile high. There's a poem that's confusing,

If I or she should chance to be
Involved in this affair,
He trusts to you to set them free
Exactly as we were.

Noreen's there without me seeing, she asks if we'd like dinner by ourselves or in the dining room.

I carry all my toys in the big envelope. Ma doesn't know there's six not five. Some persons wave when we come in so I wave back, like the girl with the no hair and tattoos all her neck. I don't mind persons very much if they don't touch me.

The woman with the apron says she heard I went outside, I don't know how she heard me. "Did you love it?"

1 **DA** district attorney in the US (*Staatsanwalt*) – 1 **life** *here*: life imprisonment – 2 **federal offense** a crime against federal (*Bundes-*) laws, not state (*Landes-*) laws in the USA – 2 **parole** when a person is temporarily let out of prison before the official period has ended – but has to go back to prison when the parole is over – 4 **battery** violently attacking sb e.g. hitting sb – 14 **negligence** not taking care of sb – 14 **recklessness** carelessness – 15 **to ban sb from sth** to forbid sb from entering a place; Jack is refering to Alice in Wonderland – 17 **to chance** *old* to happen by accident

"No," I say. "I mean, no, thanks."

I'm learning lots more manners. When something tastes yucky we say it's interesting, like wild rice that bites like it hasn't been cooked. When I blow my nose I fold the tissue so nobody sees the snot, it's a secret. If I want Ma to listen to me not some person else I say, "Excuse me," sometimes I say, "Excuse me, Excuse me," for ages, then when she asks what is it I don't remember anymore.

When we're in pajamas with masks off having some on the bed, I remember and ask, "Who's the first baby?"

Ma looks down at me.

"You told Morris there was a she that did a murder."

She shakes her head. "I meant she got murdered, kind of." Her face is away from me.

"Was it me that did it?"

"No! You didn't do anything, it was a year before you were even born," says Ma. "You know I used to say, when you came the first time, on Bed, you were a girl?"

"Yeah."

"Well, that's who I meant."

I'm even more confused.

"I think she was trying to be you. The cord—" Ma puts her face in her hands.

"The blind cord?" I look at it, there's only dark coming in the stripes.

"No, no, remember the cord that goes to the belly button?"

"You cutted it with the scissors and then I was free."

Ma's nodding. "But with the girl baby, it got tangled when she was coming out, so she couldn't breathe."

"I don't like this story."

She presses her eyebrows. "Let me finish it."

"I don't—"

"He was right there, watching." Ma's nearly shouting. "He didn't know the first thing about babies getting born, he hadn't

22 **cord** string connecting an unborn baby to the mother (*(Nabel-)schnur*) – 28 **to get tangled** *here*: to get caught

even bothered to Google it. I could feel the top of her head, it was all slippery, I pushed and pushed, I was shouting, 'Help, I can't, help me—' And he just stood there."

I wait. "Did she stay in your tummy? The girl baby?"

Ma doesn't say anything for a minute. "She came out blue."

Blue?

"She never opened her eyes."

"You should ask Old Nick for medicine for her, for Sundaytreat."

Ma shakes her head. "The cord was all knotted around her neck."

"Was she still tied in you?"

"Till he cut it."

"And then she was free?"

There's tears falling all on the blanket. Ma's nodding and crying but on mute.

"Is it all done now? The story?"

"Nearly." Her eyes are shut but the water still slides out. "He took her away and buried her under a bush in the backyard. Just her body, I mean."

She was blue.

"The *her* part of her, that went straight back up to Heaven."

"She got recycled?"

Ma nearly smiles. "I like to think that's what happened." "Why you like to think that?"

"Maybe it really was you, and a year later you tried again and came back down as a boy."

"I was me for real that time. I didn't go back."

"No way Jose." The tears are falling out again, she rubs them away. "I didn't let him in Room that time."

"Why not?"

"I heard Door, the beeping, and I roared, 'Get out.' " I bet that made him mad.

"I was ready, this time I wanted it to be just me and you."

"What color was I?"

10 **to knot** *verknoten* – 16 **on mute** without a sound – 32 **to roar** to shout

"Hot pink."

"Did I open my eyes?"

"You were born with your eyes open."

I do the most enormous yawn. "Can we go to sleep now?"

"Oh, yeah," says Ma.

* * *

In the night *bang* I fall out on the floor. My nose runs a lot but I don't know to blow it in the dark.

"This bed's too small for two," says Ma in the morning. "You'd be more comfortable in the other one."

"No."

"What if we took the mattress and put it right here beside my bed so we could hold hands even?"

I shake my head.

"Help me figure this out, Jack."

"Let's stay both in the one but keep our elbows in."

Ma blows her nose loud, I think the cold jumped from me to her but I still have it too.

We have a deal that I go in the shower with her but I keep my head out. The Band-Aid on my finger's fallen off and I can't find it. Ma brushes my hair, the tangles hurt. We have a hairbrush and two toothbrushes and all our new clothes and the little wooden train and other toys, Ma still hasn't counted, so she doesn't know I took six not five. I don't know where the stuff should go, some on the dresser, some on the table beside the bed, some in the wardrobe, I have to keep asking Ma where she put them.

She's reading one of her books with no pictures but I bring her the picture ones instead. *The Very Hungry Caterpillar* is a terrible waster, he just eats holes through strawberries and salamis and everything and leaves the rest. I can put my actual finger through the holes, I thought somebody teared the book

15 **to figure out** to find a solution – 31 **actual** Jack means "real" – 32 **to tear, tore, torn** to open by force

but Ma says it was made that way on purpose to be extra fun. I like *Go, Dog, Go* more, especially when they fight with tennis rackets.

Noreen knocks with somethings very exciting, the first are softy stretchy shoes like socks but made of leather, the second is a watch with just numbers so I can read it like Watch. I say, "The time is nine fifty-seven." It's too small for Ma, it's just mine, Noreen shows me how to tight the strap on my wrist.

"Presents every day, he'll be getting spoiled," says Ma, putting her mask up to blow her nose again.

"Dr. Clay said, whatever gives the lad a bit of a sense of control," says Noreen. When she smiles her eyes crinkle. "Probably a bit homesick, aren't you?"

"Homesick?" Ma's staring at her.

"Sorry, I didn't—"

"It wasn't a *home,* it was a soundproofed cell."

"That came out wrong, I beg your pardon," says Noreen.

She goes in a hurry. Ma doesn't say anything, she just writes in her notebook.

If Room wasn't our home, does that mean we don't have one?

This morning I give Dr. Clay a high five, he's thrilled.

"It seems a bit ridiculous to keep wearing these masks when we've already got a streaming cold," says Ma.

"Well," he says, "there are worse things out there."

"Yeah, but we have to keep pulling the masks up to blow our noses anyway—"

He shrugs. "Ultimately it's your call."

"Masks off, Jack," Ma tells me.

"Yippee."

We put them in the trash.

Dr. Clay's crayons live in a special box of cardboard that says 120 on it, that's how many all different. They've got amazing

8 **to tight** Jack means "to tighten, to fasten" – 9 **to spoil** to give a child too many presents or sweets – 12 **to crinkle** to get many lines – 21 **a high five** to greet or say goodbye to sb by clapping your hand against the other person's hand above your heads – 27 **call** request *here*: decision

names written small up the sides like Atomic Tangerine and Fuzzy Wuzzy and Inchworm and Outer Space that I never knew had a color, and Purple Mountain's Majesty and Razzmatazz and Unmellow Yellow and Wild Blue Yonder. Some are spelled wrong on purpose for a joke, like Mauvelous, that's not very funny I don't think. Dr. Clay says I can use any but I just choose the five I know to color like the ones in Room, a blue and a green and an orange and a red and a brown. He asks can I draw Room maybe but I'm already doing a rocket ship with brown. There's even a white crayon, wouldn't that be invisible?

"What if the paper was black," says Dr. Clay, "or red?" He finds me a black page to try and he's right, I can see the white on it. "What's this square all around the rocket?"

"Walls," I tell him. There's the girl me baby waving bye-bye and Baby Jesus and John the Baptist, they don't have any clothes because it's sunny with God's yellow face.

"Is your ma in this picture?"

"She's down at the bottom having a nap."

The real Ma laughs a bit and blows her nose. That remembers me to do mine because it's dripping.

"What about the man you call Old Nick, is he anywhere?"

"OK, he can be over in this corner in his cage." I do him and the bars very thick, he's biting them. There are ten bars, that's the strongest number, not even an angel could burn them open with his blowtorch and Ma says an angel wouldn't turn on his blowtorch for a bad guy anyway. I show Dr. Clay how many counting I can do up to 1,000,029 and even higher if I wanted.

"A little boy I know, he counts the same things over and over when he feels nervous, he can't stop."

"What things?" I ask.

"Lines on the sidewalk, buttons, that kind of thing."

I think that boy should count his teeth instead, because they're always there, unless they fall out.

19 **to remember** Jack means "to remind"

"You keep talking about separation anxiety," Ma's saying to Dr. Clay, "but me and Jack are not going to be separated."

"Still, it's not just the two of you anymore, is it?"

She's chewing her mouth. They talk about *social reintegration* and *self-blame*.

"The very best thing you did was, you got him out early," says Dr. Clay. "At five, they're still plastic."

But I'm not plastic, I'm a real boy.

"... probably young enough to forget," he's saying, "which will be a mercy."

That's *thanks* in Spanish I think.

I want to keep playing with the boy puppet with the tongue but time's up, Dr. Clay has to go play with Mrs. Garber. He says I can borrow the puppet till tomorrow but he still belongs to Dr. Clay.

"Why?"

"Well, everything in the world belongs to somebody."

Like my six new toys and my five new books, and Tooth is mine I think because Ma didn't want him anymore.

"Except the things we all share," says Dr. Clay, "like the rivers and the mountains."

"The street?"

"That's right, we all get to use the streets."

"I ran on the street."

"When you were escaping, right."

"Because we didn't belong to him."

"That's right." Dr. Clay's smiling. "You know who you belong to, Jack?"

"Yeah."

"Yourself."

He's wrong, actually, I belong to Ma.

The Clinic keeps having more bits in it, like there's a room with a ginormous TV and I jump up and down hoping *Dora* might be on or *SpongeBob*, I haven't met them in ages, but it's

1 **separation anxiety** fear of being separated – 5 **self-blame** to accuse oneself of sth bad – 10 **mercy** *Gnade*

only golf, three old people I don't know the names are watching.

In the corridor I remember, I ask, "What's the *mercy* for?"

"Huh?"

"Dr. Clay said I was made of plastic and I'd forget."

"Ah," says Ma. "He figures, soon you won't remember Room anymore."

"I will too." I stare at her. "Am I meant to forget?"

"I don't know."

She's always saying that now. She's gone ahead of me already, she's at the stairs, I have to run to catch up.

After lunch. Ma says it's time to try going Outside again. "If we stay indoors all the time, it's like we never did our Great Escape at all." She's sounding cranky, she's tying her laces already.

After my hat and shades and shoes and the sticky stuff again, I'm tired.

Noreen is waiting for us beside the fish tank.

Ma lets me revolve in the door five times. She pushes and we're out.

It's so bright, I think I'm going to scream. Then my shades get darker and I can't see. The air smells weird in my sore nose and my neck's all tight. "Pretend you're watching this on TV," says Noreen in my ear.

"Huh?"

"Just try it." She does a special voice: " 'Here's a boy called Jack going for a walk with his Ma and their friend Noreen.' "

I'm watching it.

"What's Jack wearing on his face?" she asks.

"Cool red shades."

"So he is. Look, they're all walking across the parking lot on a mild April day."

There's four cars, a red and a green and a black and a brownish goldy. Burnt Sienna, that's the crayon of it. Inside their windows

14 **to tie laces** i.e. of her shoes (laces = *Schnürsenkel*) – 31 **parking lot** parking area – 34 **Burnt Sienna** the name of a brown crayon

they're like little houses with seats. A teddy bear is hanging up in the red one on the mirror. I'm stroking the nose bit of the car, it's all smooth and cold like an ice cube. "Careful," says Ma, "you might set off the alarm."

I didn't know, I put my hands back under my elbows.

"Let's go onto the grass." She pulls me a little bit.

I'm squishing the green spikes under my shoes. I bend down and rub, it doesn't cut my fingers. My one Raja tried to eat is nearly grown shut. I watch the grass again, there's a twig and a leaf that's brown and a something, it's yellow.

A hum, so I look up, the sky's so big it nearly knocks me down. "Ma. Another airplane!"

"Contrail," she says, pointing. "I just remembered, that's what the streak is called."

I walk on a flower by accident, there's hundreds, not a bunch like the crazies send us in the mail, they're growing right in the ground like hair on my head. "Daffodils," says Ma, pointing, "magnolias, tulips, lilacs. Are those apple blossoms?" She smells everything, she puts my nose on a flower but it's too sweet, it makes me dizzy. She chooses a lilac and gives it to me.

Up close the trees are giant giants, they've got like skin but knobblier when we stroke them. I find a triangularish thing the big of my nose that Noreen says is a rock.

"It's millions of years old," says Ma.

How does she know? I look at the under, there's no label. "Hey, look." Ma's kneeling down.

It's a something crawling. An ant. "Don't!" I shout, I'm putting my hands around it like armor.

"What's the matter?" asks Noreen.

"Please, please, please," I say to Ma, "not this one."

"It's OK," she says, "of course I won't squish it."

"Promise."

7 **to squish** to walk while making a squelching sound in the mud – 9 **twig** *Zweig* – 13 **contrail** the line of white steam in the sky by planes flying – 17 **daffodil** a yellow flower that blooms in the spring – 22 **knobbly** *knotig* – 22 **triangularish** *inf* shaped like a triangle (but isn't a perfect triangle with three corners etc.) – 28 **armor** *AE* here: protection

"I promise."

When I take my hands away the ant is gone and I cry.

But then Noreen finds another one and another, there's two carrying a bit of something between them that's ten times their big.

A thing else comes spinning out of the sky and lands in front of me, I jump back.

"Hey, a maple key," says Ma.

"Why?"

"It's the seed of this maple tree in a little—a sort of pair of wings to help it go far."

It's so thin I can see through its little dry lines, it's thicker brown in the middle. There's a tiny hole. Ma throws it up in the air, it comes spinning down again.

I show her another one that's something wrong with. "It's just a single, it lost its other wing."

When I throw it high it still flies OK, I put it in my pocket.

But the coolest thing is, there's a huge whirry noise, when I look up it's a helicopter, much bigger than the plane—

"Let's get you inside," says Noreen.

Ma grabs me by the hand and yanks.

"Wait—," I say but I lose all my breath, they pull me along in between them, my nose is running.

When we jump back through the revolving door I'm blurry in my head. That helicopter was full of paparazzi trying to steal pictures of me and Ma.

* * *

After our nap my cold's still not fixed yet. I'm playing with my treasures, my rock and my injured maple key and my lilac that's gone floppy. Grandma knocks with more visitors, but she waits outside so it won't be too much of a crowd. The persons are two,

5 **big** Jack means "size" – 8 **maple** *Ahorn* – 18 **whirry** the blades of a helicopter make a whirring sound – 21 **to yank** *inf* to pull suddenly – 24 **blurry** *opp of* clear

they're called my Uncle that's Paul that has floppy hair just to his ears and Deana that's my Aunt with rectangular glasses and a million black braids like snakes. "We've got a little girl called Bronwyn who's going to be so psyched to meet you," she tells me. "She didn't even know she had a cousin—well, none of us knew about you till two days ago, when your grandma called with the news."

"We would have jumped in the car except the doctors said—" Paul stops talking, he puts his fist at his eyes.

"It's OK, hon," says Deana and she rubs his leg.

He clears his throat very noisy. "Just, it keeps hitting me." I don't see anything hitting him.

Ma puts her arm around his shoulder. "All those years, he thought his little sister might be dead," she tells me.

"Bronwyn?" I say it on mute but she hears.

"No, me, remember? Paul's my brother."

"Yeah I know."

"I couldn't tell what to—" His voice stops again, he blows his nose. It's way more louder than I do it, like elephants.

"But where is Bronwyn?" asks Ma.

"Well," says Deana, "we thought ..." She looks at Paul.

He says, "You and Jack can meet her another day soon. She goes to Li'l Leapfrogs."

"What's that?" I ask.

"A building where parents send kids when they're busy doing other stuff," says Ma.

"Why the kids are busy—?"

"No, when the parents are busy."

"Actually Bronwyn's wild about it," says Deana.

"She's learning Sign and hip-hop," says Paul.

He wants to take some photos to e-mail to Grandpa in Australia who's going to get on the plane tomorrow. "Don't worry, he'll be fine once he meets him," Paul says to Ma, I don't

3 **braids** *Zöpfe* – 4 **to be psyched** *inf* here: excited – 11 **to clear one's throat** *räuspern*

know who all the *hims* are. Also I don't know to go in photos but Ma says we just look at the camera as if it's a friend and smile.

Paul shows me on the little screen after, he asks which do I think is best, the first or second or third, but they're the same.

My ears are tired from all the talking.

When they're gone I thought we were just us two again but Grandma comes in and gives Ma a long hug and blows me another kiss from just a bit away so I can feel the blowing. "How's my favorite grandson?"

"That's you," Ma tells me. "What do you say when someone asks you how you are?"

Manners again. "Thank you."

They both laugh, I did another joke by accident. " 'Very well,' then 'thank you,' " says Grandma.

"Very well, then thank you."

"Unless you're not, of course, then it's OK to say, 'I'm not feeling a hundred percent today.' " She turns back to Ma. "Oh, by the way, Sharon, Michael Keelor, Joyce whatshername—they've all been calling."

Ma nods.

"They're dying to welcome you back."

"I'm—the doctors say I'm not quite up for visits yet," says Ma. "Right, of course."

The Leo man is in the door.

"Could he come in just for a minute?" Grandma asks. "I don't care," says Ma.

He's my Stepgrandpa so Grandma says I could maybe call him Steppa, I didn't know she knowed word salads. He smells funny like smoke, his teeth are crookedy and his eyebrows go all ways.

"How come all his hair is on his face not his head?"

He laughs even though I was whispering to Ma. "Search me," he says.

29 **crookedy** Jack means "crooked, uneven"

"We met on an Indian Head Massage weekend," says Grandma, "and I picked him as the smoothest surface to work on." They laugh both, not Ma.

"Can I have some?" I ask.

"In a minute," says Ma, "when they're gone."

Grandma asks, "What does he want?"

"It's OK."

"I can call the nurse."

Ma shakes her head. "He means breastfeeding."

Grandma stares at her. "You don't mean to say you're still—"

"There was no reason to stop."

"Well, cooped up in that place, I guess everything was—but even so, five years—"

"You don't know the first thing about it."

Grandma's mouth is all squeezed down. "It's not for want of asking."

"Mom—"

Steppa stands up. "We should let these folks rest."

"I guess so," says Grandma. "Bye-bye, then, till tomorrow ..."

Ma reads me again *The Giving Tree* and *The Lorax* but quietly because she's got a sore throat and a headache as well. I have some, I have lots instead of dinner, Ma falls asleep in the middle. I like looking at her face when she doesn't even know it.

I find a newspaper folded up, the visitors must have brung it. On the front there's a picture of a bridge that's broken in half, I wonder if it's true. On the next page there's the one of me and Ma and the police the time she was carrying me into the Precinct. It says *HOPE FOR BONSAI BOY*. It takes me a while to figure out all the words.

He is "Miracle Jack" to the staff at the exclusive Cumberland Clinic who have already lost their hearts to the pint-sized hero

12 **to coop up** shut into a small place – 18 **folks** *AE* people – 21 **a sore throat** an infection of the throat – 32 **pint-sized** *derog* very small

who awakened Saturday night to a brave new world. The haunting, long-haired Little Prince is the product of his beautiful young mother's serial abuse at the hands of the Garden-shed Ogre (captured by state troopers in a dramatic standoff Sunday at two a.m.). Jack says everything is "nice" and adores Easter eggs but still goes up and down stairs on all fours like a monkey. He was sealed up for all his five years in a rotting cork-lined dungeon, and experts cannot yet say what kind or degree of long-term developmental retardation—

Ma's up, she's taking the paper out of my hand. "What about your *Peter Rabbit* book?"

"But that's me, the Bonsai Boy."

"The bouncy what?" She looks at the paper again and pushes her hair out of her face, she sort of groans.

"What's *bonsai?*"

"A very tiny tree. People keep them in pots indoors and cut them every day so they stay all curled up."

I'm thinking about Plant. We never cutted her, we let her grow all she liked but she died instead. "I'm not a tree, I'm a boy."

"It's just a figure of speech." She squeezes the paper into the trash.

"It says I'm haunting but that's what ghosts do."

"The paper people get a lot of things wrong."

Paper people, that sounds like the ones in *Alice* that are really a pack of cards. "They say you're beautiful."

Ma laughs.

Actually she is. I've seen so many person faces for real now and hers is the most beautifulest.

I have to blow my nose again, the skin's getting red and hurting. Ma takes her killers but they don't zap the headache. I didn't think she'd still be hurting in Outside. I stroke her hair in

1 **brave new world** reference to the novel Brave New World by Aldous Huxley: Jack experiences a completely new world – 2 **haunting** [ˈhɑːn̬tɪŋ] strange – 3 **serial** repeated – 7 **to seal up** *here*: to lock in – 9 **retardation** delay, lateness, i.e. developing slower than other children – 20 **figure of speech** *Redewendung* – 25 **pack of cards** the 52 cards that are used to play card games – 30 **to zap** *inf* here: to stop

the dark. It's not all black in Room Number Seven, God's silver face is in the window and Ma's right, it's not a circle at all, it's pointy at both ends.

* * *

In the night there's vampire germs floating around with masks on so we can't see their faces and an empty coffin that turns into a huge toilet and flushes the whole world away.

"Shh, shh, it's only a dream." That's Ma.

Then Ajeet is all crazy putting Raja's poo in a parcel to mail to us because I kept six toys, somebody's breaking my bones and sticking pins in them.

I wake up crying and Ma lets me have lots, it's the right but it's pretty creamy.

"I kept six toys, not five," I tell her.

"What?"

"The ones the crazy fans sent, I kept six."

"It doesn't matter," she says.

"It does, I kept the sixth, I didn't send it to the sick kids." "They were for you, they were your presents."

"Then why could I only have five?"

"You can have as many as you like. Go back to sleep." I can't. "Somebody shut my nose."

"That's just the snot getting thicker, it means you'll be all better soon."

"But I can't be better if I can't breathe."

"That's why God gave you a mouth to breathe through. Plan B," says Ma.

* * *

6 **coffin** ['kɑːfɪn] a box in which a dead person is buried

When it starts getting light, we count our friends in the world, Noreen and Dr. Clay and Dr. Kendrick and Pilar and the apron woman I don't know the name and Ajeet and Naisha.

"Who are they?"

"The man and the baby and the dog that called the police," I tell her.

"Oh, yeah."

"Only I think Raja's an enemy because he bited my finger. Oh, and Officer Oh and the man police that I don't know his name and the captain. That's ten and one enemy."

"Grandma and Paul and Deana," says Ma.

"Bronwyn my cousin only I haven't seen her yet. Leo that's Steppa."

"He's nearly seventy and stinks of dope," says Ma. "She must have been on the rebound."

"What's the rebound?"

Instead of answering she asks, "What number are we at?" "Fifteen and one enemy."

"The dog was scared, you know, that was a good reason."

Bugs bite for no reason. Night-night, sleep tight, don't let the bugs bite, Ma doesn't remember to say that anymore. "OK," I say, "sixteen. Plus Mrs. Garber and the girl with tattoos and Hugo, only we don't talk to them hardly, does that count?"

"Oh, sure."

"That's nineteen then." I have to go get another tissue, they're softer than toilet paper but sometimes they rip when they're wetted. Then I'm up already so we have a getting dressed race, I win except for forgetting my shoes.

I can go down the stairs really fast on my butt now *bump bump bump* so my teeth clack. I don't think I'm like a monkey like the paper people said, but I don't know, the ones on the wildlife planet don't have stairs.

For breakfast I have four French toasts. "Am I growing?" Ma looks up and down me. "Every minute."

14 **dope** *sl* cannabis, marijuana – 15 **to be on the rebound** *inf* to start a relationship with sb very soon after the last one has ended in disappointment

When we go see Dr. Clay Ma makes me tell about my dreams. He thinks my brain is probably doing a spring cleaning.

I stare at him.

"Now you're safe, it's gathering up all those scary thoughts you don't need anymore, and throwing them out as bad dreams." His hands do the throwing.

I don't say because of manners, but actually he's got it backwards. In Room I was safe and Outside is the scary.

Dr. Clay is talking to Ma now about how she wants to slap Grandma.

"That's not allowed," I say.

She blinks at me. "I don't want to really. Just sometimes."

"Did you ever want to slap her before you were kidnapped?" asks Dr. Clay.

"Oh, sure." Ma looks at him, then laughs sort of groaning. "Great, I've got my life back."

We find another room with two things I know what they are, they're computers. Ma says, "Excellent, I'm going to e-mail a couple of friends."

"Who of the nineteen?"

"Ah, old friends of mine, actually, you don't know them yet." She sits and goes tap tap on the letters bit for a while, I watch. She's frowning at the screen. "Can't remember my password."
"What's—?"

"I'm such a—" She covers her mouth. She does a scratchy breath through her nose. "Never mind. Hey, Jack, let's find something fun for you, will we?"

"Where?"

She moves the mouse a bit and suddenly there's a picture of Dora. I go close to watch, she shows me bits to click with the little arrow so I can do the game myself. I put all the pieces of the magic saucer back together and Dora and Boots clap and sing a thank-you song. It's better than TV even.

9 **to slap** to hit – 23 **to frown** [fraʊn] *die Stirn runzeln* – 32 **saucer** ['sɑːsɚ] a small plate for putting a cup on

Ma's with the other computer looking up a book of faces she says is a new invention, she types in the names and it shows them smiling. "Are they really, really old?" I ask.

"Mostly twenty-six, like me."

"But you said they're old friends."

"That just means I knew them a long time ago. They look so different ..." She puts her eyes nearer the pictures, she mutters things like "South Korea" or "Divorced already, no way—"

There's another new website she finds with videos of songs and things, she shows me two cats dancing in ballet shoes that's funny. Then she goes to other sites with only words like *confinement* and *trafficking,* she says can I let her read for a while, so I try my Dora game again and this time I win a Switchy Star.

There's a somebody standing in the door, I jump. It's Hugo, he's not smiling. "I Skype at two."

"Huh?" says Ma.

"I Skype at two."

"Sorry, I have no idea what—"

"I Skype my mother every day at two p.m., she'll have been expecting me two minutes ago, it's written down in the schedule right here on the door."

Back in our room on the bed there's a little machine with a note from Paul, Ma says it's like the one she was listening to when Old Nick stole her, only this one's got pictures you can move with your fingers and not just a thousand songs but millions. She's put the bud things in her ears, she's nodding to a music I don't hear and singing in a little voice about being a million different people from one day to the next.

"Let me."

"It's called 'Bitter Sweet Symphony,' when I was thirteen I listened to it all the time." She puts one bud in my ear.

7 **to mutter** to speak in a low voice, unclearly – 12 **confinement** [kənˈfaɪnmənt] being kept in a small place – 12 **trafficking** illegally buying and selling goods, e.g. drugs – 21 **schedule** [ˈskedʒuːl] plan, time-table – 27 **bud** *here*: *Ohrstöpsel* – 31 **'Bitter Sweet Symphony'** Pop song by British band *The Verve* – from the album *Urban Hymns* (1997)

"Too loud." I yank it out.

"Be gentle with it, Jack, it's my present from Paul."

I didn't know it was hers-not-mine. In Room everything was ours.

"Hang on, here's the Beatles, there's an oldie you might like from about fifty years ago," she says, " 'All You Need Is Love.' "

I'm confused. "Don't persons need food and stuff?"

"Yeah, but all that's no good if you don't have somebody to love as well," says Ma, she's too loud, she's still flicking through the names with her finger. "Like, there's this experiment with baby monkeys, a scientist took them away from their mothers and kept each one all alone in a cage—and you know what, they didn't grow up right."

"Why they didn't grow?"

"No, they got bigger but they were weird, from not getting cuddles."

"What kind of weird?"

She clicks her machine off. "Actually, sorry, Jack, I don't know why I brought it up."

"What kind of weird?"

Ma chews her lip. "Sick in their heads."

"Like the crazies?"

She nods. "Biting themselves and stuff."

Hugo cuts his arms but I don't think he bites himself. "Why?" Ma puffs her breath. "See, if their mothers were there, they'd have cuddled the baby monkeys, but because the milk just came from pipes, they—It turns out they needed the love as much as the milk." "This is a bad story."

"Sorry. I'm really sorry. I shouldn't have told you."

"No, you should," I say.

"But—"

"I don't want there to be bad stories and me not know them." Ma holds me tight. "Jack," she says, "I'm a bit strange this week, aren't I?"

9 **to flick through** to look at sth quickly – 16 **cuddle** embrace; holding sb in your arms

I don't know, because everything's strange.

"I keep messing up. I know you need me to be your ma but I'm having to remember how to be me as well at the same time and it's ..."

But I thought the her and the Ma were the same. I want to go Outside again but Ma's too tired.

* * *

"What day is this morning?"

"Thursday," says Ma.

"When is Sunday?"

"Friday, Saturday, Sunday ..."

"Three away, like in Room?"

"Yeah, a week's seven days everywhere."

"What'll we ask for Sundaytreat?"

Ma shakes her head.

In the afternoon we're going in the van that says *The Cumberland Clinic,* we're driving actually outside the big gates to the rest of the world. I don't want to, but we have to go show the dentist Ma's teeth that still hurt. "Will there be persons there not friends of ours?"

"Just the dentist and an assistant," says Ma. "They've sent everybody else away, it's a special visit just for us."

We have our hats and our cool shades on, but not the sunblock because the bad rays bounce off glass. I get to keep my stretchy shoes on. In the van there's a driver with a cap, I think he's on mute. There's a special booster seat on the seat that makes me higher so the belt won't squish my throat if we brake suddenly. I don't like the tight of the belt. I watch out the window and blow my nose, it's greener today. Lots and lots of hes and shes on the sidewalks, I never saw so many, I wonder are they all real for real or just some. "Some of the women grow long hair like us," I tell Ma, "but the men don't."

24 **to bounce off** to jump back

"Oh, a few do, rock stars. It's not a rule, just a convention."

"What's a—?"

"A silly habit everybody has. Would you like a haircut?" asks Ma.

"No."

"It doesn't hurt. I had short hair before—back when I was nineteen."

I shake my head. "I don't want to lose my strong."

"Your what?"

"My muscles, like Samson in the story."

That makes her laugh.

"Look, Ma, a man putting himself on fire!"

"Just lighting his cigarette," she says. "I used to smoke." I stare at her. "Why?"

"I can't remember."

"Look, look."

"Don't shout."

I'm pointing where there's all littles walking along the street. "Kids tied together."

"They're not tied, I don't think." Ma puts her face more against the window. "Nah, they're just holding on to the string so they don't get lost. And see, the really small ones are in those wagons, six in each. They must be a day care, like the one Bronwyn goes to."

"I want to see Bronwyn. May you go us please to the kid place, where the kids and Bronwyn my cousin are," I say to the driver.

He doesn't hear me.

"The dentist is expecting us right now," says Ma.

The kids are gone, I stare out all the windows.

The dentist is Dr. Lopez, when she pulls up her mask for a second her lipstick is purple. She's going to look at me first because I have teeth too. I lie down in a big chair that moves. I stare up with my mouth wide wide open and she asks me to

1 **convention** sth that is generally accepted – 21 **string** cord – 23 **day care** kindergarden

count what I see on her ceiling. There's three cats and one dog and two parrots and—

I spit out the metal thing.

"It's just a little mirror, Jack, see? I'm counting your teeth."

"Twenty," I tell her.

"That's right." Dr. Lopez grins. "I've never met a five-year-old who could count his own teeth before." She puts the mirror in again. "Hmm, wide spacing, that's what I like to see."

"Why you like to see that?"

"It means ... plenty of room for maneuvering."

Ma's going to be a long time in the chair while the drill gets the yuck out of her teeth. I don't want to wait in the waiting room but Yang the assistant says, "Come check out our cool toys." He shows me a shark on a stick that goes *clattery clattery* and there's a stool to sit on that's shaped like a tooth too, not a human tooth but a giant one all white with no rot. I look at a book about Transformers and another one with no jacket about mutant turtles that say no to drugs. Then I hear a funny noise.

Yang blocks the door. "I think maybe your Mom would prefer—"

I duck in under his arm and there's Dr. Lopez doing a machine in Ma's mouth that screeches. "Leave her alone!"

"Is OK," Ma says but like her mouth is broken, what the dentist did to her?

"If he'd feel safer here, that's fine," says Dr. Lopez.

Yang brings the tooth stool in the corner and I watch, it's awful but it's better than not watching. One time Ma twitches in the chair and makes a moan and I stand up, but Dr. Lopez says, "A little more numbing?" and does a needle and Ma stays quiet again. It goes on for hundreds of hours. I need to blow my nose but the skin's coming off so I just press the tissue on my face.

8 **wide spacing** *here:* space between the teeth – 11 **drill** a tool which is used to make holes – 12 **yuck** *inf* here: the rotten substance – 18 **mutant** produced by a mutation – 18 **turtle** *Schildkröte* – 22 **to screech** to make a sharp sound

When Ma and me go back in the parking lot the light's all banging my head. The driver's there again reading a paper, he gets out and opens the doors for us. "Hank oo," says Ma. I wonder if she'll always talk wrong now. I'd rather sore teeth than talk like that.

All the way back to the Clinic I watch the street whizzing by, I sing the song about the ribbon of highway and the endless skyway.

* * *

Tooth's still under our pillow, I give him a kiss. I should have brung him and maybe Dr. Lopez could have fixed him too.

We have our dinner on a tray, it's called beef Stroganoff with bits that's meat and bits that look like meat but they're mushrooms, all lying on fluffy rice. Ma can't have the meats yet, just little slurps of the rice, but she's nearly talking properly again. Noreen knocks to say she has a surprise for us, Ma's Dad from Australia.

Ma's crying, she jumps up.

I ask, "Can I take my Stroganoff?"

"Why don't I bring Jack down in a few minutes, when he's finished?" asks Noreen.

Ma doesn't even say anything, she just runs off.

"He had a funeral for us," I tell Noreen, "but we weren't in the coffin."

"Glad to hear it."

I chase the little rices.

"This must be the most tiring week of your life," she says, sitting down beside me.

I blink at her. "Why?"

"Well, everything's strange, because you're like a visitor from another planet, aren't you?"

2 **to bang** *here:* to hit – 14 **mushrooms** *Pilze* – 14 **fluffy** soft, light – 15 **slurp** *inf* here *(Jack's language)*: pieces

I shake my head. "We're not visitors, Ma says we have to stay forever till we're dead."

"Ah, I suppose I mean ... a new arrival."

When I'm all done, Noreen finds the room where Ma's sitting holding hands with a person that has a cap on. He jumps up and says to Ma, "I told your mother I didn't want—"

Ma butts in. "Dad, this is Jack."

He shakes his head.

But I am Jack, was he expecting a different one?

He's looking at the table, he's all sweaty on his face. "No offense."

"What do you mean, 'no offense'?" Ma's talking nearly in a shout.

"I can't be in the same room. It makes me shudder."

"There's no *it*. He's a boy. He's five years old," she roars.

"I'm saying it wrong, I'm—it's the jet lag. I'll call you later from the hotel, OK?" The man who's Grandpa is gone past me without looking, he's nearly at the door.

There's a crash, Ma's banged the table with her hand. "It's not OK."

"OK, OK."

"Sit down, Dad."

He doesn't move.

"He's the world to me," she says.

Her Dad? No, I think the *he* is me.

"Of course, it's only natural." The Grandpa man wipes the skin under his eyes. "But all I can think of is that beast and what he—" "Oh, so you'd rather think of me dead and buried?"

He shakes his head again.

"Then live with it," says Ma. "I'm back—"

"It's a miracle," he says.

"I'm back, with Jack. That's two miracles."

10 **"No offense."** "I don't mean to hurt your feelings!" – 14 **to shudder** to tremble from fear, cold or strong dislike – 27 **beast** wild animal, *here*: an awful person – 28 **dead and buried** dead and under the ground

He puts his hand on the door handle. "Right now, I just can't—"

"Last chance," says Ma. "Take a seat."

Nobody does anything.

Then the grandpa comes back to the table and sits down. Ma points to the chair beside him so I go on it even though I don't want to be here. I'm looking at my shoes, they're all crinkly at the edges.

Grandpa takes off his cap, he looks at me. "Pleased to meet you, Jack."

I don't know which manners so I say, "You're welcome." Later on Ma and me are in Bed, I'm having some in the dark.

I ask, "Why he didn't want to see me? Was it another mistake, like the coffin?"

"Kind of." Ma puffs her breath. "He thinks—he thought I'd be better off without you."

"Somewhere else?"

"No, if you'd never been born. Imagine."

I try but I can't. "Then would you still be Ma?"

"Well, no, I wouldn't. So it's a really dumb idea."

"Is he the real Grandpa?"

"I'm afraid so."

"Why you're afraid—"

"I mean, yeah, he's it."

"Your Dad from when you were a little girl in the hammock?"
"Ever since I was a baby, six weeks old," she says. "That's when they brought me home from the hospital."

"Why she left you there, the tummy mommy? Was that a mistake?"

"I think she was tired," says Ma. "She was young." She sits up to blow her nose very noisy. "Dad will get his act together in a while," she says.

"What's his act?"

She sort of laughs. "I mean he'll behave better. More like a real grandpa."

31 **to get one's act together** *inf* to act normally, come back to one's senses

Like Steppa, only he's not a real one.

I go asleep really easy, but I wake up crying.

"It's OK, it's OK." That's Ma, kissing my head.

"Why they don't cuddle the monkeys?"

"Who?"

"The scientists, why don't they cuddle the baby monkeys?" "Oh." After a second she says, "Maybe they do. Maybe the baby monkeys learn to like the human cuddles."

"No, but you said they're weird and biting themselves." Ma doesn't say anything.

"Why don't the scientists bring the mother monkeys back and say sorry?"

"I don't know why I told you that old story, it all happened ages ago, before I was born."

I'm coughing and there's nothing to blow my nose on.

"Don't think about the baby monkeys anymore, OK? They're OK now."

"I don't think they're OK."

Ma holds me so tight my neck hurts.

"Ow."

She moves. "Jack, there's a lot of things in the world." "Zillions?"

"Zillions and zillions. If you try to fit them all in your head, it'll just burst."

"But the baby monkeys?"

I can hear her breathing funny. "Yeah, some of the things are bad things."

"Like the monkeys."

"And worse than that," says Ma.

"What worse?" I try to think of a thing worse.

"Not tonight."

"Maybe when I'm six?"

"Maybe."

She spoons me.

34 **to spoon** *inf* Jack means "to lie closely together like two spoons"

I listen to her breaths, I count them to ten, then ten of mine. "Ma?" "Yeah."

"Do you think about the worse things?"

"Sometimes," she says. "Sometimes I have to."

"Me too."

"But then I put them out of my head and I go to sleep."

I count our breaths again. I try biting myself, my shoulder, it hurts. Instead of thinking about the monkeys I think about all the kids in the world, how they're not TV they're real, they eat and sleep and pee and poo like me. If I had something sharp and pricked them they'd bleed, if I tickled them they'd laugh. I'd like to see them but it makes me dizzy that there's so many and I'm only one.

* * *

"So, you've got it?" asks Ma.

I'm lying in our bed in Room Number Seven but she's only sitting on the edge. "Me here having my nap, you in TV."

"Actually, the real me will be downstairs in Dr. Clay's office talking to the TV people," she says. "Just the picture of me will be in the video camera, then later tonight it'll be on TV."

"Why you want to talk to the vultures?"

"Believe me, I don't," she says. "I just need to answer their questions once and for all, so they'll stop asking. Back before you know it, OK? By the time you wake up, almost definitely."

"OK."

"And then tomorrow we're going on an adventure, do you remember where Paul and Deana and Bronwyn are going to take us?" "Natural History Museum to see the dinosaurs."

"That's right." She stands up.

"One song."

Ma sits down and does "Swing Low, Sweet Chariot" but it's too fast and she's still hoarse from our cold. She pulls my wrist to look at my watch with the numbers.

"Another one."

"They'll be waiting …"

"I want to come too." I sit up and wrap around Ma.

"No, I don't want them to see you," she says, putting me back down on the pillow. "Go to sleep now."

"I'm not sleepy on my own."

"You'll be exhausted if you don't have a nap. Let go of me, please." Ma's taking my hands off her. I knot them around her tighter so she can't. "Jack!"

"Stay."

I put my legs around her too.

"Get off me. I'm late already." Her hands are pressing my shoulders but I hold on even more. "You're not a baby. I said get off—"

Ma's shoving so hard, I suddenly come loose, her shove hits my head on little table *craaaaaack.*

She has her hand on her mouth.

I'm screaming.

"Oh," she says, "oh, Jack, oh, Jack, I'm so—"

"How's it going?" Dr. Clay's head, in the door. "The crew are all set up and ready for you."

I cry louder than I ever, I hold my broken head.

"I don't think this is going to work," says Ma, she's stroking my wetted face.

"You can still pull out," says Dr. Clay, coming near.

"No I can't, it's for Jack's college fund."

He twists his mouth. "We talked about whether that's a good enough reason—"

"I don't want to go to college," I say, "I want to go in TV with you."

Ma puffs a long breath. "Change of plan. You can come down just to watch if you stay absolutely quiet, OK?"

"OK."

"Not a word."

15 **to shove** to push roughly – 26 **college fund** a sum of money set aside for a college education

Dr. Clay's saying to Ma, "Do you really think that's a good idea?" But I'm getting my stretchy shoes on quick quick, my head's still wobbly.

His office is all changed around full of persons and lights and machines. Ma puts me on a chair in the corner, she kisses me the bashed bit of my head and whispers something I can't hear. She goes to a bigger chair and a man person clips a little black bug on her jacket. A woman comes over with a box of colors and starts painting Ma's face.

I recognize Morris our lawyer, he's reading pages. "We need to see the cutdown as well as the rough cut," he's telling someone. He stares at me, then he waves his fingers. "People?" He says it louder. "Excuse me? The boy is in the room, but is not to be shown on camera, no stills, snapshots for personal use, nothing, are we clear?"

Then everybody looks at me, I shut my eyes.

When I open them a different person is shaking Ma's hand, wow, it's the woman with the puffy hair from the red couch. The couch is not here, though. I never saw an actual person from TV before, I wish it was Dora instead. "The lead's your AVO over aerial footage of the shed, yeah," a man is telling her, "then we'll dissolve to a close-up on her, then the two-shot." The woman with puffy hair smiles at me extra wide. There's everybody talking and moving about, I shut my eyes again and press on my ear holes like Dr. Clay said when it gets too much. Someone's counting, "Five, four, three, two, one—" Is there going to be a rocket?

The woman with the puffy hair puts on a special voice, she has her hands together for praying. "Let me first express my gratitude, and the gratitude of all our viewers, for talking to us a

3 **wobbly** shaky – 6 **to bash** to hit hard so as to hurt; Jack means "hurt" – 11 **cutdown** the short, edited version of the whole film – 11 **rough cut** the long, unedited version – 20 **AVO** TV jargon language that only TV people understand: this abbreviation probably makes Ma and Jack even more nervous – 21 **aerial footage** ['fʊtɪdʒ] a film or photo taken from the air – 22 **to dissolve** *here (film language)*: to fade away, move over to

mere six days after your release. For refusing to be silenced any longer."

Ma does a small smile.

"Could you begin by telling us, what did you miss most in those seven long years of captivity? Apart from your family, of course."

"Dentistry, actually." Ma's voice all high and fast. "Which is ironic, because I used to hate having my teeth cleaned even."

"You've emerged into a new world. A global economic and environmental crisis, a new President—"

"We saw the inauguration on TV," says Ma.

"Well! But so much must have changed."

Ma shrugs. "Nothing seems all that totally different. But I haven't really gone out yet, except to the dentist."

The woman smiles like it's a joke.

"No, I mean everything feels different, but it's because I'm different."

"Stronger at the broken places?"

I rub my head that's still broken from the table.

Ma makes a face. "Before—I was so ordinary. I wasn't even, you know, vegetarian, I never even had a goth phase."

"And now you're an extraordinary young woman with an extraordinary tale to tell, and we're honored that it's we, that it's us—" The woman looks away, to one of the persons with the machines. "Let's try that again." She looks back at Ma and does the special voice. "And we're honored that you've chosen this show to tell it. Now, without necessarily putting it in terms of, say, Stockholm syndrome, many of our viewers are curious,

5 **captivity** the state of being a prisoner – 7 **dentistry** the work of a dentist – 9 **to emerge** to arrive, come up – 11 **inauguration** [ɪˌnɑːgjʊˈreɪʃən] the ceremony when a new president comes into power – 21 **goth** gothic; *here*: a style or fashion in which young people wear black clothes and white make-up and listen to a particular type of synthesiser-based music – 28 **Stockholm syndrome** a term used in psychology to describe the phenomenon when hostages have positive feelings towards their captors. The syndrome is named after a bank robbery in Stockholm in 1973, in which the victims, bank employees, became emotionally attached to their captors.

well, concerned to know if you found yourself in any way … emotionally dependent on your captor."

Ma's shaking her head. "I hated him."

The woman is nodding.

"I kicked and screamed. One time I hit him over the head with the lid of the toilet. I didn't wash, for a long time I wouldn't speak."

"Was that before or after the tragedy of your stillbirth?"

Ma puts her hand over her mouth.

Morris butts in, he's flicking through pages. "Clause … she doesn't want to talk about that."

"Oh, we're not going into any detail," says the woman with the puffy hair, "but it feels crucial to establish the sequence—"

"No, actually it's crucial to stick to the contract," he says.

Ma's hands are all shaking, she puts them under her legs. She's not looking my way, did she forget I'm here? I'm talking to her in my head but she's not hearing.

"Believe me," the woman is saying to Ma, "we're just trying to help *you* tell *your* story to the world." She looks down at the paper in her lap. "So. You found yourself pregnant for the second time, in the hellhole where you'd now eked out two years of your precious youth. Were there days when you felt you were being, ah, forced to bear this man's—"

Ma butts in. "Actually I felt saved."

"*Saved.* That's beautiful."

Ma twists her mouth. "I can't speak for anyone else. Like, I had an abortion when I was eighteen, and I've never regretted that."

The woman with the puffy hair has her mouth open a bit. Then she glances down at the paper and looks up at Ma again. "On that cold March day five years ago, you gave birth alone

2 **captor** sb who keeps sb else prisoner – 8 **stillbirth** This happens when a baby has died in the mother's womb. – 10 **clause** a particular section of a written legal document – 13 **crucial** very important – 13 **sequence** chain of events, scene – 21 **hellhole** *inf* a place like hell – 21 **to eke out** [i:k] to manage to survive – 27 **abortion** to end a pregnancy deliberately – 27 **to regret** to be sorry (*bedauern*)

under medieval conditions to a healthy baby. Was that the hardest thing you've ever done?"

Ma shakes her head. "The best thing."

"Well, that too, of course. Every mother says—"

"Yeah, but for me, see, Jack was everything. I was alive again, I mattered. So after that I was polite."

"Polite? Oh, you mean with—"

"It was all about keeping Jack safe."

"Was it agonizingly hard to be, as you put it, polite?"

Ma shakes her head. "I did it on autopilot, you know, Stepford Wife."

The puffy-hair woman nods a lot. "Now, figuring out how to raise him all on your own, without books or professionals or even relatives, that must have been terribly difficult."

She shrugs. "I think what babies want is mostly to have their mothers right there. No, I was just afraid Jack would get ill—and me too, he needed me to be OK. So, just stuff I remembered from Health Ed like hand-washing, cooking everything really well . . ."

The woman nods. "You breastfed him. In fact, this may startle some of our viewers, I understand you still do?"

Ma laughs.

The woman stares at her.

"In this whole story, that's the shocking detail?"

The woman looks down at her paper again. "There you and your baby were, condemned to solitary confinement—"

Ma shakes her head. "Neither of us was ever alone for a minute."

"Well, yes. But it takes a village to raise a child, as they say in Africa ..."

1 **medieval** referring to the Middle Ages, the period of European history between about 1000 AD and 1400 AD – 6 **to matter** to be important – 9 **agonizing** painful – 10 **Stepford Wife** a thriller novel by Ira Levin in which the protagonist realizes that the submissive housewives in her neighbourhood are robots created by their husbands. – 15 **to shrug** to raise your shoulders briefly to signal that you don't know sth – 18 **Health Ed** Health Education, a school subject – 20 **to startle** to surprise – 26 **solitary confinement** being kept in a closed place without being able to talk to anybody

"If you've got a village. But if you don't, then maybe it just takes two people."

"Two? You mean you and your …"

Ma's face goes all frozen. "I mean me and Jack."

"Ah."

"We did it together."

"That's lovely. May I ask—I know you taught him to pray to Jesus. Was your faith very important to you?"

"It was … part of what I had to pass on to him."

"Also, I understand that television helped the days of boredom go by a little faster?"

"I was never bored with Jack," says Ma. "Not vice versa either, I don't think."

"Wonderful. Now, you'd come to what some experts are calling a strange decision, to teach Jack that the world measured eleven foot by eleven, and everything else—everything he saw on TV, or heard about from his handful of books—was just fantasy. Did you feel bad about deceiving him?"

Ma looks not friendly. "What was I meant to tell him—Hey, there's a world of fun out there and you can't have any of it?"

The woman sucks her lips. "Now, I'm sure our viewers are all familiar with the thrilling details of your rescue—"

"Escape," says Ma. She grins right at me.

I'm surprised. I grin back but she's not looking now.

" 'Escape,' right, and the arrest of the, ah, the alleged captor. Now, did you get the sense, over the years, that this man cared—at some basic human level, even in a warped way—for his son?"

Ma's eyes have gone skinny. "Jack's nobody's son but mine."

"That's so true, in a very real sense," says the woman. "I was just wondering whether, in your view, the genetic, the biological relationship—"

18 **to deceive** to make sb believe sth that is not true – 22 **thrilling** exciting – 22 **rescue** an act of saving or setting sb free – 25 **alleged** saying sth which has no proof (*mutmaßlich*) – 27 **warped** twisted – 29 **skinny** *inf* very thin

"There was no *relationship.*" She's talking through her teeth. "And you never found that looking at Jack painfully reminded you of his origins?"

Ma's eyes go even tighter. "He reminds me of nothing but himself."

"Mmm," says the TV woman. "When you think about your captor now, are you eaten up with hate?" She waits. "Once you've faced him in court, do you think you'll ever be able to bring yourself to forgive him?"

Her mouth twists. "It's not, like, a priority," she says. "I think about him as little as possible."

"Do you realize what a beacon you've become?"

"A—I beg your pardon?"

"A beacon of hope," says the woman, smiling. "As soon as we announced we'd be doing this interview, our viewers started calling in, e-mails, text messages, telling us you're an angel, a talisman of goodness …"

Ma makes a face. "All I did was I survived, and I did a pretty good job of raising Jack. A good enough job."

"You're very modest."

"No, what I am is irritated, actually."

The puffy-hair woman blinks twice.

"All this reverential—I'm not a saint." Ma's voice is getting loud again. "I wish people would stop treating us like we're the only ones who ever lived through something terrible. I've been finding stuff on the Internet you wouldn't believe."

"Other cases like yours?"

"Yeah, but not just—I mean, of course when I woke up in that shed, I thought nobody'd ever had it as bad as me. But the thing is, slavery's not a new invention. And solitary confinement—did you know, in America we've got more than twenty-five thousand prisoners in isolation cells? Some of them for more than twenty years." Her hand is pointing at the puffy-hair woman. "As

12 **beacon** bright fire or light – 19 **to raise** to bring up (a child) (*erziehen*) – 20 **modest** *opp of* showy – 21 **irritated** angry – 23 **reverential** respectful

for kids—there's places where babies lie in orphanages five to a cot with pacifiers taped into their mouths, kids getting raped by Daddy every night, kids in prisons, whatever, making carpets till they go blind—"

It's really quiet for a minute. The woman says, "Your experiences have given you, ah, enormous empathy with the suffering children of the world."

"Not just children," says Ma. "People are locked up in all sorts of ways."

The woman clears her throat and looks at the paper in her lap. "You say *did,* you did a 'pretty good job' of raising Jack, although of course the job is far from over. But now you have lots of help from your family as well as many dedicated professionals."

"It's actually harder." Ma's looking down. "When our world was eleven foot square it was easier to control. Lots of things are freaking Jack out right now. But I hate the way the media call *him* a freak, or an idiot savant, or feral, that word—"

"Well, he's a very special boy."

Ma shrugs. "He's just spent his first five years in a strange place, that's all."

"You don't think he's been shaped—damaged—by his ordeal?" "It wasn't an ordeal to Jack, it was just how things were. And, yeah, maybe, but everybody's damaged by something."

"He certainly seems to be taking giant steps toward recovery," says the puffy-hair woman. "Now, you said just now it was 'easier to control' Jack when you were in captivity—"

"No, control *things.*"

"You must feel an almost pathological need—understandably—to stand guard between your son and the world."

1 **orphanage** a place for children whose parents are both dead – 2 **cot** a small bed for a young child – 2 **pacifier** *AE Schnuller* – 2 **to rape** to force sb to have sex against their will – 6 **empathy** the ability to put oneself in the position of another person – 13 **dedicated** very interested in or working hard – 17 **to freak sb out** *inf* to make sb very confused and nervous – 18 **savant** sb who has great knowledge (*Gelehrter*) – 18 **feral** wild – 23 **ordeal** a painful experience (physically and/or psychologically) – 29 **pathological** *here*: unnatural

"Yeah, it's called being a mother." Ma nearly snarls it.

"Is there a sense in which you miss being behind a locked door?"

Ma turns to Morris. "Is she allowed to ask me such stupid questions?"

The puffy-hair woman holds out her hand and another person puts a bottle of water into it, she takes a sip.

Dr. Clay holds his hand up. "If I may—I think we're all getting the sense that my patient is at her limit, in fact past it."

"If you need a break, we could resume taping later," the woman tells Ma.

Ma shakes her head. "Let's just get it done."

"OK, then," says the woman, with another of her wide smiles that's fake like a robot's. "There's something I'd like to return to, if I may. When Jack was born—some of our viewers have been wondering whether it ever for a moment occurred to you to ..."

"What, put a pillow over his head?"

Is that me Ma means? But pillows go under heads.

The woman waves her hand side to side. "Heaven forbid. But did you ever consider asking your captor to take Jack away?"

"Away?"

"To leave him outside a hospital, say, so he could be adopted. As you yourself were, very happily, I believe."

I can see Ma swallow. "Why would I have done that?" "Well, so he could be free."

"Free away from me?"

"It would have been a sacrifice, of course—the ultimate sacrifice—but if Jack could have had a normal, happy childhood with a loving family?"

"He had me." Ma says it one word at a time. "He had a childhood with me, whether you'd call it *normal* or not."

1 **to snarl** to make an angry sound, like a wild animal – 7 **sip** a very small amount to drink – 9 **to be at a limit** to not be able to carry on – 10 **to resume** to begin again after a break – 14 **fake** false, not natural – 25 **to swallow** *schlucken*

"But you knew what he was missing," says the woman. "Every day he needed a wider world, and the only one you could give him got narrower. You must have been tortured by the memory of everything Jack didn't even know to want. Friends, school, grass, swimming, rides at the fair …"

"Why does everyone go on about fairs?" Ma's voice is all hoarse. "When I was a kid I hated fairs."

The woman does a little laugh.

Ma's got tears coming down her face, she puts up her hands to catch them. I'm off my chair and running at her, something falls over *smaaaaaaash,* I get to Ma and wrap her all up, and Morris is shouting, "The boy is not to be shown—"

* * *

When I wake up in the morning Ma's Gone.

I didn't know she'd have days like this in the world. I shake her arm but she only does a little groan and puts her head under the pillow. I'm so thirsty, I wriggle near to try and have some but she won't turn and let me. I stay curled beside her for hundreds of hours.

I don't know what to do. In Room if Ma was being Gone I could get up on my own and make breakfast and watch TV.

I sniff, there's nothing in my nose, I think I've lost my cold.

I go pull the cord to make the blind open a bit. It's bright, the light's bouncing off a car window. A crow goes by and scares me. I don't think Ma likes the light so I do the cord back. My tummy goes *yawrrrrrrr.*

Then I remember the buzzer by the bed. I press it, nothing happens. But after a minute the door goes *tap tap.*

I open it just a bit, it's Noreen.

"Hi, pet, how are you doing today?"

"Hungry. Ma's Gone," I whisper.

5 **fair** a place of outdoor entertainment (*Jahrmarkt*) – 7 **hoarse** rough-sounding – 24 **crow** *Krähe*

"Well, let's find her, will we? I'm sure she just slipped out for a minute."

"No, she's here but she's not really."

Noreen's face goes all confused.

"Look." I point at the bed. "It's a day she doesn't get up." Noreen calls Ma by her other name and asks if she's OK. I whisper, "Don't talk to her."

She says to Ma even louder, "Anything I can get you?"

"Let me sleep." I never heard Ma say anything when she's Gone before, her voice is like some monster.

Noreen goes over to the dresser and gets clothes for me. It's hard in the mostly dark, I get both legs in one pant leg for a second and I have to lean on her. It's not so bad touching people on purpose, it's worse when it's them touching me, like electric shocks. "Shoes," she whispers. I find them and squeeze them on and do the Velcro, they're not the stretchies I like. "Good lad." Noreen's at the door, she waves her hand to make me come with her. I tight my ponytail that was coming out. I find Tooth and my rock and my maple key to put in my pocket.

"Your ma must be worn out after that interview," says Noreen in the corridor. "Your uncle's been in Reception for half an hour already, waiting for you guys to wake up."

The adventure! But no we can't because Ma's Gone.

There's Dr. Clay on the stairs, he talks to Noreen. I'm holding on tight to the rail with two hands, I do one foot down then another, I slide my hands down, I don't fall, there's just a second when it feels fally then I'm standing on the next foot. "Noreen."

"Just a tick."

"No but, I'm doing the stairs."

She grins at me. "Would you look at that!"

"Gimme some skin," says Dr. Clay.

I let go with one hand to high-five him.

"So do you still want to see those dinosaurs?"

28 **Just a tick.** *inf* "Wait a second!" – 31 **Gimme some skin** *inf* expression for: "Show me your hand (so I can do "high-five" with you)!" – 32 **to high-five** to greet by slapping the other person's hand (the slapping hands are above the people's heads)

"Without Ma?"

Dr. Clay nods. "But you'll be with your uncle and aunt all the time, you'll be perfectly safe. Or would you rather leave it till another day?"

Yeah but no because another day the dinosaurs might be gone. "Today, please."

"Good lad," says Noreen. "That way your ma can have a big snooze and you can tell her all about the dinosaurs when you come back."

"Hey, buddy." Here's Paul my Uncle, I didn't know he was let in the dining room. I think *buddy* is man talk for *sweetie.*

I have breakfast with Paul sitting beside, that's weird. He talks on his little phone, he says it's Deana on the other end. The other end is the invisible one. There's juice with no bits today, it's yum, Noreen says they ordered it specially for me.

"You ready for your first trip outside?" asks Paul.

"I've been in Outside six days," I tell him. "I've been in the air three times, I've seen ants and helicopters and dentists."

"Wow."

After my muffin I get my jacket and hat and sunblock and cool shades on. Noreen gives me a brown paper bag in case I can't breathe. "Anyway," says Paul when we're going out the revolving door, "it's probably best your ma's not coming with us today, because after that TV show last night, everybody knows her face."

"Everyone in all the world?"

"Pretty much," says Paul.

In the parking he puts out his hand beside him like I'm meant to hold it. Then he puts it down again.

Something falls on my face and I shout.

"Just a speck of rain," says Paul.

I stare up at the sky, it's gray. "Is it going to fall on us?" "It's fine, Jack."

I want to be back in Room Number Seven with Ma even if she's Gone.

31 **speck** a tiny amount

"Here we are …"

It's a green van, Deana's in the seat with the steering wheel. She waves her fingers at me through the window. I see a smaller face in the middle. The van doesn't open out, it slides a piece of it and I climb in.

"At last," says Deana. "Bronwyn, hon, can you say hi to your cousin, Jack?"

It's a girl nearly the same big as me, she's got all braids like Deana but sparkly beads on the ends and an elephant that's furry and cereals in a tub with a lid that's shape of a frog. "Hi Jack," she says very squeaky.

There's a booster for me beside Bronwyn. Paul shows me to click the buckle. The third time I do it all myself, Deana claps and Bronwyn too. Then Paul slides the van shut with a loud clunk. I jump, I want Ma, I think I might be going to cry, but I don't.

Bronwyn keeps going "Hi Jack, Hi Jack." She doesn't talk right yet, she says "Dada sing," and "Pretty doggy," and "Momma more pretzl pees," *pees* is what she says for *please*. Dada means Paul and Momma means Deana but they're the names only Bronwyn gets to say, like nobody calls Ma Ma but me.

I'm being scave but a bit more brave than scared because this isn't as bad as pretending I'm dead in Rug. Anytime a car comes at us I say in my head that it has to stay on its own side or Officer Oh will put it in jail with the brown truck. Pictures in the window are like in TV but blurrier, I see cars that are parked, a cement mixer, a motorbike and a car trailer with one two three four five cars on it, that's my best number. In a front yard a kid pushing a wheelbarrow with a littler kid in it, that's funny. There's a dog crossing a road with a human on a rope, I think it's actually tied, not like the daycare that were just holding on.

6 **hon** *inf* honey (expression of affection) – 11 **squeaky** describing a high, soft sound (The noise that a mouse makes is called a squeak.) – 12 **booster** a cushion for children – 13 **buckle** *AE* safety belt – 15 **clunk** a loud metalic noise – 22 **scave** Jack's word combination of "brave" and "scared" – 29 **wheelbarrow** a small cart used in the garden (*Schubkarre*)

Traffic lights changing to green and a woman with crutches hopping and a huge bird on a trash, Deana says that's just a gull, they eat anything and everything.

"They're omnivores," I tell her.

"My, you know some big words."

We turn where there's trees. I say, "Is this the Clinic again?"

"No, no, we just have to make a pit stop at the mall to pick up a present for a birthday party Bronwyn's going to this afternoon."

The mall means stores like Old Nick buys our groceries, but not anymore.

It's just Paul going in the mall, but he says he doesn't know what to choose, so Deana's going in instead, but then Bronwyn starts chanting, "Me with Momma, me with Momma." So it's going to be Deana pulling Bronwyn in the red wagon and Paul and me will wait in the van.

I'm staring at the red wagon. "Can I try?"

"Later, at the museum," Deana tells me.

"Listen, I'm desperate for the bathroom anyway," says Paul, "it might be faster if we all run in."

"I don't know ..."

"It shouldn't be too hectic on a weekday."

Deana looks at me, not smiling. "Jack, would you like to come in the mall in the wagon, just for a couple of minutes?"

"Oh yeah."

I ride at the back making sure Bronwyn doesn't fall out because I'm the big cousin, "like John the Baptist," I tell Bronwyn but she's not listening. When we get up to the doors they make a *pop* sound and crack open by their own, I nearly fall out of the wagon but Paul says it's all just tiny computers sending each other messages, don't worry about it.

It's all extra bright and ginormous, I didn't know inside could be as big as Outside, there's trees even. I hear music but I can't

1 **crutch** sb who broke his leg walks on crutches. – 2 **gull** a sea bird – 4 **omnivore** ['ɑːmnɪvɔːr] animal that eat everything (plants as well as meat) – 7 **pit stop** *sl* short stop – 19 **desperate** *here*: in real need

see the players with the instruments. The most amazing thing, a bag of Dora, I get down to touch her face, she's smiling and dancing at me. "Dora," I whisper to her.

"Oh, yeah," says Paul, "Bronwyn used to be all about her too but now it's Hannah Montana."

"Hannah Montana," Bronwyn sings, "Hannah Montana."

The Dora bag has straps, it's like Backpack but with Dora on it instead of Backpack's face. It has a handle too, when I try it pulls up, I think I broke it, but then it rolls, it's a wheelie bag and a backpack at the same time, that's magic.

"You like it?" It's Deana talking to me. "Would you like to keep your things in it?"

"Maybe one that's not pink," says Paul to her. "What about this one, Jack, pretty cool or what?" He's holding up a bag of Spider-Man.

I give Dora a big hug. I think she whispers, *Hola, Jack.*

Deana tries to take the Dora bag but I won't let her. "It's OK, I just have to pay the lady, you'll get it back in two seconds ..." It's not two seconds, it's thirty-seven.

"There's the bathroom," says Paul and he runs off.

The lady's wrapping the bag in paper so I can't see Dora anymore, she puts it into a big cardboard, then Deana gives it to me, swinging it on its strings. I take Dora out and put my arms in her straps and I'm wearing it, I'm actually wearing Dora.

"What do you say?" asks Deana.

I don't know what I say.

"Bronwyn pretty bag," says Bronwyn, she's waving a spangled one with hearts hanging on strings.

"Yes, hon, but you've got lots of pretty bags at home." She takes the shiny bag, Bronwyn screams and one of the hearts falls on the ground.

7 **backpack** rucksack – 9 **wheelie bag** a bag on wheels – 22 **cardboard** thick, brownish paper – 23 **string** cord – 24 **strap** a narrow band of strong material – 28 **spangled** shiny, glittery

"Sometime, could we get more than twenty feet in before the first meltdown?" asks Paul, he's back again.

"If you were here you could have distracted her," Deana tells him. "Bronwyn pretty baaaaaaaggggggg!"

Deana lifts her back into the wagon. "Let's go."

I pick up the heart and put it in my pocket with the other treasures, I walk along beside the wagon.

Then I change my mind, I put all my treasures in my Dora bag in the front zip bit instead. My shoes are sore so I take them off. "Jack!" That's Paul calling at me.

"Don't keep bawling his name out, remember?" says Deana. "Oh, right."

I see a gigantic apple made of wood. "I like that."

"Crazy, isn't it?" says Paul. "What about this drum for Shirelle?" he says to Deana.

She rolls her eyes. "Concussion hazard. Don't even try." "Can I have the apple, thank you?" I ask.

"I don't think it would fit into your bag," says Paul, grinning. Next I find a silver-and-blue thing like a rocket. "I want this, thank you."

"That's a coffeepot," says Deana, putting it back on the shelf. "We bought you a bag already, that's it for today, OK? We're just looking for a present for Bronwyn's friend, then we can get out of here."

"Excuse me, I wonder are these your older daughter's?" It's an old woman holding up my shoes.

Deana stares at her.

"Jack, buddy, what's going on?" says Paul, pointing at my socks.

"Thank you so much," says Deana, taking the shoes from the woman and kneeling down. She pushes my feet to step into the

2 **meltdown** *here*: tantrum (*Wutanfall*) – 3 **to distract** to take sb's attention away from sth – 11 **to bawl** [bɑ:l] to shout in a loud voice – 13 **gigantic** [dʒaɪˈgæntɪk] huge – 16 **concussion** [kənˈkʌʃən] *Gehirnerschütterung* – 16 **hazard** danger, risk

right then the left. “You keep saying his name,” she says to Paul through her teeth.

I wonder what’s wrong with my name.

“Sorry, sorry,” says Paul.

“Why she said older daughter?” I ask.

“Ah, it’s your long hair and your Dora bag,” says Deana. The old woman’s disappeared. “Was she a bad guy?”

“No, no.”

“But if she figured out that you were *that* Jack,” says Paul, “she might take your picture with her cell phone or something, and your mom would kill us.”

My chest starts banging. “Why Ma would—?”

“I mean, sorry—”

“She’d be really mad, that’s all he means,” says Deana.

I’m thinking of Ma lying in the dark Gone. “I don’t like her being mad.”

“No, of course not.”

“Can you back me to the Clinic now, please?”

“Very soon.”

“Now.”

“Don’t you want to see the museum? We’ll get going in just a minute. Webkinz,” Deana tells Paul, “that should be safe enough. I think there’s a toy shop past the food court …”

I wheel my bag all the time, my shoes are Velcroed too tight. Bronwyn’s hungry so we have popcorn that’s the crunchiest thing I ever ate, it sticks in my throat and makes me cough. Paul gets him and Deana lattes from the coffee shop. When bits of popcorn fall down from my bag Deana says to leave them there because we’ve got plenty and we don’t know what’s been on that floor. I made a mess, Ma will be mad. Deana gives me a wet wipe to unsticky my fingers, I put it in my Dora bag. It’s too bright here and I think we’re lost, I wish I was in Room Number Seven.

2 **through one’s teeth** angrily (*zähneknirschend*) – 22 **Webkinz** name of a shop – 23 **food court** restaurant area – 30 **mess** *inf* disorder, untidiness – 31 **wipe** Jack means “cloth”

I need to pee, Paul brings me in a bathroom that has funny floppy sinks on the wall. He waves at them. "Go ahead."

"Where's the toilet?"

"These are special ones just for us guys."

I shake my head and go out again.

Deana says I can come with her and Bronwyn, she lets me choose the cubicle. "Great job, Jack, no splashing at all."

Why would I splashing?

When she takes Bronwyn's underwear down it's not like Penis, or Ma's vagina, it's a fat little piece of body folded in the middle with no fur. I put my finger on it and press, it's squishy.

Deana bangs my hand away.

I can't stop screaming.

"Calm down, Jack. Did I—is your hand hurt?"

There's all blood coming out of my wrist.

"I'm sorry," says Deana, "I'm so sorry, it must have been my ring." She stares at her ring with the gold bits. "But listen, we don't touch each other's private parts, that is not OK. OK?"

I don't know private parts.

"All done, Bronwyn? Let Momma wipe."

She's rubbing the same bit of Bronwyn I did but she doesn't hit herself after.

When I wash my hands it hurts the blood more. Deana keeps digging in her bag for a Band-Aid. She folds up some brown paper towel and tells me to press in on the cut.

"Okelydokely?" asks Paul outside.

"Don't ask," says Deana. "Can we get out of here?"

"What about the present for Shirelle?"

"We can wrap up something of Bronwyn's that looks new."

"Not something mine," Bronwyn shouts.

They're arguing. I want to be in bed with Ma in the dark and her all soft and no invisible music and red-faced wide persons

2 **floppy** *here*: falling side walls – 7 **cubicle** one of several toilets in a row – 11 **fur** soft thin hair – usually of an animal – 26 **okelydokely** *usu* okey-doke (meaning: "OK")

going by and girls laughing with their arms knotted together and bits of them showing through their clothes. I press the cut to stop my blood falling out, I close my eyes walking along, I bang into a plant pot, actually it's not really a plant like Plant was till she died, it's plastic of one.

Then I see anybody smiling at me that's Dylan! I run and give him a huge hug.

"A book," says Deana, "perfect, give me two seconds."

"It's Dylan the Digger, he's my friend from Room," I tell Paul. " ' Heeeeeeeeere's Dylan, the sturdy digger! The loads he shovels get bigger and bigger. Watch his long arm delve into the earth—' "

"That's great, buddy. Now can you find where it goes back?"

I'm stroking Dylan's front, it's gone all smooth and shiny, how did he get here to the mall?

"Careful you don't get blood on it." Paul's putting a tissue on my hand, my brown paper must have dropped off. "Why don't you choose a different book that you've never read before?"

"Momma, Momma," Bronwyn's trying to get a jewelry out of the front of a book.

"Go pay," says Deana, putting a book in Paul's hand, she runs over to Bronwyn.

I open my Dora bag, I put Dylan in and zip him up safe.

When Deana and Bronwyn come back we walk near the fountain to hear the splashing but not get splashed. Bronwyn's saying, "Money, money," so Deana gives her a coin and Bronwyn throws it in the water.

"Want one?" That's Deana saying to me.

It must be a special trash for money that's too dirty. I take the coin and throw it in and get out the wet wipe to clean my fingers. "Did you make a wish?"

I never made a wish with trash before. "For what?"

"Whatever you'd like best in the world," says Deana.

10 **sturdy** strong – 11 **to delve into** to search deeply

What I'd like best is to be in Room but I don't think that's in the world.

There's a man talking to Paul, he's pointing at my Dora.

Paul comes and unzips it and takes out Dylan. "Ja—Buddy!" "I am so sorry," says Deana.

"He's got a copy at home, you see," says Paul, "he thought this was his one." He holds out Dylan to the man.

I run and grab him back, I say, " 'Heeeeeeeeere's Dylan, the sturdy digger! The loads he shovels get bigger and bigger.' "

"He doesn't understand," says Paul.

" 'Watch his long arm delve into the earth—' "

"Jack, sweetheart, this one belongs to the store." Deana's pulling the book out of my hand.

I hold even harder again and push him up my shirt. "I'm from somewhere else," I tell the man. "Old Nick kept me and Ma locked up and he's in jail now with his truck but the angel won't burst him out because he's a bad guy. We're famous and if you take our picture we'll kill you."

The man blinks.

"Ah, how much is the book?" says Paul.

The man says, "I'll need to scan it—"

Paul puts out his hand, I curl up on the floor around Dylan. "Why don't I get another copy for you to scan," says Paul and he runs back into the store.

Deana's looking all around shouting, "Bronwyn? Honey?" She rushes over to the fountain and looks in all along it. "Bronwyn?"

Actually Bronwyn's behind a window with dresses putting her tongue at the glass.

"Bronwyn?" Deana's screaming.

I put my tongue out too, Bronwyn laughs behind the glass.

* * *

17 **to burst** to break open *here*: to let out – 19 **to blink** to open and shut your eyes quickly (*blinzeln*)

I nearly fall asleep in the green van but not really.

Noreen says my Dora bag is magnificent and the shiny heart too and *Dylan the Digger* looks like a great read. "How were the dinosaurs?"

"We didn't have time to see them."

"Oh, that's a pity." Noreen gets me a Band-Aid for my wrist but there's no pictures on it. "Your ma's been snoozing the day away, she'll be thrilled to see you." She taps and opens the Door Number Seven.

I take off my shoes but not my clothes, I get in with Ma at last. She's warmy soft, I snuggle up but carefully. The pillow smells bad.

"See you guys at dinnertime," whispers Noreen and shuts the door.

The bad is vomit, I remember from our Great Escape. "Wake up," I say to Ma, "you did sick on the pillow."

She doesn't switch on, she doesn't groan even or roll over, she's not moving when I pull her. This is the most Gone she's ever.

"Ma, Ma, Ma."

She's a zombie, I think.

"Noreen?" I shout, I run at the door. I'm not meant to disturb the persons but—"Noreen!"

She's at the end of the corridor, she turns around. "Ma did a vomit."

"Not a bother, we'll have that cleaned up in two ticks. Let me just get the cart—"

"No, but come now."

"OK, OK."

When she switches on the light and looks at Ma she doesn't say OK, she picks up the phone and says, "Code blue, room seven, code blue—"

I don't know what's—Then I see Ma's pill bottles open on the table, they look mostly empty. Never more than two, that's the rule, how could they be mostly empty, where did the pills go?

Noreen's pressing on the side of Ma's throat and saying her other name and "Can you hear me? Can you hear me?"

But I don't think Ma can hear, I don't think she can see. I shout, "Bad idea bad idea bad idea."

Lots of persons run in, one of them pulls me outside in the corridor. I'm screaming "Ma" as loud as I can but it's not loud enough to wake her.

Living

I'm in the house with the hammock. I'm looking out the window for it, but Grandma says it would be in the backyard, not the front, anyway it's not hung up yet because it's only the tenth of April. There's bushes and flowers and the sidewalk and the street and the other front yards and the other houses, I count eleven of bits of them, that's where neighbors live like Beggar My Neighbor. I suck to feel Tooth, he's right in the middle of my tongue. The white car is outside not moving, I rode in it from the Clinic even though there was no booster, Dr. Clay wanted me to stay for *continuity* and *therapeutic isolation* but Grandma shouted that he wasn't allowed keep me like a prisoner when I do have a family. My family is Grandma Steppa Bronwyn Uncle Paul Deana and Grandpa, only he shudders at me. Also Ma. I move Tooth into my cheek. "Is she dead?"

"No, I keep telling you. Definitely not." Grandma rests her head on the wood around the glass.

Sometimes when persons say *definitely* it sounds actually less true. "Are you just playing she's alive?" I ask Grandma. "Because if she's not, I don't want to be either."

There's all tears running all down her face again. "I don't—I can't tell you any more than I know, sweetie. They said they'd call as soon as they had an update."

"What's an update?"

"How she is, right this minute."

"How is she?"

"Well, she's not well because she took too much of the bad medicine, like I told you, but they've probably pumped it all out of her stomach by now, or most of it."

"But why she—?"

"Because she's not well. In her head. She's being taken care of," says Grandma, "you don't need to worry."

"Why?"

"Well, it doesn't do any good to."

God's face is all red and stuck on a chimney. It's getting darker. Tooth is digging into my gum, he's a bad hurting tooth.

"You didn't touch your lasagna," Grandma says, "would you like a glass of juice or something?"

I shake my head.

"Are you tired? You must be tired, Jack. Lord knows I am. Come downstairs and see the spare room."

"Why is it spare?"

"That means we don't use it."

"Why you have a room you don't use?"

Grandma shrugs. "You never know when we might need it." She waits while I do the stairs down on my butt because there's no banister to hold. I pull my Dora bag behind me *bumpity bump*. We go through the room that's called the living room, I don't know why because Grandma and Steppa are living in all the rooms, except not the spare.

An awful *waah waah* starts, I cover my ears. "I'd better get that," says Grandma.

She comes back in a minute and brings me into a room. "Are you ready?"

"For what?"

"To go to bed, honey."

"Not here."

She presses around her mouth where the little cracks are. "I know you're missing your ma, but just for now you need to sleep on your own. You'll be fine, Steppa and I will be just upstairs. You're not afraid of monsters, are you?"

It depends on the monster, if it's a real one or not and if it's where I am.

"Hmm. Your ma's old room is beside ours," says Grandma, "but we've converted it into a fitness suite, I don't know if there'd be space for a blow-up ..."

I go up the stairs with my feet this time, just pressing onto the walls, Grandma carries my Dora bag. There's blue squishy mats

1 **chimney** *Schornstein* – 7 **spare** not used or needed – 31 **suite** *here*: room – 32 **blow-up**... air mattress

and dumbbells and abs crunchers like I saw in TV. "Her bed was here, right where her crib was when she was a baby," says Grandma, pointing to a bicycle but stuck to the ground. "The walls were covered in posters, you know, bands she liked, a giant fan and a dreamcatcher ..."

"Why it catched her dreams?"

"What's that?"

"The fan."

"Oh, no, they were just decorations. I feel just terrible about dropping it all off at the Goodwill, it was a counselor at the grief group that advised it ..."

I do a huge yawn, Tooth nearly slips out but I catch him in my hand.

"What's that?" says Grandma. "A bead or something? Never suck on something small, didn't your—?"

She's trying to bend my fingers open to get him. My hand hits her hard in the tummy.

She stares.

I put Tooth back in under my tongue and lock my teeth.

"Tell you what, why don't I put a blow-up beside our bed, just for tonight, until you're settled in?"

I pull my Dora bag. The next door is where Grandma and Steppa sleep. The blow-up is a big bag thing, the pump keeps popping out of the hole and she has to shout for Steppa to help. Then it's all full like a balloon but a rectangle and she puts sheets over it. Who's the *they* that pumped Ma's stomach? Where do they put the pump? Won't she burst?

"I said, where's your toothbrush, Jack?"

I find it in my Dora bag that has my everything. Grandma tells me to put on my pj's that means pajamas. She points at the blow-up and says, "Pop in," persons are always saying *pop* or *hop* when it's something they want to pretend is fun. Grandma

1 **dumbbell** ['dʌmbel] *Hantel* – 1 **abs crunchers** sports apparatus to strengthen the stomach muscles – 10 **Goodwill** name of a charity place where people can bring things they no longer need – 10 **counselor** a person who gives advice in a crisis – 10 **grief group** a group of people who meet regularly because they have all gone through a terrible crisis – 25 **rectangle** *Rechteck*

leans down with her mouth out like to kiss but I put my head under the duvet. "Sorry," she says. "What about a story?"

"No."

"Too tired for a story, OK, then. Night-night."

It goes all dark. I sit up. "What about the Bugs?"

"The sheets are perfectly clean."

I can't see her but I know her voice. "No, the *Bugs*."

"Jack, I'm ready to drop here—"

"The Bugs that don't let them bite."

"Oh," says Grandma. "Night-night, sleep tight … That's right, I used to say that when your ma was—"

"Do it all."

"Night-night, sleep tight, don't let the bugs bite."

Some light comes in, it's the door opening. "Where are you going?"

I can see Grandma's shape all black in the hole. "Just downstairs."

I roll off the blow-up, it wobbles. "Me too."

"No, I'm going to watch my shows, they're not for children."

"You said you and Steppa in the bed and me beside on the blow-up."

"That's later, we're not tired yet."

"You said you were tired."

"I'm tired of—" Grandma's nearly shouting. "I'm not sleepy, I just need to watch TV and not think for a while."

"You can not think here."

"Just try lying down and closing your eyes."

"I can't, not all my own."

"Oh," says Grandma. "Oh, you poor creature."

Why am I poor and creature?

She bends down beside the blow-up and touches my face. I get away.

"I was just closing your eyes for you."

"You in the bed. Me on the blow-up."

2 **duvet** bed cover with feathers inside

I hear her puff her breath. "OK. I'll lie down for just a minute …"

I see her shape on top of the duvet. Something drops *clomp,* it's her shoe. "Would you like a lullaby?" she whispers.

"Huh?"

"A song?"

Ma sings me songs but there's no more of them anymore. She smashed my head on the table in Room Number Seven. She took the bad medicine, I think she was too tired to play anymore, she was in a hurry to get to Heaven so she didn't wait, why she didn't wait for me?

"Are you crying?"

I don't say anything.

"Oh, honey. Well, better out than in."

I want some, I really really want some, I can't get to sleep without. I suck on Tooth that's Ma, a bit of her anyway, her cells all brown and rotten and hard. Tooth hurted her or he was hurted but not anymore. Why is it better out than in? Ma said we'd be free but this doesn't feel like free.

Grandma's singing very quietly, I know that song but it sounds wrong. " 'The wheels on the bus go—' "

"No, thanks," I say, and she stops.

* * *

Me and Ma in the sea, I'm tangled in her hair, I'm all knotted up and drowning—

Just a bad dream. That's what Ma would say if she was here but she's not.

I lie counting five fingers five fingers five toes five toes, I make them wave one by one. I try the talking in my head, *Ma? Ma? Ma?* I can't hear her answering.

When it starts being lighter I put the duvet over my face to dark it. I think this must be what Gone feels like.

4 **lullaby** ['lʌləbaɪ] a song for children to help them go to sleep – 24 **tangled** *here*: caught

Persons are walking around whispering. "Jack?" That's Grandma near my ear so I curl away. "How are you doing?"

I remember manners. "Not a hundred percent today, thank you." I'm mumbly because Tooth is stuck to my tongue.

When she's gone I sit up and count my things in my Dora bag, my clothes and shoes and maple key and train and drawing square and rattle and glittery heart and crocodile and rock and monkeys and car and six books, the sixth is *Dylan the Digger* from the store.

Lots of hours later the *waah waah* means the phone. Grandma comes up. "That was Dr. Clay, your ma is stable. That sounds good, doesn't it?"

It sounds like horses.

"Also, there's blueberry pancakes for breakfast."

I lie very still like I'm a skeleton. The duvet smells dusty. *Ding-dong ding-dong* and she goes downstairs again.

Voices under me. I count my toes then my fingers then my teeth all over again. I get the right numbers every time but I'm not sure.

Grandma comes up again out of breath to say that my Grandpa's here to say good-bye.

"To me?"

"To all of us, he's flying back to Australia. Get up now, Jack, it won't do you any good to wallow."

I don't know what that is. "He wants me not born."

"He wants what?"

"He said I shouldn't be and then Ma wouldn't have to be Ma."

Grandma doesn't say anything so I think she's gone downstairs. I take my face out to see. She's still here with her arms wrapped around her tight. "Never you mind that a-hole."

"What's a—?"

"Just come on down and have a pancake."

"I can't."

4 **to mumble** to speak unclearly – 24 **to wallow** to lie about unhappily (Grandma thinks Jack is sad.) – 31 **a-hole** *vulg* asshole

"Look at you," says Grandma.

How do I do that?

"You're breathing and walking and talking and sleeping without your Ma, aren't you? So I bet you can eat without her too."

I keep Tooth in my cheek for safe. I take a long time on the stairs.

In the kitchen, Grandpa the real one has purple on his mouth. His pancake is all in a puddle of syrup with more purples, they're blueberries.

The plates are normal white but the glasses are wrong-shaped with corners. There's a big bowl of sausages. I didn't know I was hungry. I eat one sausage then two more.

Grandma says she doesn't have the juice that's pulp-free but I have to drink something or I'll choke on my sausages. I drink the pulpy with the germs wiggling down my throat. The refrigerator is huge all full of boxes and bottles. The cabinets have so many foods in, Grandma has to go up steps to look in them all.

She says I should have a shower now but I pretend I don't hear. "What's stable?" I ask Grandpa.

"Stable?" A tear comes out of his eye and he wipes it. "No better, no worse, I guess." He puts his knife and his fork together on his plate.

No better no worse than what?

Tooth tastes all sour of juice. I go back upstairs to sleep.

* * *

"Sweetie," says Grandma. "You are not spending another entire day in front of the goggle box."

"Huh?"

9 **puddle** a small amount of water lying on the ground (*Pfütze*) – 14 **pulp-free** *ohne Fruchtfleisch* – 29 **goggle box** *sl* television

She switches off the TV. "Dr. Clay was just on the phone about your developmental needs, I had to tell him we were playing Checkers."

I blink and rub my eyes. Why she told him a lie? "Is Ma—?"

"She's still stable, he says. Would you like to play checkers for real?"

"Your bits are for giants and they fall off."

She sighs. "I keep telling you, they're regular ones, and the same with the chess and the cards. The mini magnetic set you and your Ma had was for traveling."

But we didn't travel.

"Let's go to the playground."

I shake my head. Ma said when we were free we'd go together.

"You've been outside before, lots of times."

"That was at the Clinic."

"It's the same air, isn't it? Come on, your ma told me you like climbing."

"Yeah, I climb on Table and on our chairs and on Bed thousands of times."

"Not on my table, mister."

I meant in Room.

Grandma does my ponytail very tight and tucks it down my jacket, I pull it out again. She doesn't say anything about the sticky stuff and my hat, maybe skin doesn't get burned in this bit of the world? "Put on your sunglasses, oh, and your proper shoes, those slipper things don't have any support."

My feet are squished walking even when I loose the Velcro. We're safe as long as we stay on the sidewalk but if we go on the street by accident we'll die. Ma isn't dead, Grandma says she wouldn't lie to me. She lied to Dr. Clay about Checkers. The sidewalk keeps stopping so we have to cross the street, we'll be fine as long as we hold hands. I don't like touching but Grandma says too bad. The air is all blowy in my eyes and the sun so dazzling around the edges of my shades. There's a pink thing

22 **to tuck** to put or push

that's a hair elastic and a bottle top and a wheel not from a real car but a toy one and a bag of nuts but the nuts are gone and a juice box that I can hear still some juice sploshing in and a yellow poo. Grandma says it's not from a human but from some disgusting dog, she tugs at my jacket and says, "Come away from that." The litter shouldn't be there, except for the leaves that the tree can't help dropping. In France they let their dogs do their business everywhere, I can go there someday.

"To see the poo?"

"No, no," says Grandma, "the Eiffel Tower. Someday when you're really good at climbing stairs."

"Is France in Outside?"

She looks at me strange.

"In the world?"

"Everywhere's in the world. Here we are!"

I can't go in the playground because there's kids not friends of mine.

Grandma rolls her eyes. "You just play at the same time, that's what kids do."

I can see through the fence in the diamonds of wire. It's like the secret fence in the walls and Floor that Ma couldn't dig through, but we got out, I saved her, only then she didn't want to be alive anymore. There's a big girl hanging upside down off a swing. Two boys on the thing I don't remember the name that does up and down, they're banging it and laughing and falling off I think on purpose. I count my teeth to twenty and one more time. Holding the fence makes white stripes on my fingers. I watch a woman carry a baby to the climber and it crawls through the tunnel, she does faces at it through the holes in the sides and pretends she doesn't know where it is. I watch the big girl but she only swings, sometimes with her hair nearly in the mud, sometimes right side up. The boys chase and do bang with their hands like guns, one falls down and cries. He runs out the gate and into a house, Grandma says he must live there,

3 **to splosh** *inf* to splash – 5 **to tug** *here*: to pull – 6 **litter** waste

how does she know? She whispers, "Why don't you go play with the other boy now?" Then she calls out, "Hi there." The boy looks over at us, I go into a bush, it pricks me in the head.

After a while she says it's chillier than it looks and maybe we should be getting home for lunch.

It takes hundreds of hours and my legs are breaking.

"Maybe you'll enjoy it more next time," says Grandma. "It was interesting."

"Is that what your ma says to say when you don't like something?" She smiles a bit. "I taught her that."

"Is she dying by now?"

"No." She nearly shouts. "Leo would have called if there was any news."

Leo is Steppa, it's confusing all the names. I only want my one name Jack.

At Grandma's house, she shows me France on the globe that's like a statue of the world and always spinning. This whole entire city we're in is just a dot and the Clinic's in the dot too. So is Room but Grandma says I don't need to think about that place anymore, put it out of my mind.

For lunch I have lots of bread and butter, it's French bread but there's no poo on it I don't think. My nose is red and hot, also my cheeks and my top bit of my chest and my arms and the back of my hands and my ankles above my socks.

Steppa tells Grandma not to upset herself.

"It wasn't even that sunny," she keeps saying, wiping her eyes.

I ask, "Is my skin going to fall off?"

"Just little bits of it," says Steppa.

"Don't frighten the boy," Grandma says. "You'll be fine, Jack, don't worry. Put on more of this nice cool after-sun cream, now ..."

It's hard to reach behind me but I don't like other persons' fingers so I manage.

3 **to prick** *here*: to scratch – 17 **to spin** to turn around fast

Grandma says she should call the Clinic again but she's not up to it right now.

Because I'm burned I get to lie on the couch and watch cartoons, Steppa's in the recliner reading his *World Traveler* magazine.

* * *

In the night Tooth is coming for me, bouncing on the street *crash crash crash,* ten feet tall all moldy and jaggedy bits falling off, he smashes at the walls. Then I'm floating in a boat that's nailed shut and *the worms crawl in, the worms crawl out—*

A hiss in the dark that I don't know it then it's Grandma. "Jack. It's OK."

"No."

"Go back to sleep."

I don't think I do.

At breakfast Grandma takes a pill. I ask if it's her vitamin. Steppa laughs. She tells him, "You should talk." Then she says to me, "Everybody needs a little something."

This house is hard to learn. The doors I'm let go in anytime are the kitchen and the living room and the fitness suite and the spare room and the basement, also outside the bedroom that's called the landing, like where airplanes would land but they don't. I can go in the bedroom unless the door's shut when I have to knock and wait. I can go in the bathroom unless it won't open, that means anybody else is in it and I have to wait. The bath and sink and toilet are green called avocado, except the seat is wood so I can sit on that. I should put the seat up and down again after as a courtesy to ladies, that's Grandma. The toilet has a lid on the tank like the one that Ma hit on Old Nick. The soap is a hard ball and I have to rub and rub to make it work. Outsiders are not like us, they've got a million of things and different kinds of each thing, like all different chocolate

8 **moldy** *AE* mouldy *schimmelig* – 8 **jaggedy** Jack means "jagged" (*gezackt*) – 22 **landing** *Treppenabsatz* – 28 **courtesy** an act of politeness

bars and machines and shoes. Their things are all for different doing, like nailbrush and toothbrush and sweeping brush and toilet brush and clothes brush and yard brush and hairbrush. When I drop some powder called talc on the floor I sweep it up but Grandma comes in and says that's the toilet brush and she's mad I'm spreading germs.

It's Steppa's house too but he doesn't make the rules. He's mostly in his den which is his special room for his own.

"People don't always want to be with people," he tells me. "It gets tiring."

"Why?"

"Just take it from me, I've been married twice."

The front door I can't go out without telling Grandma but I wouldn't anyway. I sit on the stairs and suck hard on Tooth.

"Go play with something, why don't you?" says Grandma, squeezing past.

There's lots, I don't know which. My toys from the crazy wellwishers that Ma thought there was only five but actually I took six. There's chalks all different colors that Deana brought around only I didn't see her, they're too smudgy on my fingers. There's a giant roll of paper and forty-eight markers in a long invisible plastic. A box of boxes with animals on that Bronwyn doesn't use anymore, I don't know why, they stack to a tower more than my head.

I stare at my shoes instead, they're my softies. If I wiggle I can sort of see the toes under the leather. *Ma!* I shout it very loud in my head. I don't think she's there. No better no worse. Unless everybody's lying.

There's a tiny brown thing under the carpet where it starts being the wood of the stairs. I scrape it out, it's a metal. A coin. It's got a man face and words, IN GOD WE TRUST LIBERTY 2004. When I turn it over there's a man, maybe the same one

4 **talc** talcum powder for the body – 8 **den** *inf* a small comfortable room where a person can be alone – 20 **smudgy** Jack means "dirty"

but he's waving at a little house and says UNITED STATES OF AMERICA E PLURIBUS UNUM ONE CENT.

Grandma's on the bottom step staring at me.

I jump. I move Tooth to the back of my gums. "There's a bit in Spanish," I tell her.

"There is?" She frowns.

I show her with my finger.

"It's Latin. E PLURIBUS UNUM. Hmm, I think that means 'United we stand' or something. Would you like some more?"

"What?"

"Let me look in my purse ..."

She comes back with a round flat thing that if you squish, it suddenly opens like a mouth and there's different moneys inside. A silvery has a man with a ponytail like me and FIVE CENTS but she says everybody calls it a nickel, the little silvery is a dime, that is ten.

"Why is the five more bigger than the ten one if it's five?" "That's just how it is."

Even the one cent is bigger than the ten, I think how it is is dumb.

On the biggest silvery there's a different man not happy, the back says NEW HAMPSHIRE 1788 LIVE FREE OR DIE. Grandma says New Hampshire is another bit of America, not this bit.

"*Live free,* does that mean not costing anything?"

"Ah, no, no. It means ... nobody being the boss of you."

There's another the same front but when I turn it over there's pictures of a sailboat with a tiny person in it and a glass and more Spanish, GUAM E PLURIBUS UNUM 2009 and Guahan ITano' ManChamorro. Grandma squeezes up her eyes at it and goes to get her glasses.

"Is that another bit of America?"

2 **E Pluribus Unum** *Lat* Out of many, one. This motto appears on U.S. coins and on the Great Seal (*Siegel*) of the U.S.A. – 15 **nickel** *USA* a penny (one cent) – 16 **dime** *USA* 10 cents – 28 **GUAM E PLURIBUS UNUM** motto on a 25 cent coin of Guam. Guam is an organized, unincorporated territory of the United States located in the Western Pacific Ocean – 28 **Guahan ITano' ManChamorro Guam –** Land of the Chamorro. The Chamorro are the indigenous people of Guam

"Guam? No, I think it's somewhere else."

Maybe it's how Outsiders spell Room.

The phone starts its screaming in the hall, I run upstairs to get away.

Grandma comes up, crying again. "She's turned the corner." I stare at her.

"Your ma."

"What corner?"

"She's on the mend, she's going to be fine, probably."

I shut my eyes.

* * *

Grandma shakes me awake because she says it's been three hours and she's afraid I won't sleep tonight.

It's hard to talk with Tooth in so I put him in my pocket instead. My nails have still got soap in. I need something sharp to get it out, like Remote.

"Are you missing your ma?"

I shake my head. "Remote."

"You miss your … moat?"

"*Remote.*"

"The TV remote?"

"No, my Remote that used to make Jeep go *vrumm zoom* but then it got broke in Wardrobe."

"Oh," says Grandma, "well, I'm sure we can get them back." I shake my head. "They're in Room."

"Let's make a little list."

"To flush down the toilet?"

Grandma looks all confused. "No, I'll call the police."

"Is it an emergency?"

She shakes her head. "They'll bring your toys over here, once they've finished with them."

I stare at her. "The police can go in Room?"

"They're probably there right this minute," she tells me, "collecting evidence."

"What's evidence?"

"Proof of what happened, to show the judge. Pictures, fingerprints ..."

While I'm writing the list, I think about the black of Track and the hole under Table, all the marks me and Ma made. The judge looking at my picture of the blue octopus.

Grandma says it's a shame to waste such a nice spring day, so if I put on a long shirt and my proper shoes and hat and shades and lots of sunblock I can come out in the backyard.

She squirts sunblock into her hands. "You say go and stop, whenever you like. Like remote control."

That's kind of funny.

She starts rubbing it on my back of hands.

"Stop!" After a minute I say, "Go," and she starts again. "Go." She stops. "You mean keep going?"

"Yeah."

She does my face. I don't like it near my eyes but she's careful. "Go."

"Actually we're all done, Jack. Ready?"

Grandma goes out first through both doors, the glass one and the net one, she waves me out and the light is zigzaggy. We're standing on the deck that's all wooden like the deck of a ship. There's fuzz on it, little bundles. Grandma says it's some kind of pollen from a tree.

"Which one?" I'm staring up at all the differents.

"Can't help you there, I'm afraid."

In Room we knowed what everything was called but in the world there's so much, persons don't even know the names.

Grandma's in one of the wooden chairs wiggling her butt in. There's sticks that break when I stand on them and some yellow tiny leaves and mushy brown ones that she says she asked Leo to deal with back in November.

25 **fuzz** *inf* a hairy substance – 25 **bundle** a number of things held together

"Does Steppa have a job?"

"No, we retired early but of course now our stocks are decimated ..."

"What does that mean?"

She's leaning her head back on the top of the chair, her eyes are shut. "Nothing, don't worry about it."

"Will he die soon?"

Grandma opens her eyes at me.

"Or will it be you first?"

"I'll have you know I'm only fifty-nine, young man."

Ma's only twenty-six. She's turned the corner, does that mean she's coming back yet?

"Nobody's going to die," says Grandma, "don't you fret." "Ma says everybody's going to die sometime."

She squeezes up her mouth, it's got lines around it like sun rays. "You've only just met most of us, mister, so don't be in a hurry to say bye-bye."

I'm looking down into the green bit of the yard. "Where's the hammock?"

"I suppose we could dig it out of the basement, since you're so keen." She gets up with a grunt.

"Me too."

"Sit tight, enjoy the sunshine, I'll be back before you know it." But I'm not sitting, I'm standing.

It's quiet when she's gone, except there's squeaky sounds in the trees, I think it's birds but I don't see. The wind makes the leaves go swishy swishy. I hear a kid shout, maybe in another yard behind the big hedge or else he's invisible. God's yellow face has a cloud on top. Colder suddenly. The world is always changing brightness and hotness and soundness, I never know how it's going to be the next minute. The cloud looks kind of gray blue, I wonder has it got rain inside it. If rain starts dropping on me I'll run in the house before it drowns my skin.

2 **to retire** to stop working because of old age – 2 **stocks** *Wertpapiere* – 3 **to decimate** to destroy (*here*: to lose drastically in value) – 13 **to fret** *inf* to worry – 20 **basement** cellar – 21 **grunt** a short, deep, rough sound – 33 **to drown** Jack means "to get completely covered in water"

There's something going *zzzzz*, I look in the flowers and it's the most amazing thing, an alive bee that's huge with yellow and black bits, it's dancing right inside the flower. "Hi," I say. I put out my finger to stroke it and—

Arghhhhhh,

my hand's exploding the worst hurt I ever. "Ma," I'm screaming, *Ma* in my head, but she's not in the backyard and she's not in my head and she's not anywhere, I'm all alone in the hurt in the hurt in the hurt in—

"What did you do to yourself?" Grandma rushes across the deck.

"I didn't, it was the bee."

When she spreads the special ointment it doesn't hurt quite as much but still a lot.

I have to use my other hand for helping her. The hammock hangs on hooks in two trees at the very back of the yard, one is a shortish tree that's only twice my tall and bent over, one is a million times high with silvery leaves. The rope bits are kind of squished from being in the basement, we need to keep pulling till the holes are the right size. Also two of the ropes are broken so there's extra holes that we have to not sit in. "Probably moths," says Grandma.

I didn't know moths grow big enough to break ropes.

"To be honest, we haven't put it up for years." She says she won't risk climbing in, anyway she prefers some back support.

I stretch out and fill the hammock all myself. I wriggle my feet in my shoes, I put them through the holes, and my hands, but not my right one because that's still agonizing from the bee. I think about the little Ma and little Paul that swinged in the hammock, it's weird, where are they now? The big Paul is with Deana and Bronwyn maybe, they said we'd go see the dinosaurs another day but I think they were lying. The big Ma is at the Clinic turning the corner.

13 **ointment** an oily substance which is used to heal the skin – 16 **hook** a piece of metal for hanging things on (*Haken*) – 22 **moth** an insect (*Motte*)

I push the ropes, I'm a fly inside a web. Or a robber Spider-Man catched. Grandma pushes and I swing so I'm dizzy but a cool kind of dizzy.

"Phone." That's Steppa on the deck, shouting.

Grandma runs up the grass, she leaves me all on my own again in the outside Outside. I jump down off the hammock and nearly fall because one shoe gets stuck. I pull my foot out, the shoe falls off. I run after, I'm nearly as fast as her.

In the kitchen Grandma's talking on the phone. "Of course, first things first, he's right here. There's somebody wants to talk to you." That's me she's telling, she holds out the phone but I don't take it. "Guess who?"

I blink at her.

"It's your ma."

It's true, here's Ma's voice in the phone. "Jack?"

"Hi."

I don't hear anything else so I pass it back to Grandma.

"It's me again, how are you doing, really?" Grandma asks. She nods and nods and says, "He's keeping his chin up."

She gives me the phone again, I listen to Ma say sorry a lot. "You're not poisoned with the bad medicine anymore?" I ask. "No, no, I'm getting better."

"You're not in Heaven?"

Grandma covers her mouth.

Ma makes a sound I can't tell if it's a cry or a laugh. "I wish." "Why you wish you're in Heaven?"

"I don't really, I was just joking."

"It's not a funny joke."

"No."

"Don't wish."

"OK. I'm here at the clinic."

"Were you tired of playing?"

I don't hear anything, I think she's gone. "Ma?"

"I was tired," she says. "I made a mistake."

19 **to keep one's chin up** *inf* to try to stay cheerful in a difficult situation

"You're not tired anymore?"

She doesn't say anything. Then she says, "I am. But it's OK."

"Can you come here and swing in the hammock?"

"Pretty soon," she says.

"When?"

"I don't know, it depends. Is everything OK there with Grandma?"

"And Steppa."

"Right. What's new?"

"Everything," I say.

That makes her laugh, I don't know why. "Have you been having fun?"

"The sun burned my skin off and a bee stinged me."

Grandma rolls her eyes.

Ma says something I don't hear. "I've got to go now, Jack, I need some more sleep."

"You'll wake up after?"

"I promise. I'm so—" Her breath sounds all raggedy. "I'll talk to you again soon, OK?"

"OK."

There's no more talking so I put the phone down. Grandma says, "Where's your other shoe?"

* * *

I'm watching the flames dancing all orange under the pasta pot. The match is on the counter with its end all black and curly. I touch it to the fire, it makes a hiss and gets a big flame again so I drop it on the stove. The little flame goes invisible nearly, it's nibbling along the match little by little till it's all black and a small smoke goes up like a silvery ribbon. The smell is magic. I take another match from the box, I light the end in the fire and this time I hold on to it even when it hisses. It's my own little

18 **raggedy** Jack means "ragged" (old and torn) – 28 **to nibble** to eat with small bites – 29 **ribbon** a long narrow strip

flame I can carry around with me. I wave it in a circle, I think it's gone out but it comes back. The flame's getting bigger and messy all along the match, it's two different flames and there's a little line of red along the wood between them—

"Hey!"

I jump, it's Steppa. I don't have the match anymore.

He stamps on my foot.

I howl.

"It was on your sock." He shows me the match all curled up, he rubs my sock where there's a black bit. "Didn't your ma ever teach you not to play with fire?"

"There wasn't."

"There wasn't what?"

"Fire."

He stares at me. "I guess your stove was electric. Go figure."

"What's up?" Grandma comes in.

"Jack's just learning kitchen tools," says Steppa, stirring the pasta. He holds a thing up and looks at me.

"Grater," I remember.

Grandma's setting the table.

"And this?"

"Garlic masher."

"Garlic *crusher*. Way more violent than mashing." He grins at me. He didn't tell Grandma about the match, that's kind of lying but not getting me into trouble is a good reason. He's holding up something else.

"Another grater?"

"Citrus zester. And this?"

"Ah … a whisk."

Steppa dangles a long pasta in the air and slurps it. "My elder brother pulled a pot of rice down on himself when he was three, and his arm was always rippled like a chip."

8 **to howl** to shout in pain – 15 **"Go figure"** *inf* "Go and figure it out.", meaning: "I should have known." or: "Yes, but there's no point in me trying to work out why this is true." – 19 **grater** a kitchen tool (*Raspel, Reibe*) – 22 **garlic** *Knoblauch* – 28 **zester** a tool which is used to grate a lemon – 29 **whisk** a small tool for beating eggs or whipping cream – 32 **rippled** wavy – 32 **chip** *AE* potato chip

"Oh, yeah, I saw them in TV."

Grandma stares at me. "Don't tell me you've never had potato chips?" Then she gets up on the steps and moves things in a cabinet.

"E.T.A. two minutes," says Steppa.

"Oh, a handful won't hurt." Grandma climbs down with a scrunched bag and opens it out.

The chips have got all lines on them, I take one and eat the edge of it. Then I say, "No, thanks," and put it back in the bag.

Steppa laughs, I don't know what's funny. "The boy's saving himself for my tagliatelle carbonara."

"Can I see the skin instead?"

"What skin?" asks Grandma.

"The brother's."

"Oh, he lives in Mexico. He's your, I guess, your great-uncle." Steppa throws all the water into the sink so it makes a big cloud of wet air.

"Why is he great?"

"It just means he's Leo's brother. All our relatives, you're related to them now too," says Grandma. "What's ours is yours."

"LEGO," says Steppa.

"What?" she says.

"Like LEGO. Bits of families stuck together."

"I saw that in TV too," I tell them.

Grandma's staring at me again. "Growing up without LEGO," she tells Steppa, "I literally can't imagine it."

"Bet there's a couple billion children in the world managing somehow," says Steppa.

"I guess you're right." She's looking confused. "We must have a box of it kicking around down in the basement, though ..."

5 **E.T.A.** *abb* **"Estimated Time of Arrival"** (usually used for journeys; Steppa is saying that the chips will arrive in two minutes – whereas he has taken much longer to cook the pasta) – 27 **literally** really

Steppa cracks an egg with one hand so it plops over the pasta. "Dinner is served."

* * *

I'm riding lots on the bike that doesn't move, I can reach the pedals with my toes if I stretch. I zoom it for thousands of hours so my legs will get super strong and I can run away back to Ma and save her again. I lie down on the blue mats, my legs are tired. I lift the free weights, I don't know what's free about them. I put one on my tummy, I like how it holds me down so I won't fall off the spinny world.

Ding-dong, Grandma shouts because it's a visitor for me, that's Dr. Clay.

We sit on the deck, he'll warn me if there's any bees. Humans and bees should just wave, no touching. No patting a dog unless its human says OK, no running across roads, no touching private parts except mine in private. Then there's special cases, like police are allowed shoot guns but only at bad guys. There's too many rules to fit in my head, so we make a list with Dr. Clay's extra-heavy golden pen. Then another list of all the new things, like free weights and potato chips and birds. "Is it exciting seeing them for real, not just on TV?" he asks.

"Yeah. Except nothing in TV ever stinged me."

"Good point," says Dr. Clay, nodding. " 'Human kind cannot bear very much reality.' "

"Is that a poem again?"

"How did you guess?"

"You do a weird voice," I tell him. "What's humankind?"

"The human race, all of us."

"Is that me too?"

1 **to plop** *inf* to fall with a plopping sound – 5 **to zoom** *inf* to move quickly – 10 **spinny** Jack means "a world that turns around fast" – 15 **human** Jack means "the dog's owner" – 23 **'Human kind cannot bear very much reality.'** a quote from the famous poem: 'Burnt Norton' (1935), which is one of a series of 'The Four Quartets', by T.S. Eliot, a British/U.S. American poet (1888–1965)

"Oh, for sure, you're one of us."

"And Ma."

Dr. Clay nods. "She's one too."

But what I actually meant was, maybe I'm a human but I'm a me-and-Ma as well. I don't know a word for us two. Roomers? "Is she coming to get me soon?"

"As soon as she possibly can," he says. "Would you feel more comfortable staying at the clinic instead of here at your Grandma's?"

"With Ma in Room Number Seven?"

He shakes his head. "She's in the other wing, she needs to be on her own for a while."

I think he's wrong, if I was sick I'd need Ma with me even more. "But she's working really hard to get better," he tells me.

I thought people are just sick or better, I didn't know it was work.

For good-bye, me and Dr. Clay do high five, low five, back five.

When I'm on the toilet I hear him on the porch with Grandma. Her voice is twice the high of his. "For Pete's sake, we're only talking about a minor sunburn and a bee sting," she says. "I raised two children, don't give me *acceptable standard of care.*"

* * *

In the night there's a million of tiny computers talking to each other about me. Ma's gone up the beanstalk and I'm down on earth shaking it and shaking it so she'll fall down—

No. That was only dreaming.

"I've had a brainwave," says Grandma in my ear, she's leaning down with her bottom half still in her bed. "Let's drive to the playground before breakfast so there'll be no other kids there."

17 **high five, low five, back five** when two people clap hands with each other – 21 **minor** *here*: little – 25 **beanstalk** *Bohnenstange* – 28 **brainwave** *inf* a sudden clever idea

Our shadows are really long and stretchy. I wave my giant fists. Grandma nearly sits on a bench, but there's wet on it, so she leans against the fence instead. There's a small wet on everything, she says it's dew that looks like rain but not out of the sky, it's a kind of sweat that happens in the night. I draw a face on the slide. "It doesn't matter if you get your clothes wet, feel free."

"Actually I feel cold."

There's a bit with all sand in, Grandma says I could sit in that and play with it.

"What?"

"Huh?" she says.

"Play what?"

"I don't know, dig it or scoop it or something."

I touch it but it's scratchy, I don't want it all over me.

"What about the climber, or the swings?" says Grandma. "Are you going to?"

She does a little laugh, she says she'd probably break something. "Why you'd—?"

"Oh, not on purpose, just because I'm heavy."

I go up some steps, standing like a boy not like a monkey, they're metal with rough orange bits called rust and the holding-on bars make my hands frozen. At the end there's a tiny house like for elves, I sit at the table and the roof's right over my head, it's red and the table is blue.

"Yoo-hoo."

I jump, it's Grandma waving through the window. Then she goes around the other side and waves again. I wave back, she likes that.

At the corner of the table I see something move, it's a tiny spider. I wonder if Spider is still in Room, if her web is getting bigger and bigger. I tap tunes, like Hum but only tapping and

4 **dew** small drops of water which form during the night (*Tau*) – 6 **slide** Children slide down it in a playground (*Rutsche*) – 14 **to scoop** to take up or out – 16 **swing** Children play on it in a playground (*Schaukel*) – 23 **bar** a long piece of solid metal – 32 **to tap** to hit the floor lightly and rhythmically with one's foot

Ma in my head has to guess, she guesses most of them right. When I do them on the floor with my shoe it's different-sounding because it's metal. The wall says something I can't read, all scribbled and there's a drawing that I think is a penis but it's as big as the person.

"Try the slide, Jack, it looks like a fun one."

That's Grandma calling at me. I go out of the little house and look down, the slide is silver with some little stones on.

"Whee! Come on, I'll catch you at the bottom."

"No, thanks."

There's a ladder of rope like the hammock but flopping down, it's too sore for my fingers. There's lots of bars to hang from if I had more stronger arms or I really was a monkey. There's a bit I show Grandma where robbers must have took the steps away.

"No, look, there's a fireman's pole there instead," she says. "Oh, yeah, I saw that in TV. But why they live up here?" "Who?"

"The firemen."

"Oh, it isn't one of their real poles, just a play one."

When I was four I thought everything in TV was just TV, then I was five and Ma unlied about lots of it being pictures of real and Outside being totally real. Now I'm in Outside but it turns out lots of it isn't real at all.

I go back in the elf house. The spider's gone somewhere. I take off my shoes under the table and stretch my feet.

Grandma's at the swings. Two are flat but the third has a rubbery bucket with holes for legs. "You couldn't fall out of this one," she says. "Want a go?"

She has to lift me, it feels strange with her hands squeezing in my armpits. She pushes me at the back of the bucket but I don't like that, I keep twisting around to see, so she pushes me from in front instead. I'm swinging faster faster higher higher, it's the strangest thing I ever.

"Put your head back."

"Why?"

12 **sore** painful – 15 **pole** a long straight round stick or post – 26 **rubbery** strong and elastic like rubber (*Gummi*) – 26 **bucket** an open container usually with a handle

"Trust me."

I put my head back and everything flips upside down, the sky and trees and houses and Grandma and all, it's unbelievable.

There's a girl on the other swing, I didn't even see her coming in. She's swinging not at the same time as me, she's back when I'm forward. "What's your name?" she asks.

I pretend I don't hear.

"This is Ja—Jason," says Grandma.

Why she's calling me that?

"I'm Cora and I'm four and a half," says the girl. "Is she a baby?" "He's a boy and he's five, actually," says Grandma.

"Then why is she in the baby swing?"

I want to get out now but my legs are stuck in the rubber, I kick, I pull at the chains.

"Easy, easy," says Grandma.

"Is she having a fit?" asks the girl Cora.

My foot kicks Grandma by accident.

"Stop that."

"My friend's little brother has fits.",

Grandma yanks me under my arms, my foot goes twisty then I'm out.

She stops at the gate and says, "Shoes, Jack."

I try hard and remember. "They're in the little house."

"Scoot back and get them, then." She waits. "The little girl won't bother you."

But I can't climb when she might be watching.

So Grandma does it and her bum gets stuck in the elf house, she's mad. She Velcros my left shoe up way too tight so I pull it off again and the other one as well. I go in my socks to the white car. She says I'll get glass in my foot but I don't.

My pants are wet from the dew and my socks as well. Steppa's in his recliner with a huge mug, he says, "How did it go?"

"Little by little," says Grandma, going upstairs.

16 **fit** an attack with with strange uncontrolled movements of the body – 20 **to yank** to pull suddenly – 24 **to scoot** *inf* to go quickly – 32 **recliner** a very comfortable armchair in which you can lie back or down

He lets me try his coffee, it makes me shudder.

"Why are places to eat called coffee shops?" I ask him.

"Well, coffee's the most important thing they sell because most of us need it to keep us going, like gas in the car."

Ma only drinks water and milk and juice like me, I wonder what keeps her going. "What do kids have?"

"Ah, kids are just full of beans."

Baked beans keep me going all right but green beans are my enemy food. Grandma made them a few dinners ago and I just pretended I didn't see them on my plate. Now I'm in the world, I'm never going to eat green beans again.

* * *

I'm sitting on the stairs listening to the ladies.

"Mmm. Knows more math than me but can't go down a slide," says Grandma.

That's me, I think.

They're her book club but I don't know why because they're not reading books. She forgot to cancel them so they all came at 03:30 with plates of cakes and stuff. I have three cakes on a little plate but I have to stay out of the way. Also Grandma gave me five keys on a key ring that says *POZZO'S HOUSE OF PIZZA*, I wonder how a house is made of pizza, wouldn't it flop? They're not actually keys to anywhere but they jingle, I got them for promising not to take the key out of the liquor cabinet anymore. The first cake is called coconut, it's yucky. The second is lemon and the third is I don't know but I like it the best.

"You must be worn to the bone," says one of the ladies with the highest voice.

"Heroic," says another.

7 **full of beans** *inf* full of life – 22 **to flop** to fall in an awkward way – 23 **to jingle** to make a pleasant sound like little bells – 24 **liquor cabinet** a cupboard for strong alcoholic drinks – 27 **to be worn to the bone** *inf* to be exhausted

Also I have the camera on borrow, not Steppa's fancy-schmancy one with the giant circle but the one hidden in the eye of Grandma's cell phone, if it rings I have to shout to her and not answer it. So far I have ten pictures, one of my softy shoes, two of the light in the ceiling in the fitness suite, three of the dark in the basement (only the picture came out too bright), four of my hand inside with its lines, five of a hole beside the refrigerator I was hoping it might be a mouse hole, six of my knee in pants, seven of the carpet in the living room up close, eight was meant to be Dora when she was in TV this morning but it's all zigzaggy, nine is Steppa not smiling, ten is out the bedroom window with a gull going by only the gull's not in the photo. I was going to take one of me in the mirror but then I'd be a paparazzi.

"Well, he looks like a little angel from the photos," one of the ladies is saying.

How did she see my ten photos? And I don't look a bit like an angel, they're massive with wings.

"You mean that bit of grainy footage outside the police station?" says Grandma.

"Oh, no, the close-ups, from when they were doing the interview with …"

"My daughter, yes. But close-ups of *Jack?* " She sounds furious. "Oh, honey, they're all over the Internet," says another voice. Then lots are talking all at once. "Didn't you know?" "Everything gets leaked, these days."

"The world's one big oyster."

"Terrible."

"Such horrors, in the news every day, sometimes I just feel like staying in bed with the drapes closed."

"I still can't believe it," says the deep voice. "I remember saying to Bill, seven years back, how could something like this happen to a girl we *know?*"

1 **on borrow** Jack means that he has borrowed (*leihen*) it from Grandma – 1 **fancy-schmancy** *inf* very good and expensive – 19 **grainy** *here*: not clear – 26 **to leak** to let in and out of a hole or crack – 27 **the world is one big oyster** *die Welt steht offen* – 30 **drapes** *AE* curtains

"We all thought she was dead. Of course we never liked to say—"

"And you had such faith."

"Who could have imagined—?"

"Any more tea for anyone?" That's Grandma.

"Well, I don't know. I spent a week in a monastery in Scotland once," says another voice, "it was so peaceful."

My cakes are gone except the coconut. I leave the plate on the step and go up to the bedroom and look at my treasures. I put Tooth back in my mouth for a suck. He doesn't taste like Ma.

* * *

Grandma's finded a big box of LEGOs in the basement that belongs to Paul and Ma. "What would you like to make?" she asks me. "A house? A skyscraper? Maybe a town?"

"Might want to lower your sights a little," says Steppa behind his newspaper.

There's so many tiny pieces all colors, it's like a soup. "Well," says Grandma, "go wild. I've got ironing to do."

I look at the LEGOs but I don't touch in case I break them.

After a minute Steppa puts his paper down. "I haven't done this in too long." He starts grabbing pieces just anyhow and squishing them together so they stick.

"Why you haven't—?"

"Good question, Jack."

"Did you play LEGO with your kids?"

"I don't have any kids."

"How come?"

Steppa shrugs. "Just never happened."

I watch his hands, they're lumpy but clever. "Is there a word for adults when they aren't parents?"

6 **monastery** a building in which monks live – 16 **to lower one's sights** to be less ambitious – 30 **lumpy** uneven

Steppa laughs. "Folks with other things to do?"

"Like what things?"

"Jobs, I guess. Friends. Trips. Hobbies."

"What's hobbies?"

"Ways of spending the weekend. Like, I used to collect coins, old ones from all over the world, I stored them in velvet cases."

"Why?"

"Well, they were easier than kids, no stinky diapers."

That makes me laugh.

He holds out the LEGO bits, they've magically turned into a car. It's got one two three four wheels that turn and a roof and a driver and all.

"How you did that?"

"One piece at a time. You pick one now," he says.

"Which?"

"Anything at all."

I choose a big red square.

Steppa gives me a small bit with a wheel. "Stick that on."

I put it so the bump is under the other bump's hole and I press hard.

He hands me another wheel bit, I push that on.

"Nice bike. *Vroom!*"

He says it so loud I drop the LEGO on the floor and a wheel comes off. "Sorry."

"No need for sorry. Let me show you something." He puts his car on the floor and steps on it, *crunch*. It's in all pieces. "See?" says Steppa. "No problemo. Let's start again."

* * *

Grandma says I smell.

"I wash with the cloth."

"Yeah, but dirt hides in the cracks. So I'm going to run a bath, and you're going to get in it."

6 **to store** to keep – 8 **diaper** *AE* Babies wear diapers. (*Windel*)

She makes the water very high and steamy and she pours in bubble stuff for sparkly hills. The green of the bath is nearly hidden but I know it's still there. "Clothes off, sweetie." She stands with her hands on her hips. "You don't want me to see? You'd rather I was outside the door?"

"No!"

"What's the matter?" She waits. "Do you think without your ma in the bath you'll drown or something?"

I didn't know persons could drown in baths.

"I'll sit right here all the time," she says, patting the lid of the toilet.

I shake my head. "You be in the bath too."

"Me? Oh, Jack, I have my shower every morning. What if I sit right on the edge of the bath like this?"

"In it."

Grandma stares at me. Then she groans, she says, "OK, if that's what it takes, just this once... . But I'm wearing my swimsuit."

"I don't know to swim."

"No, we won't actually be swimming, I just, I'd rather not be naked if that's all right with you."

"Does it make you scared?"

"No," she says, "I just—I'd rather not, if you don't mind."

"Can I be naked?"

"Of course, you're a kid."

In Room we were sometimes naked and sometimes dressed, we never minded.

"Jack, can we just get in this bath before it's cold?"

It's not nearly cold, there's still steam flying off it. I start taking off my clothes. Grandma says she'll be back in a sec.

Statues can be naked even if they're adults, or maybe they have to be. Steppa says that's because they're trying to look like

2 **sparkly** shiny – 10 **to pat** to hit gently and repeatedly with the palm of your hand – 18 **swimsuit** In the U.S., public nudity is taboo, e.g. it is usual to wear swimsuits in a public sauna. Jack does not know this and is confused. – 23 **if you don't mind** if that is alright – 30 **sec** *abb* second

old statues that were always naked because the old Romans thought bodies are the most beautiful thing. I lean against the bath but the hard outside is cold on my tummy. There's that bit in *Alice,*

They told me you had been to her
And mentioned me to him,
She gave me a good character
But said I could not swim.

My fingers are scuba divers. The soap falls in the water and I play it's a shark. Grandma comes in with a stripey thing on like underwear and T-shirt stuck together with beads, also a plastic bag on her head she says is called a shower cap even though we're having a bath. I don't laugh at her, only inside.

When she climbs in the bath the water gets higher, I get in too and it's nearly spilling. She's at the smooth end, Ma always sat at the faucet end. I make sure I don't touch Grandma's legs with my legs. I bang my head on a faucet.

"Careful."

Why do persons only say that after the hurt?

Grandma doesn't remember any bath games except "Row, Row, Row Your Boat," when we try that it makes a slosh on the floor.

She doesn't have any toys. I play the nailbrush is a submarine that brushes the seabed, it finds the soap that's a gooey jellyfish.

After we dry ourselves, I'm scratching my nose and a bit comes off in my nail. In the mirror there's little scaly circles where some of me is peeling off.

Steppa's come in for his slippers. "I used to love this ..." He touches my shoulder and suddenly there's a strip of all thin and white,

9 **scuba diver** *Taucher* – 11 **beads** tiny balls which (*here*) function as buttons – 15 **to spill** *AE* to pour by accident over the edge of a container – 16 **faucet** *AE* tap – 24 **jellyfish** a sea creature with a nearly transparent body (*Qualle*) – 27 **scaly** *schuppig*

I didn't feel it go. He holds it out for me to take. "That's a goody."

"Stop that," says Grandma.

I rub the white thing and it rolls up, a tiny dried ball of me. "Again," I say.

"Hang on, let me find a long bit on your back ..."

"Men," says Grandma, making a face.

* * *

This morning the kitchen's empty. I get the scissors from the drawer and cut my ponytail all off.

Grandma comes in and stares. "Well, I'm going to just tidy you up, if I may," she says, "and then you can get the brush and pan. Really we should keep a piece, as it's your first haircut ..."

Most goes in the trash but she takes three long bits and makes a braid that's a bracelet for me with green thread on the end.

She says go look in a mirror but first I check my muscles, I still have my strong.

* * *

The newspaper at the top says *Saturday April 17,* that means I've been at Grandma and Steppa's house one whole week. I was one week in the Clinic before, that equals two weeks I've been in the world. I keep adding it up to check, because it feels like a million years and Ma's still not coming for me.

Grandma says we have to get out of this house. Nobody would know me now my hair's all short and going curly. She tells me to take my shades off because my eyes must be used to Outside now and besides the shades will only attract attention.

We cross lots of roads holding hands and not letting the cars squish us. I don't like the holding hands, I pretend they're some

2 **goody** *inf* a good one – 15 **braid** *Zopf* – 15 **bracelet** a band worn round the wrist (*Armband*) – 29 **to squish** *here*: Jack means "crush"

boy else's she's holding. Then Grandma has a good idea, I can hold on to the chain of her purse instead.

There's lots of every kind of thing in the world but it all costs money, even stuff to throw away, like the man in the line ahead of us in the convenience store buys a something in a box and rips the box and puts it in the trash right away. The little cards with numbers all over are called a lottery, idiots buy them hoping to get magicked into millionaires.

In the post office we buy stamps, we send Ma a picture I did of me in a rocket ship.

We go in a skyscraper that's Paul's office, he says he's crazy busy but he makes a Xerox of my hands and buys me a candy bar out of the vending machine. Going down in the elevator pressing the buttons, I play I'm actually inside a vending machine.

We go in a bit of the government to get Grandma a new Social Security card because she lost the old one, we have to wait for years and years. Afterwards she takes me in a coffee shop where there's no green beans, I choose a cookie bigger than my face.

There's a baby having some, I never saw that. "I like the left," I say, pointing. "Do you like the left best?" But the baby's not listening.

Grandma's pulling me away. "Sorry about that."

The woman puts her scarf over so I can't see the baby's face. "She wanted to be private," Grandma whispers.

I didn't know persons could be private out in the world.

We go in a Laundromat just to see. I want to climb in a spinny machine but Grandma says it would kill me.

We walk to the park to feed the ducks with Deana and Bronwyn. Bronwyn throws all her breads in at one go and the plastic bag too and Grandma has to get it out with a stick.

2 **purse** bag – 5 **convenience store** a shop where you can buy everything – 8 **to get magicked** Jack means "to become a millionaire by magic" – 12 **Xerox** photocopy – 12 **candy bar** *AE* a bar of chocolate or sweets – 13 **vending machine** a machine in a public place from which articles can be bought by putting a coin into it – 27 **laundromat** *AE* a public place where people do their washing – 27 **spinny machine** Jack means "spin drier"

Bronwyn wants my breads, Grandma says I have to give her half because she's little. Deana says she's sorry about the dinosaurs, we'll definitely make it to the Natural History Museum one of these days.

There's a store that's only shoes outside, bright spongy ones with holes all over them and Grandma lets me try on a pair, I choose yellow. There's no laces or Velcro even, I just put my foot in. They're so light it's like not having any on. We go in and Grandma pays five dollar papers for the shoes, that's the same as twenty quarters, I tell her I love them.

When we come out there's a woman sitting on the ground with her hat off. Grandma gives me two quarters and points to the hat.

I put one in the hat and I run after Grandma.

When she's doing my seat belt she says, "What's that in your hand?"

I hold up the second coin, "It's NEBRASKA, I'm keeping it for my treasures."

She clicks her tongue and takes it back. "You should have given it to the street person like I told you to."

"OK, I'll—"

"Too late now."

She starts the car. All I can see is the back of her yellowy hair. "Why she's a street person?"

"That's where she lives, on the street. No bed even."

Now I feel bad I didn't give her the second quarter.

Grandma says that's called having a conscience.

In a store window I see squares that are like Room, cork tiles, Grandma lets me go in to stroke one and smell it but she won't buy it.

We go in a car wash, the brushes swish us all over but the water doesn't come in our tight windows, it's hilarious.

In the world I notice persons are nearly always stressed and have no time. Even Grandma often says that, but she and

5 **spongy** soft, like a sponge (*Schwamm*) – 12 **quarter** *USA* 25 cents – 32 **hilarious** [hɪˈleriəs] very funny

Steppa don't have jobs, so I don't know how persons with jobs do the jobs and all the living as well. In Room me and Ma had time for everything. I guess the time gets spread very thin like butter over all the world, the roads and houses and playgrounds and stores, so there's only a little smear of time on each place, then everyone has to hurry on to the next bit.

Also everywhere I'm looking at kids, adults mostly don't seem to like them, not even the parents do. They call the kids gorgeous and so cute, they make the kids do the thing all over again so they can take a photo, but they don't want to actually play with them, they'd rather drink coffee talking to other adults. Sometimes there's a small kid crying and the Ma of it doesn't even hear.

In the library live millions of books we don't have to pay any moneys for. Giant insects are hanging up, not real, made of paper. Grandma looks under C for *Alice* and she's there, the wrong shape but the same words and pictures, that's so weird. I show Grandma the scariest picture with the Duchess. We sit on the couch for her reading me *The Pied Piper,* I didn't know he was a book as well as a story. My best bit is when the parents hear the laughing inside the rock. They keep shouting for the kids to come back but the kids are in a lovely country, I think it might be Heaven. The mountain never opens up to let the parents in.

There's a big boy doing a computer of Harry Potter, Grandma says not to stand too near, it's not my turn.

There's a tiny world on a table with train tracks and buildings, a little kid is playing with a green truck. I go up, I take a red engine. I zoom it into the kid's truck a bit, the kid giggles. I do it faster so the truck falls off the track, he giggles more.

"Good sharing, Walker." That's a man on the armchair looking at a thing like Uncle Paul's BlackBerry.

I think the kid must be Walker. "Again," he says.

5 **smear** mark or spot – 9 **gorgeous** [ˈgɔːrdʒəs] wonderful – 9 **cute** [kjuːt] sweet – 18 **scary** frightening – 26 **my turn** if it is your turn to do sth, you then have the right or obligation to do it (*an der Reihe sein*)

This time I balance my engine on the little truck, then I take an orange bus and crash it into both of them.

"Gently," says Grandma, but Walker is saying, "Again," and jumping up and down.

Another man comes in and kisses the first one and then Walker. "Say bye-bye to your friend," he tells him.

Is that me?

"Bye-bye." Walker flaps his hand up and down.

I think I'll give him a hug. I do it too fast and knock him down, he bangs on the train table and cries.

"I'm *so* sorry," Grandma keeps saying, "my grandson doesn't—he's learning about boundaries—"

"No harm done," says the first man. They go off with the little boy doing *one two three whee* swinging between them, he's not crying anymore. Grandma watches them, she's looking confused.

"Remember," she says on the way to the white car, "we don't hug strangers. Even nice ones."

"Why not?"

"We just don't, we save our hugs for people we love."

"I love that boy Walker."

"Jack, you never saw him before in your life."

* * *

This morning I spread a bit of syrup on my pancake. It's actually good the two together.

Grandma's tracing around me, she says it's fine to draw on the deck because the next time it rains the chalk will all get washed away. I watch the clouds, if they start raining I'm going to run inside supersonic fast before a drop hits me. "Don't get chalk on me," I tell her.

"Oh, don't be such a worrywart."

12 **boundary** limit – 26 **to trace** *here*: to draw (when Grandma has finished there will be the outline shape of Jack on the ground) – 27 **deck** *AE* patio, terrace – 31 **worrywart** *AE, inf* a person who worries too much about little things

She pulls me up to standing and there's a kid shape on the patio, it's me. I have a huge head, no face, no insides, blobby hands.

"Delivery for you, Jack." That's Steppa shouting, what does he mean?

When I go in the house he's cutting a big box. He pulls out something huge and he says, "Well, this can go in the trash for starters."

She unrolls. "Rug," I give her a huge hug, "she's our Rug, mine and Ma's."

He lifts up his hands and says, "Suit yourself."

Grandma's face is twisting. "Maybe if you took it outside and gave it a good beating, Leo …"

"No!" I'm shouting.

"OK, I'll use the vacuum, but I don't like to think what's in here …" She rubs Rug between her fingers.

I have to keep Rug on my blow-up in the bedroom, I'm not to drag her all around the house. So I sit with her over my head like a tent, her smell is just like I remember and the feel. Under there I've got other things the police brung too. I give Jeep and Remote especially big kisses, and Meltedy Spoon. I wish Remote wasn't broken so he could make Jeep go. Wordy Ball is flatter than I remember and Red Balloon is hardly at all. Spaceship is here but his rocket blaster's missing, he doesn't look very good. No Fort or Labyrinth, maybe they were too big to go in the boxes. I have my five books, even *Dylan*. I get out the other *Dylan*, the new one I took from the mall because I thought he was my one but the new is way shinier. Grandma says there's thousands of each book in the world so thousands of persons can be reading the same at the same minute, it makes me dizzy. New Dylan says, "Hello, Dylan, nice to meet you."

"I'm Jack's Dylan," says Old Dylan.

"I'm Jack's one too," says New.

2 **blobby** Jack means: "indistinct, not clear" (probably "without fingers") – 4 **delivery** *here*: sth brought e.g. in the post – 7 **for starters** *inf* to begin with – 11 **"Suit yourself."** *inf* "Do what you like!" – 18 **to drag** to pull along

"Yeah, but actually I was Jack's first."

Then Old and New bash each other with corners till a page of New rips and I stop because I've ripped a book and Ma will be mad. She's not here to be mad, she doesn't even know, I'm crying and crying and I zip away the books in my Dora bag so they don't get cried on. The two Dylans cuddle up together inside and say sorry.

I find Tooth under the blow-up and suck him till he feels like he's one of mine.

The windows are making funny noises, it's drops of rain. I go close, I'm not very scared so long as the glass is between. I put my nose right on it, it's all blurry from the rain, the drops melt together and turn into long rivers down down down the glass.

* * *

Me and Grandma and Steppa are all three going in the white car on a surprise trip. "But how do you know which way?" I ask Grandma when she's driving.

She winks at me in the mirror. "It's only a surprise for *you*."

I watch out the window for new things. A girl in a wheelchair with her head back between two padded things. A dog sniffing another dog's butt, that's funny. There's a metal box for mailing mail in. A plastic bag blowing.

I think I sleep a bit but I'm not sure.

We're stopped in a parking lot that has dusty stuff all over the lines.

"Guess what?" asks Steppa, pointing.

"Sugar?"

"Sand," he says. "Getting warmer?"

"No, I'm cold."

"He means, are you figuring out where we are? Someplace me and your Grandpa used to bring your ma and Paul when they were little?"

20 **padded things** Jack probably means "cushions"

I look a long way. "Mountains?"

"Sand dunes. And in between those two, the blue stuff?"

"Sky."

"But underneath. The darker blue at the bottom."

My eyes are hurting even through my shades.

"The sea!" says Grandma.

I go behind them along the wooden path, I carry the bucket. It's not like I thought, the wind keeps putting tiny stones in my eyes. Grandma spreads out a big flowery rug, it's going to get all sandy but she says that's OK, it's a picnic blanket.

"Where's the picnic?"

"It's a bit early in the year for that."

Steppa says why don't we go down to the water.

I've got sand in my shoes, one of them comes off. "That's an idea," says Steppa. He takes his both off and puts his socks in them, he swings them from the laces.

I put my socks in my shoes too. The sand is all damp and strange on my feet, there's prickly bits. Ma never said the beach was like this.

"Let's go," says Steppa, he starts running at the sea.

I stay far back because there's huge growing bits with white stuff on top, they roar and crash. The sea never stops growling and it's too big, we're not meant to be here.

I go back to Grandma on the picnic blanket. She's wriggling her bare toes, they're all wrinkly.

We try to build a sand castle but it's the wrong kind of sand, it keeps crumbling.

Steppa comes back with his pants rolled up and dripping. "Didn't feel like paddling?"

"There's all poo."

"Where?"

"In the sea. Our poos go down the pipes to the sea, I don't want to walk in it."

18 **prickly** *stachelig* – 25 **wrinkly** full of wrinkles, lines on the skin because of old age

Steppa laughs. "Your mother doesn't know much about plumbing, does she?"

I want to hit him. "Ma knows about everything."

"There's like a big factory where the pipes from all the toilets go." He's sitting on the blanket with his feet all sandy. "The guys there scoop out all the poo and scrub every drop of water till it's good enough to drink, then they put it back in the pipes so it pours out our faucets again."

"When does it go to the sea?"

He shakes his head. "I think the sea's just rain and salt."

"Ever taste a tear?" asks Grandma.

"Yeah."

"Well, that's the same as the sea."

I still don't want to walk in it if it's tears.

But I go back down near the water with Steppa to look for treasure. We find a white shell like a snail, but when I curl my finger inside, he's gone out. "Keep it," says Steppa.

"But what about when he comes home?"

"Well," says Steppa, "I don't think he'd leave it lying around if he still needed it."

Maybe a bird ate him. Or a lion. I put the shell in my pocket, and a pink one, and a black one, and a long dangerous one called a razor shell. I'm allowed take them home because finders keepers, losers weepers.

We have our lunch at a diner which doesn't mean just have dinner but food anytime at all. I have a BLT that's a hot sandwich of lettuce and tomato with bacons hidden inside.

Driving home I see the playground but it's all wrong, the swings are on the opposite side.

2 **plumbing** *here*: *Abwassersystem* – 6 **to scoop** to take out (usually with a spoon) – 6 **to scrub** to clean – 11 **tear** [tɪr] a drop of liquid that flows from the eye – 16 **snail** a soft creature with a shell on its back (*Schnecke*) – 23 **razor** a sharp instrument to remove hair that grows on a man's face – 24 **finders keepers, losers weepers** (children's rhyme) *Wers findet, dem gehörts, wers verloren hat, kann heulen.* – 25 **diner** ['daɪnɚ] *USA* a small, cheap restaurant where you get simple food all day long – 27 **lettuce** *Blattsalat*

"Oh, Jack, that's a different one," says Grandma. There's playgrounds in every town."

Lots of the world seems to be a repeat.

* * *

"Noreen tells me you've had a haircut." Ma's voice is tiny on the phone.

"Yeah. But I still have my strong." I'm sitting under Rug with the phone, all in the dark to pretend Ma's right here. "I have baths on my own now," I tell her. "I've been on swings and I know money and fire and street persons and I've got two *Dylan the Digger*s and a conscience and spongy shoes."

"Wow."

"Oh and I've seen the sea, there's no poo in it, you were tricking me."

"You had so many questions," says Ma. "And I didn't have all the answers, so I had to make some up."

I hear her crying breath.

"Ma, can you come get me tonight?"

"Not quite yet."

"Why not?"

"They're still fiddling with my dosage, trying to figure out what I need."

Me, she needs me. Can't she figure that out?

* * *

I want to eat my pad thai with Meltedy Spoon but Grandma says it's unhygienic.

11 **conscience** ['kɑːntʃənts] the part of your mind that tells you what you are doing is right or wrong (*Gewissen*) – 21 **to fiddle** *here*: to experiment – 21 **dosage** the amount of pills a person has to take – 25 **pad thai** a meal that originates in Thailand

Later I'm in the living room channel surfing, that means looking at all the planets as fast as a surfer, and I hear my name, not in real but in TV.

"… need to listen to Jack."

"We're all Jack, in a sense," says another man sitting at the big table.

"Obviously," says another one.

Are they called Jack too, are they some of the million?

"The inner child, trapped in our personal Room one oh one," says another of the men, nodding.

I don't think I was ever in that room.

"But then perversely, on release, finding ourselves alone in a crowd …"

"Reeling from the sensory overload of modernity," says the first one.

"*Post*-modernity."

There's a woman too. "But surely, at a symbolic level, Jack's the child sacrifice," she says, "cemented into the foundations to placate the spirits."

Huh?

"I would have thought the more relevant archetype here is Perseus—born to a walled-up virgin, set adrift in a wooden box, the victim who returns as hero," says one of the men.

"Of course Kaspar Hauser famously claimed he'd been happy in his dungeon, but perhaps he really meant that nineteenth-century German society was just a bigger dungeon."

"At least Jack had TV."

12 **on release** when set free – 14 **Reeling from the sensory overload of modernity** The man's theory is that Jack is in a state of shock because modern life contains so many elements that stimulate the senses and the brain. – 18 **sacrifice** *Opfer* – 18 **to cement** to fix in one place, to make firm with cement – 19 **to placate** ['pleɪkeɪt] to calm down (*beschwichtigen*) – 19 **spirits** *here*: the "gods" – 22 **Perseus** in Greek mythology the son of Zeus, who was sent on a fatal mission and returned as a hero – 22 **walled up** imprisoned – 22 **adrift** loose – 24 **Kaspar Hauser** a famous foundling who appeared out of nowhere in Nuremberg in 1828 and claimed he had been hidden in a dark room all his life. His way of speaking and his understanding of the world were limited.

Another man laughs. “Culture as a shadow on the wall of Plato’s cave.”

Grandma comes in and switches it right off, scowling. “It was about me,” I tell her.

“Those guys spent too much time at college.”

“Ma says I have to go to college.”

Grandma’s eyes roll. “All in good time. Pj’s and teeth now.”

She reads me *The Runaway Bunny* but I’m not liking it tonight. I keep thinking what if it was the mother bunny that ran away and hid and the baby bunny couldn’t find her.

* * *

Grandma’s going to buy me a soccer ball, it’s very exciting. I go look at a plastic man with a black rubber suit and flippers, then I see a big stack of suitcases all colors like pink and green and blue, then an escalator. I just step on for a second but I can’t get back up, it zooms me down down down and it’s the coolest thing and scary as well, coolary, that’s a word sandwich, Ma would like it. At the end I have to jump off, I don’t know to get back up to Grandma again. I count my teeth five times, one time I get nineteen instead of twenty. There’s signs everywhere that all say the same thing, *Just Three Weeks to Mother’s Day, Doesn’t She Deserve the Best?* I look at plates and stoves and chairs, then I’m all floppy so I lie down on a bed.

2 **Plato** Greek philosopher and educator (c. 427-347 B.C.). His parable of the cave is an allegory written as a fictional dialogue between Plato’s teacher Socrates and Plato’s brother Glaucon. In the dialogue, Socrates describes a group of prisoners who have lived chained to the wall of a cave all of their lives, facing a blank wall. The prisoners watch shadows projected on the wall by things passing in front of a fire behind them. The shadows are taken to be reality. Socrates then supposes that one prisoner is freed and permitted to stand up. When shown the things that had cast the shadows he does not recognize them for what they are. He believes the shadows on the wall to be more real than what he sees. – 2 **cave** a deep natural hollow place (*Höhle*) – 3 **to scowl** [skaʊl] to frown angrily – 7 **pj’s** Grandma’s way of saying “pyjamas” (*Schlafanzug*) – 15 **escalator** moving staircase (particularly in big shops) – 22 **to deserve** to be worthy of (*etwas verdient haben*) – 23 **floppy** *here*: exhausted

A woman says I'm not allowed so I sit up. "Where's your mom, little guy?"

"She's in the Clinic because she tried to go to Heaven early." The woman's staring at me. "I'm a bonsai."

"You're a what?"

"We were locked up, now we're rap stars."

"Oh my go—you're that boy! The one—Lorana," she shouts, "get over here. You'll never believe it. It's the boy, Jack, the one on TV from the shed."

Another person comes over, shaking her head. "The shed one's smaller with long hair tied back, and all kind of hunched."

"It's him," she says, "I swear it's him."

"No way," says the other one.

"Jose," I say.

She laughs and laughs. "This is unreal. Can I have an autograph?"

"Lorana, he won't know how to sign his name."

"Yes I will," I say, "I can write anything there is."

"You're something else," she tells me. "Isn't he something else?" she says to the other one.

The only paper is old labels from the clothes, I'm writing *JACK* on lots for the women to give to their friends when Grandma runs up with a ball under her arm and I've never seen her so mad. She shouts at the women about *lost child procedures,* she tears my autographs into bits. She yanks me by the hand. When we're rushing out of the store the gate goes *aieeee aieee,* Grandma drops the soccer ball on the carpet.

In the car she won't look at me in the mirror. I ask, "Why you threw away my ball?"

"It was setting off the alarm," says Grandma, "because I hadn't paid."

"Were you robbing?"

12 **hunched** with his body pulled into a round shape (*gekrümmt*) – 26 **procedure** a set of actions necessary for doing sth *here*: *Vorschrift*

"No, Jack," she shouts, "I was running around the building like a lunatic looking for you." Then she says, more quietly, "Anything could have happened."

"Like an earthquake?"

Grandma stares at me in the little mirror. "A stranger might snatch you, Jack, that's what I'm talking about."

A stranger's a not-friend, but the women were my new friends.

"Why?"

"Because they might want a little boy of their own, all right?" It doesn't sound all right.

"Or to hurt you, even."

"You mean him?" Old Nick, but I can't say it.

"No, he can't get out of jail, but somebody like him," says Grandma.

I didn't know there was somebody like him in the world. "Can you go back and get my ball now?" I ask.

She switches on the engine and drives out of the parking lot fast so the wheels screech.

In the car I get madder and madder.

When we get back to the house I put everything in my Dora bag, except my shoes don't fit so I throw them in the trash and I roll Rug up and drag her down the stairs behind me.

Grandma comes into the hall. "Did you wash your hands?"

"I'm going back to the Clinic," I shout at her, "and you can't stop me because you're a, you're a stranger."

"Jack," she says, "put that stinky rug back where it was." "You're the stinky," I roar.

She's pressing on her chest. "Leo," she says over her shoulder, "I swear, I've had just about as much—"

Steppa comes up the stairs and picks me up.

I drop Rug. Steppa kicks my Dora bag out of the way. He's carrying me, I'm screaming and hitting him because it's all-

2 **lunatic** a mad person – 6 **to snatch sb** to take hold of sb and take them away – 19 **to screech** to make an unpleasant, loud, high sound

owed, it's a special case, I can kill him even, I'm killing and killing him—

"Leo," wails Grandma downstairs, "Leo—"

Fee fie foe fum, he's going to rip me in pieces, he's going to wrap me in Rug and bury me and *the worms crawl in, the worms crawl out—*

Steppa drops me on the blow-up, but it doesn't hurt.

He sits down on the end so it all goes up like a wave. I'm still crying and shaking and my snot's getting on the sheet.

I stop crying. I feel under the blow-up for Tooth, I put him in my mouth and suck hard. He doesn't taste like anything anymore.

Steppa's hand is on the sheet just beside me, it's got hairs on the fingers.

His eyes are waiting for my eyes. "All fair and square, water under the bridge?"

I move Tooth to my gum. "What?"

"Want to have pie on the couch and watch the game?" "OK."

* * *

I pick up branches fallen off the trees, even enormous heavy ones. Me and Grandma tie them into bundles with string for the city to take them. "How does the city—?"

"The guys from the city, I mean, the guys whose job it is."

When I grow up my job is going to be a giant, not the eating kind, the kind that catches kids that are falling into the sea maybe and puts them back on land.

I shout, "Dandelion alert," Grandma scoops it out with her trowel so the grass can grow, because there isn't room for everything.

3 **to wail** to shout, making a long and often high-pitched sound – 15 **all fair and square** fairly, in accordance with the rules – 15 **water under the bridge** past events which one can no longer be changed – 18 **pie** [paɪ] a dish filled with pastry and either meat or fruit (e.g. apple pie) – 27 **dandelion** *Löwenzahn* – 27 **alert** warning – 28 **trowel** [traʊəl] a garden tool like a small spade

When we're tired we go in the hammock, even Grandma. "I used to sit like this with your ma when she was a baby."

"Did you give her some?"

"Some what?"

"From your breast."

Grandma shakes her head. "She used to bend back my fingers while she had her bottle."

"Where's the tummy mommy?"

"The—oh, you know about her? I have no idea, I'm afraid."

"Did she get another baby?"

Grandma doesn't say anything. Then she says, "That's a nice thought."

* * *

I'm painting at the kitchen table in Grandma's old apron that has a crocodile and *I Ate Gator on the Bayou*. I'm not doing proper pictures, just splotches and stripes and spirals, I use all the colors, I even mix them in puddles. I like to make a wet bit then fold the paper over like Grandma showed me, so when I unfold it it's a butterfly.

There's Ma in the window.

The red spills. I try and wipe it up but it's all on my foot and the floor. Ma's face isn't there anymore, I run to the window but she's gone. Was I just imagining? I've got red on the window and the sink and the counter. "Grandma?" I shout. "Grandma?"

Then Ma's right behind me.

I run to nearly at her. She goes to hug me but I say, "No, I'm all painty."

She laughs, she undoes my apron and drops it on the table. She holds me hard all over but I keep my sticky hands and foot away. "I wouldn't know you," she says to my head.

"Why you wouldn't—?"

"I guess it's your hair."

15 **bayou** ['baɪu:] a small river with a slow current – 16 **splotch** *AE* an irregular mark or spot – 21 **to spill** to pour out by accident (*verschütten*)

"Look, I have some long in a bracelet, but it keeps getting catched on things."

"Can I have it?"

"Sure."

The bracelet gets some paint on it sliding off my wrist. Ma puts it on hers. She looks different but I don't know how. "Sorry I made you red on your arm."

"It's all washable," says Grandma, coming in.

"You didn't tell him I was coming?" asks Ma, giving her a kiss. "I thought it best not, in case of a hitch."

"There's no hitches."

"Good to hear it." Grandma wipes her eyes and starts cleaning the paint up. "Now, Jack's been sleeping on a blow-up mattress in our room, but I can make you up a bed on the couch ..."

"Actually, we better head off."

Grandma stands still for a minute. "You'll stay for a bit of supper?"

"Sure," says Ma.

Steppa makes pork chops with risotto, I don't like the bone bits but I eat all the rice and scrape the sauce with my fork. Steppa steals a bit of my pork.

"Swiper no swiping."

He groans, "Oh, man!"

Grandma shows me a heavy book with kids she says were Ma and Paul when they were small. I'm working on believing, then I see one of the girl on a beach, the one Grandma and Steppa took me there, and her face is Ma's exact face. I show Ma.

"That's me, all right," she says, turning the page. There's one of Paul waving out of a window in a gigantic banana that's actually a statue, and one of them both eating ice cream in cones with Grandpa but he looks different and Grandma too, she has dark hair in the picture.

2 **catched** Jack means "caught" – 5 **to slide off** to go smoothly over a surface – 10 **hitch** a difficulty which delays sth for a while – 19 **pork chop** *Schweinekotelett* – 20 **to scrape** *here*: to clean or make smooth – 22 **to swipe** *inf* to steal – 31 **cone** *here*: *Eishörnchen*

"Where's one of the hammock?"

"We were in it all the time, so probably nobody ever thought of taking a picture," says Ma.

"It must be terrible to not have any," Grandma tells her. "Any what?" says Ma.

"Pictures of Jack when he was a baby and a toddler," she says. "I mean, just to remember him by."

Ma's face is all blank. "I don't forget a day of it." She looks at her watch, I didn't know she had one, it's got pointy fingers.

"What time are they expecting you at the clinic?" asks Steppa. She shakes her head. "I'm all done with that." She takes something out of her pocket and shakes it, it's a key on a ring. "Guess what, Jack, you and me have our own apartment."

Grandma says her other name. "Is that such a good idea, do you think?"

"It was my idea. It's OK, Mom. There's counselors there around the clock."

"But you've never lived away from home before ..."

Ma's staring at Grandma, and so is Steppa. He lets out a big whoop of laughing.

"It's not funny," says Grandma, whacking him in the chest. "She knows what I mean."

Ma takes me upstairs to pack my stuff.

"Close your eyes," I tell her, "there's surprises." I lead her into the bedroom. "Ta-da." I wait. "It's Rug and lots of our things, the police gave them back."

"So I see," says Ma.

"Look, Jeep and Remote—"

"Let's not cart broken stuff around with us," she says, "just take what you really need and put it in your new Dora bag."

"I need all of it."

Ma breathes out. "Have it your way."

What's my way?

6 **toddler** a small child who has just learnt to walk – 8 **blank** empty – 16 **counselor** an adviser *here*: *Sozialarbeiter* – 20 **whoop** a loud, joyful cry – 21 **to whack** *inf* to beat – 29 **to cart** *inf* to take or remove – 32 **your way** the way you want it

"There's boxes it all came in."

"I said OK."

Steppa puts all our stuff into the back of the white car.

"I must get my license renewed," says Ma when Grandma's driving along.

"You might find you're a bit rusty."

"Oh, I'm rusty at everything," says Ma.

I ask, "Why you're—?"

"Like the Tin Man," Ma says over her shoulder. She lifts her elbow and does a squeak. "Hey, Jack, will we buy a car of our own someday?"

"Yeah. Or actually a helicopter. A super zoomer helicopter train car submarine."

"Now, that sounds like a ride."

It's hours and hours in the car. "How come it's so long?" I ask. "Because it's all the way across the city," says Grandma. "It's practically the next state."

"Mom …"

The sky's getting dark.

Grandma parks where Ma says. There is a big sign. INDEPENDENT LIVING RESIDENTIAL FACILITY. She helps us carry all our boxes and bags in the building that's made of brown bricks, except I pull my Dora on its wheels. We go in a big door with a man called the doorman that smiles. "Does he lock us in?" I whisper to Ma.

"No, just other people out."

There's three women and a man called Support Staff, we're very welcome to buzz down anytime we need help with anything at all, buzzing is like calling on the phone. There's lots of floors, and apartments on each one, mine and Ma's is on six. I tug at her sleeve, I whisper, "Five."

"What's that?"

4 **licence** *here*: driver's license – 6 **rusty** *here*: out of practise, no longer fit – 10 **squeak** a short very high soft sound – 21 **residential facility** a building in which people live for a certain period of time – 23 **brick** baked clay blocks used to build houses with (*Ziegelstein*) – 25 **to lock** to shut with a key – 27 **Support Staff** a group of people who help – 31 **to tug** to pull

"Can we be on five instead?"

"Sorry, we don't get to choose," she says.

When the elevator bangs shut Ma shivers.

"You OK?" asks Grandma.

"Just one more thing to get used to."

Ma has to tap in the secret code to make the elevator shake. My tummy feels odd when it ups. Then the doors open and we're on six already, we flew without knowing it. There's a little hatch that says *INCINERATOR,* when we put trash in it it'll fall down down down and go up in smoke. On the doors it's not numbers it's letters, ours is the B, that means we live in Six B. Six is not a bad number like nine, it's the upside down of it actually. Ma puts the key in the hole, when she turns it she makes a face because of her bad wrist. She's not all fixed yet. "Home," she says, pushing the door open.

How is it home if I've never been here?

An apartment's like a house but all squished flat. There's five rooms, that's lucky, one is the bathroom with a bath so we can have baths not showers. "Can we have one now?"

"Let's get settled in first," says Ma.

The stove does flames like at Grandma's. The next to the kitchen is the living room that has a couch and a low-down table and a super-big TV in it.

Grandma's in the kitchen unpacking a box. "Milk, bagels, I don't know if you've started drinking coffee again... . He likes this alphabet cereal, he spelled out *Volcano* the other day."

Ma puts her arms on Grandma and stops her moving for a minute. "Thanks."

"Should I run out for anything else?"

"No, I think you've thought of everything. 'Night, Mom." Grandma's face is twisted. "You know—"

"What?" Ma waits. "What is it?"

3 **to shiver** to shake slightly – 6 **to tap in** to enter, to hit lightly – 7 **when it ups** Jack means "when it goes up" – 9 **hatch** an opening in the wall (*Luke*) – 9 **incinerator** [ɪnˈsɪnəreɪt̬ɚ] a machine that burns unwanted things – 24 **bagel** [ˈbeɪgəl] a ring shaped bread roll – 26 **cereal** Cornflakes are an example of (breakfast) cereal.

"I didn't forget a day of you either."

They aren't saying anything so I go try the beds for which is bouncier. When I'm doing somersaults I hear them talking a lot. I go around opening and shutting everything.

After Grandma's gone back to her house Ma shows me how to do the bolt, that's like a key that only us on the inside can open or shut.

In bed I remember, I pull her T-shirt up.

"Ah," says Ma, "I don't think there's any in there."

"Yeah, there must be."

"Well, the thing about breasts is, if they don't get drunk from, they figure, *OK, nobody needs our milk anymore, we'll stop making it.*"

"Dumbos. I bet I can find some ..."

"No," says Ma, putting her hand between, "I'm sorry. That's all done. Come here."

We cuddle hard. Her chest goes *boom boom* in my ear, that's the heart of her.

I lift up her T-shirt.

"Jack—"

I kiss the right and say, "Bye-bye." I kiss the left twice because it was always creamier. Ma holds my head so tight I say, "I can't breathe," and she lets go.

* * *

God's face comes up all pale red in my eyes. I blink and make the light come and go. I wait till Ma's breathing is on. "How long do we stay here at the Independent Living?"She yawns. "As long as we like."

"I'd like to stay for one week."

She stretches her whole self. "We'll stay for a week, then, and after that we'll see."

3 **somersault** *Purzelbaum* – 6 **bolt** a metal bar used to fasten (lock) a door – 17 **to cuddle** to hold each other lovingly

I curl her hair like a rope. "I could cut yours and then we'd be the same again."

Ma shakes her head. "I think I'm going to keep mine long."

When we're unpacking there's a big problem, I can't find Tooth.

I look in all my stuff and then all around in case I dropped him last night. I'm trying to remember when I had him in my hand or in my mouth. Not last night but maybe the night before at Grandma's I think I was sucking him. I have a terrible thought, maybe I swallowed him by accident in my sleep.

"What happens to stuff we eat if it's not food?"

Ma's putting socks in her drawer. "Like what?"

I can't tell her I maybe lost a bit of her. "Like a little stone or something."

"Oh, then it just slides on through."

We don't go down in the elevator today, we don't even get dressed. We stay in our Independent Living and learn all the bits. "We could sleep in this room," says Ma, "but you could play in the other one that gets more sunshine."

"With you."

"Well, yeah, but sometimes I'll be doing other things, so maybe during the day our sleeping room could be my room."

What other things?

Ma pours us our cereal, not even counting. I thank Baby Jesus. "I read a book at college that said everyone should have a room of their own," she says.

"Why?"

"To do their thinking in."

"I can do my thinking in a room with you." I wait. "Why you can't think in a room with me?"

Ma makes a face. "I can, most of the time, but it would be nice to have somewhere to go that's just mine, sometimes."

"I don't think so."

She does a long breath. "Let's just try it for today. We could make nameplates and stick them on the doors ..."

"Cool."

We do all different color letters on pages, they say *JACK'S ROOM* and *MA'S ROOM,* then we stick them up with tape, we use all we like.

I have to poo, I look in it but I don't see Tooth.

We're sitting on the couch looking at the vase on the table, it's made of glass but not invisible, it's got all blues and greens. "I don't like the walls," I tell Ma.

"What's wrong with them?"

"They're too white. Hey, you know what, we could buy cork squares from the store and stick them up all over."

"No way Jose." After a minute, she says, "This is a fresh start, remember?"

She says *remember* but she doesn't want to remember Room.

I think of Rug, I run to get her out of the box and I drag her behind me. "Where will Rug go, beside the couch or beside our bed?"

Ma shakes her head.

"But—"

"Jack, it's all frayed and stained from seven years of—I can smell it from here. I had to watch you learn to crawl on that rug, learn to walk, it kept tripping you up. You pooed on it once, another time the soup spilled, I could never get it really clean." Her eyes are all shiny and too big.

"Yeah and I was born on her and I was dead in her too."

"Yeah, so what I'd really like to do is throw it in the incinerator."

"No!"

"If for once in your life you thought about me instead of—"

"I do," I shout. "I thought about you always when you were Gone."

Ma shuts her eyes just for a second. "Tell you what, you can keep it in your own room, but rolled up in the wardrobe. OK? I don't want to have to see it."

20 **frayed** to have loose threads (*ausgefranst*) – 20 **stained** full of spots and marks – 22 **to trip up** to fall

She goes out to the kitchen, I hear her splash the water. I pick up the vase, I throw it at the wall and it goes in a zillion pieces.

"Jack—" Ma's standing there.

I scream, "I don't want to be your little bunny."

I run into *JACK'S ROOM* with Rug pulling behind me getting caught on the door, I drag her into the wardrobe and put her all around me, I sit there for hours and hours and Ma doesn't come.

My face is all stiff where the tears dried. Steppa says that's how they make salt, they catch waves in little ponds then the sun dries them up.

There's a scary sound *bzz bzz bzz,* then I hear Ma talking. "Yeah, I guess, as good a time as any." After a minute I hear her outside the wardrobe, she says, "We've got visitors."

It's Dr. Clay and it's Noreen. They've brought a food called takeout that's noodles and rice and slippery yellow yummy things.

The splintery bits of the vase are all gone, Ma must have disappeared them down the incinerator.

There's a computer for us, Dr. Clay is setting it up so we can do games and send e-mails. Noreen shows me how to do drawings right on the screen with the arrow turned into a paintbrush. I do one of me and Ma in the Independent Living.

"What's all this white scribbly stuff?" asks Noreen.

"That's the space."

"Outer space?"

"No, all the space inside, the air."

"Well, celebrity is a secondary trauma," Dr. Clay is saying to Ma. "Have you given any further thought to new identities?"

Ma shakes her head. "I can't imagine … I'm me and Jack's Jack, right? How could I start calling him Michael or Zane or something?"

4 **bunny** (*used especially by children*) rabbit – 15 **takeout** *AE* a meal bought from a shop to be taken home – 17 **splinter** *Splitter* – 21 **arrow** a thin stick with a point at one end and feathers at the other end (*Pfeil*) – 23 **scribbly stuff** meaningless marks or drawings – 27 **celebrity** [sə'lebrət̬i] a famous person – 27 **secondary** not the main one, i.e. the second one

Why she'd call me Michael or Zane?

"Well, what about a new surname at least," says Dr. Clay, "so he attracts less attention when he starts school?"

"When I start school?"

"Not till you're ready," says Ma, "don't worry."

I don't think I'll ever be ready.

In the evening we have a bath and I lie my head on Ma's tummy in the water nearly sleeping.

We practice being in the two rooms and calling out to each other, but not too loud because there's other persons living in the other Independent Livings that aren't Six B. When I'm in *JACK'S ROOM* and Ma's in *MA'S ROOM*, that's not so bad, only when she's in other rooms but I don't know which, I don't like that.

"It's OK," she says, "I'll always hear you."

We eat more of the takeout hotted again in our microwave, that's the little stove that works super fast by invisible death rays.

"I can't find Tooth," I tell Ma.

"My tooth?"

"Yeah, your bad one that fell out that I kept, I had him all the time but now I think he's lost. Unless maybe I swallowed him, but he's not sliding out in my poo yet."

"Don't worry about it," says Ma.

"But—"

"People move around so much out in the world, things get lost all the time."

"Tooth's not just a thing, I have to have him."

"Trust me, you don't."

"But—"

She holds on to my shoulders. "Bye-bye rotten old tooth. End of story."

She's nearly laughing but I'm not.

18 **ray** a narrow beam of light or stream of energy (*Strahl*)

I think maybe I did swallow him by accident. Maybe he's not going to slide out in my poo, maybe he's going to be hiding inside me in a corner forever.

* * *

In the night, I whisper, "I'm still switched on."

"I know," says Ma. "Me too."

Our bedroom is *MA'S ROOM* that's in the Independent Living that's in America that's stuck on the world that's a blue and green ball a million miles across and always spinning. Outside the world there's Outer Space. I don't know why we don't fall off. Ma says it's gravity, that's an invisible power that keeps us stuck to the ground, but I can't feel it.

God's yellow face comes up, we're watching out the window. "Do you notice," says Ma, "it's a bit earlier every morning?"

There's six windows in our Independent Living, they all show different pictures but some of the same things. My favorite is the bathroom because there's a building site, I can look down on the cranes and diggers. I say all the *Dylan* words to them, they like that.

In the living room I'm doing my Velcro because we're going out. I see the space where the vase used to be till I threw it. "We could ask for another for Sundaytreat," I tell Ma, then I remember.

Her shoes have laces that she's tying. She looks at me, not mad. "You know, you won't ever have to see him again."

"Old Nick." I say the name to see if it sounds scary, it does but not very.

"I'll have to just one more time," says Ma, "when I go to court. It won't be for months and months."

"Why will you have to?"

"Morris says I could do it by video link, but actually I want to look him in his mean little eye."

11 **gravity** the natural force by which objects are attracted to each other – 17 **building site** an area where new houses are being built – 32 **mean** cruel, nasty

Which one is that? I try and remember his eyes. “Maybe *he'll* ask *us* for Sundaytreat, that would be funny.”

Ma does not a nice laugh. She's looking in the mirror, putting black lines around her eyes and purple on her mouth.

“You're like a clown.”

“It's just makeup,” she says, “so I'll look better.”

“You look better always,” I tell her.

She grins at me in the mirror. I put my nose up at the end and my fingers in my ears and wiggle them.

We hold hands but the air is really warm today so they get slippy. We look in the windows of stores, only we don't go in, we just walk. Ma keeps saying that things are ludicrously expensive or else they're junk. “They sell men and women and children in there,” I tell her.

“What?” She spins around. “Oh, no, see, it's a clothes shop, so when it says *Men, Women, Children,* it just means clothes for all those people.”

When we have to cross a street we press the button and wait for the little silver man, he'll keep us safe. There's a thing that looks just concrete, but kids are there squeaking and jumping to get wet, it's called a splash pad. We watch for a while but not too long because Ma says we might seem freaky.

We play I Spy. We buy ice cream that's the best thing in the world, mine is vanilla and Ma's is strawberry. Next time we can have different flavors, there's hundreds. A big lump is cold all the way down and my face aches, Ma shows me to put my hand over my nose and sniff in the warm air. I've been in the world three weeks and a half, I still never know what's going to hurt.

I have some coins that Steppa gave me, I buy Ma a clip for her hair with a ladybug on it but just a pretend one.

She says thanks over and over.

12 **ludicrously** ['lu:dɪkrəsli] ridiculously – 13 **junk** trash, rubbish – 22 **freaky** *inf* strange – 23 **I Spy** a game in which you have to find out (by guessing) what the other person is looking at (has “spied”). You know the first letter. The “spier” says: “I spy with my little eye, something beginning with [say a letter].” – 25 **lump** a mass of sth – 26 **to ache** [eɪk] to hurt – 29 **clip** a small plastic object to fasten things with – 30 **ladybug** *AE Marienkäfer* – 30 **pretend** Jack means “not a real one”

"You can have it forever even when you're dead," I tell her. "Will you be dead before I do?"

"That's the plan."

"Why that's the plan?"

"Well, by the time you're one hundred, I'll be one hundred and twenty-one, and I think my body will be pretty worn out." She's grinning. "I'll be in Heaven getting your room ready."

"Our room," I say.

"OK, our room."

Then I see a phone booth and go in to play I'm Superman changing into his costume, I wave at Ma through the glass. There's little cards with smiley pictures that say *Busty Blonde 18* and *Filipina Shemale,* they're ours because finders keepers losers weepers, but when I show Ma she says they're dirty and makes me throw them in the trash.

For a while we get lost, then she sees the name of the street where the Independent Living is so we weren't really lost. My feet are tired. I think people in the world must be tired all the time.

In the Independent Living I go bare feet, I won't ever like shoes.

The persons in Six C are a woman and two big girls, bigger than me but not all the way big. The woman wears shades all the time even in the elevator and has a crutch to hop with, the girls don't talk I think but I waved my fingers at one and she smiled.

* * *

There's new things every single day.

Grandma brought me a watercolor set, it's ten colors of ovals in a box with an invisible lid. I rinse the little brush clean after each so they don't mix and when the water goes dirty I just get

6 **worn out** *here*: no longer functioning – 10 **booth** a small enclosed place for one person – 12 **busty** with big breasts – 24 **crutch** a stick with a piece that fits under the arm, for supporting a person who has difficulties walking

more. The first time I hold my picture up to show Ma it drips, so after that we dry them flat on the table.

We go to the hammock house and I do amazing LEGO with Steppa of a castle and a zoomermobile.

Grandma can come see us just in the afternoons now because in the mornings she's got a job in a store where people buy new hair and breasts after theirs fall off. Ma and me go peek at her through the door of the store, Grandma doesn't seem like Grandma. Ma says everybody's got a few different selves.

Paul comes to our Independent Living with a surprise for me that's a soccer ball, like the one Grandma threw away in the store. I go down to the park with him, not Ma because she's going to a coffee shop to meet one of her old friends.

"Great," he says. "Again."

"No, you," I say.

Paul does a huge kick, the ball bounces off the building and away in some bushes. "Go for it," he shouts.

When I kick, the ball goes in the pond and I cry.

Paul gets it out with a branch. He kicks it far far. "Want to show me how fast you can run?"

"We had Track around Bed," I tell him. "I can, I did a there-and-back in sixteen steps."

"Wow. I bet you can go even faster now."

I shake my head. "I'll fall over."

"I don't think so," says Paul.

"I always do these days, the world is trippy-uppy."

"Yeah, but this grass is really soft, so even if you do fall, you won't hurt yourself."

There's Bronwyn and Deana coming, I spot them with my sharp eyes.

* * *

7 **to peek** to take a quick look – 16 **to bounce** to spring back – 18 **pond** a small lake – 19 **branch** a tree has many branches (*Ast*) – 26 **is trippy-uppy** Jack means "makes me fall over a lot"

It's a bit hotter every day, Ma says it's unbelievable for April.

Then it rains. She says it might be fun to buy two umbrellas and go out with the rain bouncing off the umbrellas and not wetting us at all, but I don't think so.

The next day it's dry again so we go out, there's puddles but I'm not scared of them, I go in my spongy shoes and my feet get splashed through the holes, that's OK.

Me and Ma have a deal, we're going to try everything one time so we know what we like.

I already like going to the park with my soccer ball and feeding the ducks. I really like the playground now except when that boy came down the slide right after me and kicked me in the back. I like the Natural History Museum except the dinosaurs are just dead ones with bones.

In the bathroom I hear people talking Spanish only Ma says the word for it is Chinese. There's hundreds of different foreign ways to talk, that makes me dizzy.

We look in another museum that's paintings, a bit like our masterpieces that came with the oatmeal but way way bigger, also we can see the stickiness of the paint. I like walking past the whole room of them, but then there's lots of other rooms and I lie down on the bench and the man in the uniform comes over with a not-friendly face so I run away.

Steppa comes to the Independent Living with a super thing for me, a bike they were saving for Bronwyn but I get it first because I'm bigger. It's got shiny faces in the spokes of the wheels. I have to wear a helmet and knee pads and wrist pads when I ride it in the park for if I fall off, but I don't fall off, I've got balance, Steppa says I'm a natural. The third time we go, Ma lets me not wear the pads and in a couple of weeks she's going to take off the stabilizers because I won't need them anymore.

Ma finds a concert that's in a park, not our near park but one where we have to get a bus. I like going on the bus a lot, we look down on people's different hairy heads in the street. At the

26 **spoke** the thin metal strips which hold a bicycle wheel together (*Speichen*)

concert the rule is that the music persons get to make all the noise and we aren't allowed make even one squeak except clapping at the end.

Grandma says why doesn't Ma take me to the zoo but Ma says she couldn't stand the cages.

We go to two different churches. I like the one with the multicolored windows but the organ is too loud.

Also we go to a play, that's when adults dress up and play like kids and everybody else watches. It's in another park, it's called *Midsummer Night*. I'm sitting on the grass with my fingers on my mouth to remember it to stay shut. Some fairies are fighting over a little boy, they say so many words they all smoosh together. Sometimes the fairies disappear and persons all in black move the furniture around. "Like we did in Room," I whisper to Ma, she nearly laughs.

But then the persons sitting near us start calling out, "How now spirit," and "All hail Titania," I get mad and say shush, then I really shout at them to be quiet. Ma pulls me by the hand all the way back to the trees bit and tells me that was called audience participation, it's allowed, it's a special case.

When we get home to the Independent Living we write everything down that we tried, the list's getting long. Then there's things we might try when we're braver.

Going up in an airplane
Having some of Ma's old friends over for dinner
Driving a car
Going to the North Pole
Going to school (me) and college (Ma)
Finding our really own apartment that's not an Independent Living

5 **cage** wild animals in a zoo are kept in a cage – 7 **organ** musical instrument made of pipes (often found in churches) – 8 **play** *Theaterstück* – 11 **fairy** (pl: fairies) a small figure with magical powers – 12 **to smoosh** Jack means: "fall together in one big mess" – 20 **participation** the act of taking part in an event or activity – 23 **brave** courageous (*mutig*)

Inventing something
Making new friends
Living in another country not America
Having a playdate at another kid's house like Baby Jesus and John the Baptist
Taking swimming lessons
Ma going out dancing in the night and me staying at Steppa and Grandma's on the blow-up.
Having jobs
Going to the moon

Most important there's *getting a dog called Lucky*, every day I'm ready but Ma says she's got enough on her plate at the moment, maybe when I'm six.

"When I'll have a cake with candles?"

"Six candles," she says, "I swear."

In the night in our bed that's not Bed, I rub the duvet, it's puffed-upper than Duvet was. When I was four I didn't know about the world, or I thought it was only stories. Then Ma told me about it for real and I thought I knowed everything. But now I'm in the world all the time, I actually don't know much, I'm always confused.

"Ma?"

"Yeah?"

She still smells like her, but not her breasts, they're just breasts now.

"Do you sometimes wish we didn't escape?"

I don't hear anything. Then she says, "No, I never wish that."

* * *

"It's perverse," Ma is telling Dr. Clay, "all those years, I was craving company. But now I don't seem up to it."

4 **playdate** children's meeting (at which they play together) – 12 **on one's plate** *inf* to deal with – 30 **to crave** to long for

He's nodding, they're sipping their steamy coffee, Ma drinks it now like adults do to keep going. I still drink milk but sometimes it's chocolate milk, it tastes like chocolate but it's allowed. I'm on the floor doing a jigsaw with Noreen, it's super hard with twenty-four pieces of a train.

"Most days … Jack's enough for me."

"'The Soul selects her own Society—Then—shuts the Door—'" That's his poem voice.

Ma nods. "Yeah, but it's not how I remember myself." "You had to change to survive."

Noreen looks up. "Don't forget, you'd have changed anyway. Moving into your twenties, having a child—you wouldn't have stayed the same."

Ma just drinks her coffee.

* * *

One day I wonder if the windows open. I try the bathroom one, I figure out the handle and push the glass. I'm scared of the air but I'm being scave, I lean out and put my hands through it. I'm half in half out, it's the most amazing—

"Jack!" Ma pulls me all in by the back of my T-shirt.

"Ow."

"It's a six-story drop, if you fell you'd smash your skull."

"I wasn't falling," I tell her, "I was being in and out at the same time."

"You were being a nutcase at the same time," she tells me, but she's nearly smiling.

I go after her into the kitchen. She's beating eggs in a bowl for French toast. The shells are smashed, we just throw them in the trash, bye-bye. I wonder if they turn into the new eggs. "Do we come back after Heaven?"

I think Ma doesn't hear me.

"Do we grow in tummies again?"

7 **to select** to choose – 21 **skull** the bone of the head – 24 **nutcase** *inf* a silly person – 31 **tummy** *inf* stomach

"That's called reincarnation." She cutting the bread. "Some people think we might come back as donkeys or snails."

"No, humans in the same tummies. If I grow in you again—" Ma lights the flame. "What's your question?"

"Will you still call me Jack?"

She looks at me. "OK."

"Promise?"

"I'll always call you Jack."

* * *

Tomorrow is May Day, that means summer's coming and there's going to be a parade. We might go just to look. "Is it only May Day in the world?" I ask.

We're having granola in our bowls on the sofa not spilling. "What do you mean?" says Ma.

"Is it May Day in Room too?"

"I suppose so, but nobody's there to celebrate it."

"We could go there."

She clangs her spoon into her bowl. "Jack."

"Can we?"

"Do you really, really want to?"

"Yeah."

"Why?"

"I don't know," I tell her.

"Don't you like it outside?"

"Yeah. Not everything."

"Well, no, but mostly? You like it more than Room?"

"Mostly." I eat all the rest of my granola and the bit of Ma's that she left in her bowl. "Can we go back sometime?"

"Not to live."

I shake my head. "Just to visit for one minute."

Ma leans her mouth on her hand. "I don't think I can." "Yeah, you can." I wait. "Is it dangerous?"

13 **granola** *AE* muesli

"No, but just the idea of it, it makes me feel like …"

She doesn't say like what. "I'd hold your hand."

Ma stares at me. "What about going on your own, maybe?"

"No."

"With someone, I mean. With Noreen?"

"No."

"Or Grandma?"

"With you."

"I can't—"

"I'm choosing for both of us," I tell her.

She gets up, I think she's mad. She takes the phone in *MA'S ROOM* and talks to somebody.

Later in the morning the doorman buzzes and says there's a police car here for us.

"Are you still Officer Oh?"

"I sure am," says Officer Oh. "Long time no see."

There's tiny dots on the windows of the police car, I think it's rain. Ma's chewing her thumb. "Bad idea," I tell her, pulling her hand away.

"Yeah." She takes her thumb back and nibbles it again. "I wish he was dead." She's nearly whispering.

I know who she means. "But not in Heaven."

"No, outside it."

"Knock knock knock, but he can't come in."

"Yeah."

"Ha ha."

Two fire trucks go by with sirens. "Grandma says there's more of him."

"What?"

"Persons like him, in the world."

"Ah," says Ma.

"Is it true?"

"Yeah. But the tricky thing is, there's far more people in the middle."

16 **"Long time no see."** *inf* "We haven't seen each other for a long time."

"Where?"

Ma's staring out the window but I don't know at what. "Somewhere between good and bad," she says. "Bits of both stuck together." The dots on the window join up into little rivers.

When we stop, I only know we're there because Officer Oh says "Here we are." I don't remember which house Ma came out of, the night of our Great Escape, the houses all have garages. None of them looks especially like a secret.

Officer Oh says, "I should have brought umbrellas."

"It's only sprinkling," says Ma. She gets out and holds out her hand to me.

I don't undo my seat belt. "The rain will fall on us—"

"Let's get this over with, Jack, because I am not coming back again."

I click it open. I put my head down and squeeze my eyes half shut, Ma leads me along. The rain is on me, my face is wetting, my jacket, my hands a bit. It doesn't hurt, it's just weird.

When we get up close to the door of the house, I know it's Old Nick's house because there's a yellow ribbon that says in black letters *CRIME SCENE DO NOT CROSS*. A big sticker with a scary wolf face that says *BEWARE OF THE DOG*. I point to it, but Ma says, "That's only pretend."

Oh, yeah, the trick dog that was having the fit the day Ma was nineteen.

A man police I don't know opens the door inside, Ma and Officer Oh duck under the yellow ribbon, I only have to go a bit sideways.

The house has lots of rooms with all stuff like fat chairs and the hugest TV I ever saw. But we go right through, there's another door at the back and then it's grass. The rain's still falling but my eyes stay open.

22 **Beware of the dog.** *fml* be careful of the dog. („*Vorsicht: bissiger Hund.*")

“Fifteen-foot hedge all the way around,” Officer Oh is saying to Ma, “neighbors thought nothing of it. ‘A man’s entitled to his privacy,’ et cetera.”

There’s bushes and a hole with more yellow tape on sticks all around it. I remember something. “Ma. Is that where—?”

She stands and stares. “I don’t think I can do this.”

But I’m walking over to the hole. There’s brown things in the mud. “Are they worms?” I ask Officer Oh, my chest is *thump thump thumping.*

“Just tree roots.”

“Where’s the baby?”

Ma’s beside me, she makes a sound.

“We dug her up,” says Officer Oh.

“I didn’t want her to be here anymore,” Ma says, her voice is all scratchy. She clears her throat and asks Officer Oh, “How did you find where—?”

“We’ve got soil-sensitive probes.”

“We’ll put her somewhere better,” Ma tells me.

“Grandma’s garden?”

“Tell you what, we could—we could turn her bones into ash and sprinkle it under the hammock.”

“Will she grow again then and be my sister?”

Ma shakes her head. Her face is all stripey wet.

There’s more rain on me. It’s not like a shower, softer.

Ma’s turned around, she’s looking at a gray shed in the corner of the yard. “That’s it,” she says.

“What?”

“Room.”

“Nah.”

“It is, Jack, you’ve just never seen it from the outside.”

1 **fifteen foot** One foot equals 12 inches or about 0.305 metres. – 1 **hedge** a row of bushes planted close together (*Hecke*) – 2 **to be entitled to** to have the right to – 10 **root** the part of a plant that grows in the soil (*Wurzel*) – 17 **probe** a long thin metal instrument used to search inside a hole (*Sonde*)

We follow Officer Oh, we step over more yellow tape. "Notice the central air unit is concealed in these bushes," she tells Ma. "And the entrance is at the back, out of any sight lines."

I see silvery metal, it's Door I think but the side of him I never saw, he's halfway open already.

"Will I come in with you?" says Officer Oh.

"No," I shout.

"OK."

"Just me and Ma."

But Ma's dropped my hand and she's bending over, she makes a strange noise. There's stuff on the grass, on her mouth, it's vomit I can smell. Is she poisoned again? "Ma, Ma—"

"I'm OK." She wipes her mouth with a tissue Officer Oh gives her.

"Would you prefer—?" says Officer Oh.

"No," says Ma and she takes my hand again. "Come on."

We step in through Door and it's all wrong. Smaller than Room and emptier and it smells weird. Floor's bare, that's because there's no Rug, she's in my wardrobe in our Independent Living, I forgot she couldn't be here at the same time. Bed's here but there's no sheets or Duvet on her. Rocker's here and Table and Sink and Bath and Cabinet but no plates and cutlery on top, and Dresser and TV and Bunny with the purple bow on him, and Shelf but nothing on her, and our chairs folded up but they're all different. Nothing says anything to me. "I don't think this is it," I whisper to Ma.

"Yeah, it is."

Our voices sound not like us. "Has it got shrunk?"

"No, it was always like this."

Spaghetti Mobile's gone, and my octopus picture, and the masterpieces, and all the toys and Fort and Labyrinth. I look under Table but there's no web. "It's gone darker."

"Well, it's a rainy day. You could put the light on." Ma points to Lamp.

2 **central air unit** an apparatus to circulate air – 2 **to conceal** [kənˈsiːl] to hide

But I don't want to touch. I look closer, I'm trying to see it how it was. I find my birthday numbers marked beside Door, I stand against them and put my hand flat at the top of my head and I'm taller than the black 5. There's thin dark on everything. "Is that the dust of our skins?" I ask.

"Fingerprinting powder," says Officer Oh.

I bend and look in Under Bed for Eggsnake curled up like he's sleeping. I can't see his tongue, I reach down all careful till I feel the little prick of the needle.

I straighten up. "Where did Plant be?"

"You've forgotten already? Right here," says Ma, tapping the middle of Dresser and I see a circle that's more coloredy than the rest.

There's the mark of Track around Bed. The little hole rubbed in Floor where our feet used to go under Table. I guess this really was Room one time. "But not anymore," I tell Ma.

"What?"

"It's not Room now."

"You don't think so?" She sniffs. "It used to smell even staler. The door's open now, of course."

Maybe that's it. "Maybe it's not Room if Door's open."

Ma does a tiny smile. "Do you—?" She clears her throat. "Would you like the door closed for a minute?"

"No."

"OK. I need to go now."

I walk to Bed Wall and touch it with one finger, the cork doesn't feel like anything. "Is good night in the day?"

"Huh?"

"Can we say good night when it's not night?"

"I think it would be good-bye."

"Good-bye, Wall." Then I say it to the three other walls, then "Good-bye, Floor." I pat Bed, "Good-bye, Bed." I put my head down in Under Bed to say "Good-bye, Eggsnake." In Wardrobe I whisper, "Good-bye, Wardrobe." In the dark there's the picture

11 **to tap** to hit lightly – 19 **to sniff** to draw air into the nose with a sound – 19 **stale** no longer fresh

of me Ma did for my birthday, I look very small. I wave her over and point to it.

I kiss her face where the tears are, that's how the sea tastes.

I pull the me picture down and zip it into my jacket. Ma's nearly at Door, I go over. "Lift me up?"

"Jack—"

"Please."

Ma sits me up on her hip, I reach up.

"Higher."

She holds me by my ribs and lifts me up up up, I touch the start of Roof. I say, "Good-bye, Roof."

Ma puts me down *thump.*

"Good-bye, Room." I wave up at Skylight. "Say good-bye," I tell Ma. "Good-bye, Room."

Ma says it but on mute.

I look back one more time. It's like a crater, a hole where something happened. Then we go out the door.

Acknowledgments

I would like to thank my beloved Chris Roulston and my agent, Caroline Davidson, for their responses to the first draft, as well as Caroline (aided by Victoria X. Kwee and Laura Macdougall) and my U.S. agent, Kathy Anderson, for their exuberant commitment to this novel from day one. Judy Clain at Little, Brown, Sam Humphreys at Picador, and Iris Tupholme at HarperCollins Canada for their intelligent editing. Also my friends Debra Westgate, Liz Veecock, Arja Vainio-Mattila, Tamara Sugunasiri, Hélène Roulston, Andrea Plumb, Chantal Phillips, Ann Patty, Sinéad McBrearty, and Ali Dover for their suggestions about everything from child development to plot development. Above all, my brother-in-law Jeff Miles for his unnervingly insightful advice on the practicalities of Room.

Additional material

1. Review by Susanna Rustin

Reprinted from: The Guardian, Saturday 7 August 2010.

Emma Donoghue's novel *Room* is told, in the present tense, in the voice of a five-year-old boy who has undergone a terrible ordeal. Jack and his "Ma", who was abducted at the age of 19 from her college car park in an unnamed north American town, have been locked in a soundproofed garden shed all his life. Their captor, "Old Nick", delivers their food, a weekly "Sundaytreat" (new trousers, painkillers), and takes grotesque satisfaction in raping Ma while Jack counts the creaks in the bedsprings from the wardrobe which serves as his bedroom.

Since this deprived, stunted, deeply boring routine is all that Jack knows, he regards it as normal, and his narration is taken up with describing the daily details and rituals of the life which we, unlike him, understand to be a perverse form of captivity. These are some of the novel's most creative passages, and parents of young children will relish Donoghue's account, in Jack's voice, of the games, books, activities, jokes and mealtimes; the endless repetition, the fun and the tedium, but in Jack and Ma's case with no respite at all.

So they do Phys Ed (running around the room, jumping on the bed), they work on craft projects, they sunbathe under the skylight, and they stand on the table and "open wide our teeth and shout holler howl yowl shriek screech scream".

6 **ordeal** a difficult or painful experience – 6 **to abduct** to kidnap – 11 **creak** sound e.g. of a badly oiled door – 13 **deprived** without comfortable living conditions (*ärmlich*) – 13 **stunted** *verkümmert* – 18 **to relish** to enjoy – 20 **tedium** boredom – 21 **respite** pause, rest – 23 **craft** things done with one's hands – 25 **to holler** *inf* to shout – 25 **to howl** to make a long loud sound of pain or anger – 25 **to yowl** to make a long loud cry of pain or sadness – 25 **to shriek** to shout sth with a wild high cry – 25 **to screech** to make an unpleasant high sharp sound

This is ordinary life twisted to the very edge of endurance, and it is immediately clear that Ma has made Jack her lifeline – that as long as "Old Nick" leaves him alone, she can manage to keep herself going. More than keep herself going: Jack is full of life, curiosity, affection. What pushes her over the limit is a nasty episode with Old Nick, coupled with the realisation that Jack has reached an age at which he is a plausible ally in an escape. Having briefed him on the real world, until now denied as a television fantasy, Ma sets about persuading him to play dead so that Old Nick will carry him out to the truck wrapped up in a rug for burial, from where he can run and get help.

The second half of the novel deals with Jack's arrival "Outside": police, hospitals, the media, fan mail, Ma's family, including a new step-grandfather and three-year-old cousin. Jack catches his first cold, and has to negotiate stairs. There is something of Craig Raine's Martian postcard about all this, and it's not hard to see why the idea of describing the world as if seen for the very first time presented Donoghue with an irresistible challenge.

She clearly enjoys research, having previously written several novels based on historical sources, including the much-feted *Slammerkin*. Here she makes fertile use of the science of captivity, so we learn how easily Jack burns in the sun, how he can't judge distance, how he can't bear to be separated from his mother who, now that they are free, wants to stop breastfeeding at last.

1 **endurance** the power to remain alive or in existence (*Ausdauer*) – 7 **ally** a person who helps or supports you (*Verbündeter*) – 10 **to wrap up** *here*: to cover up – 11 **burial** the ceremony of putting a dead body into a grave – 15 **to negotiate** *here*: to manage – 16 **Craig Raine's Martian postcard** In Craig Raine's surrealist poem *A Martian Sends A Postcard Home*, everyday objects are described as if they were strange or exotic. – 21 **much-feted** highly praised – 22 **Slammerkin** a novel by Emma Donoghue – 22 **fertile** *fruchtbar*

The immediacy of the present tense, coupled with such a compelling storyline, works to dispel resistance to the notion of a novel narrated by a preschooler. Plenty of reported speech means Jack's task as storyteller is not as onerous as it might be, and for much of the time we simply watch the action unfold in dialogue. Jack's language is simple, his grammar imperfect, and Donoghue adds a sprinkling of childish mistakes: "You cutted the cord", "[Ma] goes to Thermostat to hot the air", "ten times their big". The building blocks of his world are turned into proper nouns and lose the definite article: Room, Skylight, Wardrobe.

Since Jack has spent every minute of his life in the company of his mother, his precocity is plausible, up to a point. But there are some observations he makes that clearly belong to an adult: "everywhere I'm looking at kids, adults mostly don't seem to like them, not even the parents do. They call the kids gorgeous and so cute, they make the kids do the thing all over again so they can take a photo, but they don't actually want to play with them."

At the heart of the book is a parable of the mother-child relationship, in which total intimacy and togetherness must give way to separation. Donoghue has deliberately toned down the horror, but nonetheless at times the world according to Jack feels too charming – an echo of those "dungeon tot" headlines. He finds his first trip to the car wash "hilarious"; he can hardly believe his friend Dora the Explorer from TV is printed on backpacks; he puts on "cool shades to watch God's yellow face in our window". Sometimes he seems to be played for laughs, as when he judges the *Very Hungry Caterpillar* "a terrible waster" of food.

2 **to dispel** to drive away (*vertreiben*) – 2 **notion** idea – 3 **preschooler** a child that does not yet go to school – 3 **reported speech** *direkte Rede* – 4 **onerous** difficult – 5 **to unfold** to become clear, to develop – 13 **precocity** [prɪ'kɑːsət̬i] *Frühreife* – 22 **to give way** to allow sth new, to make room for – 22 **to tone down** to reduce, to moderate – 24 **dungeon tot** a small child from a dark underground prison – 27 **cool shades** *inf* sunglasses – 29 **Very Hungry Caterpillar** a figure from a book – 30 **waster** sb who uses things wastefully

Because the novel depends on his ability to express himself, Jack can't lose it – or not without ruffling the book's surface more than its author wants him to. When difficulties are examined, they seem technical, resolvable. Completely missing from the prose is any sense of panic, disorientation, depression, the nameless terror conjured up by a string of associations "like all the half-comprehended notions that float dim through children's brains" described in *Jane Eyre*. Donoghue's reader is asked to believe that Jack is, as his mother says at one point, "OK. More or less." Although I was impressed by her book, I couldn't.

2 **to ruffle** to make a smooth surface uneven (*zerzausen*) – 6 **to conjure up** to bring up (*heraufbeschwören*) – 7 **notion** idea – 7 **to float** to move easily and lightly – 7 **dim** unclear (*verschwommen*) – 8 **Jane Eyre** novel by Charlotte Bronte, written in 1847

2. The trial of Josef Fritzl. 'Light out. Rape. Light on. Rape. In front of the children. Birth. Death. Rape.'

Kate Connolly, in St Pölten, Austria. Reprinted from The Guardian, Tuesday 17 March 2009

She pulled back the lid of the brown cardboard box, and invited the jurors to take a sniff at the objects inside. It was, said Christiane Burkheiser, a chance for the jury to experience for themselves the rancid stink that pervaded every inch of the underground prison beneath the family home in Amstetten, west of Vienna, where Josef Fritzl held his daughter for 24 years and allegedly raped her repeatedly.

It was one of the more dramatic moments of the opening yesterday of the long-awaited trial of the Austrian electrical engineer. No one in the public gallery could see what was in the box – children's toys, books, clothing perhaps – but the crumpled looks on the jurors' faces left little to the imagination.

The state prosecutor had felt the full impact of the cellar prison when she visited it herself. "I've seen the cellar dungeon twice," Burkheiser said. "It has a morbid atmosphere, which starts with having to crawl in on your hands and knees through the 83 cm entranceway. And it's sinister. It's really bad. It's incredibly damp, a damp that creeps into you after just a few minutes."

1 **trial** hearing and judging a person in a court – 1 **rape** sex against a person's will (*Vergewaltigung*) – 6 **lid** top of a bottle or box that can be lifted up or removed – 7 **juror** [ˈdʒʊrɚ] a member of a jury in a court – 7 **sniff** the act of smelling sth (*Schnuppern*) – 9 **rancid** [ˈræntsɪd] smelling extremely sour and unpleasant – 9 **to pervade** to spread through every part of – 12 **allegedly** *mutmaßlich* – 17 **crumpled** a face crumples as a result of a sudden shock – 19 **state prosecutor** *Staatsanwalt* – 20 **dungeon** [ˈdʌndʒən] a dark underground prison – 21 **morbid** depressing, deathly, extremely unpleasant – 23 **sinister** threatening (*unheimlich*) – 24 **damp** slightly wet (*feucht*)

Fritzl sat listening impassively on a suede-upholstered chair, wearing grey trousers and a black and white check jacket that was slightly too large for him.

Minutes earlier he had shuffled into room 119 of the St Pölten district court, flanked by six police officers and clutching tightly at a royal blue folder to shield his face from the clicking cameras.

The 73-year-old looked a shadow of his former self as he walked across the creaking oak floor. Gone were his healthy suntan and the confident gait shown in video footage of him on holiday or in snapshots enjoying barbecues in the garden – while his daughter, and the offspring he fathered during years of sexual abuse, languished beneath his feet.

Fritzl refused to answer the questions fired at him by two Austrian reporters.

"If you had your chance again, would you do it all the same way?" one reporter asked, provoking nervous laughter from the public gallery. Fritzl kept his shield in place, although at times he was seen to apparently grin as his grey moustache twitched behind the folder. When he finally sat after cameras had been ordered from the court, he placed the file on the table in front of him and held his hands to the side of his head like blinkers instead.

Burkheiser, for 25 minutes, laid out her emotional arguments, sometimes using a laser pointer to indicate masking tape she had stuck to the walls of the wood-panelled courtroom to illustrate the narrowness of entrances, the low heights of ceilings that Elisabeth and her children had had to endure.

1 **impassive** without emotion – 1 **suede-upholstered** [sweɪd] covered with soft leather – 2 **check** a pattern of squares on clothes (*Karomuster*) – 4 **to shuffle** to walk by dragging one's feet along slowly – 5 **district court** *Kreisgericht* – 5 **to clutch** to hold tightly – 6 **folder** *Ordner* – 9 **creaking** sounding like a badly oiled door – 10 **gait** [geɪt] the way sb walks (*Gang*) – 10 **footage** here: film – 13 **sexual abuse** *sexueller Missbrauch* – 13 **to languish** to experience long suffering – 19 **to twitch** to move quickly and suddenly – 22 **blinker** *Scheuklappen* – 24 **to lay out** *here*: to present – 25 **masking tape** *Abklebeband*

The space constraints and the damp were, she said, minor compared with the other hardships and sufferings. For years Elisabeth had had no sink, no warm water, no daylight. She had "got her air from the cracks in the walls". Sometimes she went without light for days at a time – "no lamp, not even a torch or candles". And there were also the repeated rapes.

"But do you know what the worst thing was?" she asked the jury of four men and four women. "The uncertainty: when will he return, when will he turn on the electricity, when will he go again, what will happen if he doesn't return?" she whispered, as if to maximise the impact of telling a scary bedtime tale.

She said they should not be fooled by Fritzl's polite demeanour, the image he projected of "a nice old man from next door". She said the trials of the cellar inhabitants were best encapsulated in a single paragraph, which she delivered in staccato fashion: "Light out. Rape. Light on. Mould. Rape. In front of the children. The uncertainty. Birth. Death. Rape."

She detailed the births over 12 years of Elisabeth's children, the three who stayed in the cellar and the three who were taken upstairs to live with their "grandparents" – Fritzl and his wife, Rosemarie. She also told of the birth in 1996 of a twin, Michael, who died after suffering from severe breathing difficulties, which she said would probably have been avoided had Fritzl sought medical help.

"That, ladies and gentlemen, is murder."

Then turning to Fritzl, who has admitted disposing of the body in an incinerator, she squinted her eyes and, whispering, said: "Herr Fritzl, your own flesh and blood. To treat it that way?"

The accused moved his head slightly but did not appear to express any emotion.

1 **constraint** restriction – 11 **scary** frightening – 12 **to fool** to deceive, to trick – 13 **demeanour** [dɪˈmiːnɚ] outward behaviour – 15 **to encapsulate** to sum up the main points in a short form – 15 **in staccato** in short, separate sounds – 16 **mould** a soft greenish growth on bread, cheese (*Schimmel*) – 24 **to seek** to try and find – 26 **to dispose of** to get rid of, to destroy – 27 **incinerator** a furnace for burning rubbish – 27 **to squint** here: to almost close

Rudolf Mayer, Fritzl's lawyer and a veteran presence at Austria's more obscure criminal cases, urged the jury to take a less passionate view of his client.

"You need to keep emotion out of this," he said, arguing that it was wrong to call him a monster, as he has repeatedly been referred to in the media.

"A man who put so much effort into keeping two families cannot be called a monster," he said. "If I only want a daughter as a sex slave, I don't let her bring children into the world. You'd let them starve," he said.

In an indirect reference to the Belgian criminal Marc Dutroux, who kidnapped and murdered four girls in 1996, Mayer said the "Belgian case" was an example of monstrous behaviour, but it was unfair to put the label on Fritzl.

"When his eldest daughter was seriously ill, he put her in his Mercedes and took her to hospital," he said, referring to Kerstin, 19, whose hospitalisation last April caused suspicious police to close in and was the catalyst that brought Fritzl's underground empire crashing down.

The charges:

- Murder – maximum sentence of life imprisonment
- Enslavement – 20 years
- Rape – 15 years
- Deprivation of liberty – 10 years
- Coercion – five years
- Incest – one year

1 **veteran presence** here: a very experienced and well-known person / lawyer – 2 **to urge** to try hard to persuade (*eindringlich bitten*) – 10 **to starve** to die of hunger – 11 **reference** *Hinweis* – 11 **Marc Dutroux** a serial killer who kidnapped and sexually abused six children, murdering four of them between 1995 and 1996 – 17 **suspicious** suspecting wrongdoing, not trusting – 18 **catalyst** sth that causes a change to happen – 24 **deprivation of liberty** *Freiheitsberaubung* – 25 **coercion** [koʊ'ɜːrʒən] forcing sb to do sth that they do not want to do (*Nötigung*)

3. Interviews with the author about Room

For copyright reasons, we were unfortunately unable to reprint the interview with Emma Donoghue that appeared in the original edition of the book, but it should be available online.

You will find a link to this and several other interviews by going to www.klett.de and entering the code: k3bp6b into the search field near the top of the page and pressing "Enter".

(Editor's note: these were all reliable, live links in January 2012, but we cannot absolutely guarantee that they still will be now!)